The Twelfth Man
A Story of Texas A&M Football

The Twelfth Man
A Story of Texas A&M Football

by
Wilbur Evans
and
H. B. McElroy

THE STRODE PUBLISHERS
Huntsville, Alabama 35802

Copyright 1974
By Wilbur Evans
and H. B. McElroy
All Rights In This Book
Reserved Including The Right
To Reproduce This Book Or Parts
Thereof In Any Form—Printed in U.S.A.
Library of Congress Catalog Number 74-81347
Standard Book Number 87397-034-9

Dedicated to
all of those who fashioned the Texas A&M
football story on the field and to all
others whose loyalty transcends
the scoreboard

Contents

Foreword

1. Stand Up, Stand Up For A&M 11
2. The Aggie: As Student, As Former Student 19
3. First Coach Did Not Choose To Run; He Quit 23
4. Faculty Wins Battle But Not The War 30
5. Wanted: Final Destination To Resemble
   College Station 35
6. Kyle Field: Named For Whom? 41
7. Big Little Man: So Much For So Many So Long 45
8. Three In A Row Over Varsity Spiced Uncle
   Charley's Stay 52
9. Gig 'Em! Charley Moran 58
10. Varsity Finally Shows At Kyle Field 63
11. The Great Score Branded In Bevo's Hide 69
12. Dough Kept Coming Back 72

13. Unscored On, Unbeaten Through 25 Games......... 77
14. Sight of Centre Orange Had Aggies Seeing Red 85
15. The Glory Years Return In 1925 And 1927 95
16. His Name Was Bible—So Was His Word 103
17. Gig 'Em! Joel Hunt 108
18. From Pink Slip To Rose Bowl 114
19. Reveille: A Treasured Tradition 119
20. If Shoe Fits, It'll Take Size 15 124
21. Gig 'Em! Joe Routt 133
22. Hitting The Jackpot 137
23. Gig 'Em! Dick Todd 143
24. Nineteen In A Row 148
25. Gig 'Em! John Kimbrough 163
26. Stopover To West Point 169
27. "It's How You Show Up At Showdown That Counts" 173
28. Played Best Against The Best 177
29. Junction: A Tale By The Bear 185
30. Gig 'Em! Jack Pardee 196
31. "Went According To Prayer" 201
32. Gig 'Em! John David Crow................... 213
33. Gig 'Em! Charley Krueger 217
34. The Big One Got Away 222
35. Texas Special's Longest Run 231
36. Beat The Clock And The Teacher............... 236
37. Gig 'Em! Edd Hargett...................... 247
38. Return Of The Native...................... 251
39. Freshmen Add Fresh Flavor 256
    Appendix 263

Foreword

On December 1, 1970, Dr. Jack K. Williams had just ended the exciting, yet demanding day on which he assumed the presidency of Texas A&M University. With all of the ceremonies concluded, what better way to relax than take his house guests to the living room of his campus home?

Among the guests was the Honorable Olin E. Teague, Class of 1932, and now congressman from the district that encompasses Texas A&M.

This was at the time of so much student unrest at a number of universities, but A&M students had not staged any demonstrations or protest marches. The guests had hardly settled for a quiet visit, however, when a first appeared in the making. The steadily increasing racket out front was enough to make Tiger Teague and others wonder if there was a back door to the place.

Then suddenly the crescendo changed to music quite discernible. One did not have to look to identify the Texas Aggie Band, for it was playing "The Aggie War Hymn." It was quite obvious this was not a march of protest, and the relieved guests followed the president out the front door to listen.

It appeared that the entire student body had followed the 267-man band. Gleaming red light flares glowed from the drum major's baton, and every voice in that crowd seemed to be singing.

The "march" turned into a pep rally—a welcome to the new president and his family to the realm of The Twelfth Man.

It was "yell practice" right in his own back yard.

When it ended, President Williams expressed his appreciation and love for Texas A&M. "You're the greatest," he told them. "I only hope I can be as good a president as you are students."

A news account of the students' march reached the newspapers and caught the eye of George W. Strake, Jr., a non-Aggie. He called Dr. Williams to compliment the students and offered a grant of $5,000 from the Strake Foundation for scholarship aid. Mr. Strake was advised that while scholarship money is always welcome, it was felt that since it was a student activity which Mr. Strake admired, the money should be granted to the Student Activities Committee, the body which makes recommendations on the spending of all funds in the Student Activities program.

Mr. Strake agreed, and the check was sent. A year later and still impressed by the student body (The Twelfth Man) the grant was renewed.

And Dr. Williams still declares, "That Twelfth Man. It's the greatest."

Stand Up,
Stand Up For A&M

It could have happened at some other school, but it seems most unlikely that it would; where else would a football coach look up into the grandstand and summon one of the spectators to come down and help prevent a dramatic upset? Where, but at Texas A&M, would you find enough enthusiasm, pride, and loyalty to keep the students—and *even their dates*—standing throughout every football game, simply as a symbol of their willingness to volunteer for frontline duty?

Enthusiasm, pride, loyalty—these are traits to be found in almost any successful college football program. But when these qualities become almost a religion, as they have at Texas A&M, they create a rather miraculous atmosphere which can be best described as "The Twelfth Man" spirit. It is a spirit which has worked wonders not only on the football fields across the nation but on battlefields throughout the world.

It might have been born in 1902, when A&M whipped "Varsity" (The University of Texas) for the first time; or that day at the 1914 State Fair, when a 7-9 half-time deficit was wiped out as the Aggies trounced LSU, 63-9; or Thanksgiving Day of 1915, when it became obvious that the will-to-win offsets such tangible factors as size, speed, and reputation.

But actually the tradition began on January 2, 1922. That was the day an underdog Aggie eleven "rose to the occasion," in the vernacular of Dana X. Bible, and whipped nationally-awed Centre College, 22-14, in the Dixie Classic at Dallas' Fair Park—a forerunner of today's Cotton Bowl Classic. It was a monumental triumph because it projected Texas A&M and the Southwest Conference into the national football picture. It also was a game and a day that was to become even more memorable to Aggie fans through the birth of "The Twelfth Man," the symbol of a transcendent school spirit.

Actually, Centre was a pinch-hitter in Joe Utay's Dixie Classic, so named because it was to determine the championship of the entire Southland, just as the Dixie Series functioned in organized baseball. The enterprising Utay had caught the Rose Bowl committee flat-footed by committing Washington and Jefferson to play the Aggies, but he acquiesced when Rose Bowl officials appealed to him to release the Presidents and permit them to oppose California in Pasadena.

The plan to showcase Southwest Conference football was conceived at the start of the 1921 season, and Penn State was the No. 1 objective, but by late November the interest had shifted to Washington and Jefferson, because of its superior record. Penn State had been tied by Harvard, 21-21, in midseason and wound up its regular campaign in a scoreless stalemate with Pittsburgh.

It was no disturbing task for Utay to find a replacement for W. and J. He had been Athletic Director while Charley Moran was coaching A&M to 1912 successes, and this gave him a good entree with the man who had fashioned the Praying Colonels into a national power over a three-season span.

Uncle Charley was pleased to bring his talk-of-the-nation team to Texas for two reasons. It gave him an opportunity to vindicate himself with those who had dismissed him at A&M, and the Dixie Classic provided a convenient stop-over for his team that would be returning from a season finale with Arizona. Furthermore, it would serve as a homecoming for a team blessed with Texans, headed by all-Americans Red Roberts and Bo McMillin, the latter to be married a few hours before the kickoff, and Bill James, destined to win the hearts of so many A&M and Texas fans.

Centre was undefeated for the season and numbered among its victims mighty Harvard, which had a 25-victory string going until McMillin scored the only touchdown of the game. The Colonels, who were to yield 22 points to the Aggies, had given up only 6 points to 10 opponents.

Leaders The Day The Legend Was Born

Captain Heinie Weir, left, who was injured in the 1922 Dixie Classic, and Coach Dana X. Bible, who called King Gill from the stands to don the injured player's uniform.

In arranging the Classic, Dallas officials were striving to set an annual precedent.

"Every indication points to the fact that Texas weather and the increase in avid interest of football by leaps and bounds have served to maintain interest in the most picturesque of college sports well over a month beyond the annual conclusion of the season on Thanksgiving," wrote Bill Ruggles in the *Dallas News.* "The eleven regarded as making the best showing in the Southwest Conference each year will be invited to compete against an eleven that has gained national prominence with an undefeated record and a strong schedule." That format was developed for the Cotton Bowl two decades later when the Southwest Conference took over the direction of the New Year's Day classic.

Although champion of the Conference for a third time over a five-season span, A&M was hardly a frightening foe when it lined up against the Colonels. The Aggies had lost early in the fall to LSU and had ended the regular season by playing successive stalemates with Rice and Texas, failing even to score in the latter game. It was a team made up largely of players who had come up from the ROTC company teams, since the backbone of the crew that had won twenty-four of twenty-six tests over a three-season span had departed.

"We really didn't have much of a football team," recalls Dr. Sam Houston Sanders, now a distinguished man of medicine in Memphis, Tennessee, who was an all-Conference halfback that season. "Most of the best players had graduated the year before, and we had just been coming along. These guys did have guts and determination, and whatever Coach Bible asked us to do we did it. I don't know how we accomplished what we did."

A master psychologist even at that early stage in his remarkable coaching career, Bible exploited the role of underdog from the beginning.

"It was the biggest game A&M had ever had," he recalls with enthusiasm. "It likewise was the greatest opportunity and the greatest challenge to be playing for the championship of the entire South."

Sanders remembers well "Coach Bible's talk" with the squad regarding the invitation to play the Dallas game. "Coach told us, 'We've been invited to play a postseason game, and I'll

Aggies stop Praying Colonels short of goal line.

leave the decision up to you. I am not going to advise you what to do, but if you choose to play, we're going to limit the squad to as few members as we need. And remember this: you're going to miss the Christmas holidays, and some of you will be late starting other sports.'"

And a small squad it was: only eighteen players bivouacked in the Dallas University dormitories and held their workouts there. A&M's manpower shortage was compounded by recurring injuries that had plagued Bible's squad throughout the season.

Harry Pinson had broken a leg in the finale with Texas, and Floyd (Buck) Buckner, who shared the fullback role with him, suffered a like injury in practice before the squad headed to Dallas. Captain Heinie Weir, who had missed most of the season because of a broken leg, reinjured the leg on the third play from scrimmage against Centre and was followed to the sidelines by the spectacular Sanders and Bugs Morris, who shared field general duties.

It was the injury toll that led to the origin of the Twelfth

Man tradition. Bible remembered that King Gill, a reserve halfback who had given up football for basketball after Thanksgiving Day, was up in the press box serving as a spotter for the late Jinx Tucker of the *Waco News-Tribune.*

That part of the story rightfully belongs to Gill, now a retired ophthalmologist living in Rockport, and it is his to tell: "I rode to the stadium in the same taxi with Coach Bible, and since I was not dressing for the game, he asked me to assist in spotting players for Jinx Tucker. Near the end of the first half, when Coach Bible realized he had only one able-bodied backfield substitute available, he sent word to me to come down to the bench.

"It was not until I arrived on the field that I learned Coach wanted me to put on a uniform and be ready to play if he needed me. There were no dressing rooms at the stadiums in those days. So, Heinie Weir (injured early) and I went under the stands and I put on his uniform and he dressed in my clothes.

"I'll never forget what Coach Bible said to me. He said 'Boy, it looks like we may not have enough players to finish the game. You may have to go in and stand around for a while.' 'Yes sir,' I said.

"I don't guess A&M has ever played more inspired ball. All of our remaining players managed to survive from that point forward and went on to win the game."

Bill Ruggles, reporting for the *Dallas News,* capsuled it expertly when he acknowledged: "They rose to the supreme height of the glory of the old Aggie spirit that has immortalized College Station teams."

Yes, accounts of the heroics of Cap Murrah, Puny Wilson, Sanders, T. L. Miller, et al, will be reviewed in greater detail further along, as will the impact of the Aggie victory nationwide.

As for King Gill, he won immortality simply by being at the right place at the right time and merely by climbing into a uniform. The fact that he did not play that day is irrelevant, as he was to become a hero in three sports and earn seven letters.

Gill's role in the genesis of The Twelfth Man long has been established and documented, but few are those who remember that King's designation was the inspiration of Harry W. (Red) Thompson, A&M's head yell leader of 1921 from Hubbard,

King Gill
As the Twelfth Man

King Gill
As the Hall of Famer

Harry W. (Red) Thompson: Yell leader coined Twelfth Man designation.

Texas. It was Thompson whom Coach Bible sent into the stands to find Gill and bring him down to the bench.

Fired by the stirring victory and inspired by a student answering the call for duty, Thompson scheduled a yell practice on the steps of the YMCA as soon as the team and students returned to the campus. It was on this occasion that he referred to Gill as the Twelfth Man and that from that night forward the student body would be so designated. To this day it implies that if the Aggies on the field can not get the job done, someone will climb out of the grandstand and help them.

Since that hallowed day, the fabled Twelfth Man has been summoned on several occasions by A&M coaches, and the Corps of Cadets soon adopted the custom, now an inspiring ritual, to stand throughout all football games, signifying readiness as the Twelfth Man.

Sacred as it has become, the Twelfth Man tradition prompts good-natured razzing as well. Impervious as they have become to the Aggie Joke, A&M fans laughed also when sportswriter Bill Corum rationalized: "Standing gives the Cadets a big advantage. They can get to the goalposts quickly in case of victory, or retreat with equal facility."

The Aggie: As Student, As Former Student

The camaraderie and student unity at A&M, great from the very beginning of the institution, truly reached the pitch of the one great "fraternity" during the depression decade of the 1930s and the early 1940s. The "Farmers" of the early Twentieth Century had, by 1930, become the "Aggies" of the modern era. The modern Aggie was of the same mold as the old "Farmer" species, perhaps even a little more so. He was loyal, dedicated, and determined—so much so that at times he appeared bull-headed, immature, and irrational, inspiring many of the contemporary "Aggie Jokes." The A&M man became an ethnic species of his own, and proud of it. Aggies began to take great pleasure in the unique distinction of being Aggies.

According to the 1933-34 YMCA-sponsored Students' Handbook, an Aggie:

> Speaks to every cadet and every professor at every opportunity. Learns the college songs and yells as soon as possible. Thanks the driver of a car who has given him a ride and helps the driver if he has trouble while the cadet is with him. Attends all athletic contests that are possible for him to attend and backs the team through thick and thin. Keeps his shoes shined, his hair combed and his uniform pressed. Never "razzes" a referee or umpire. Dresses neatly and is a gentleman while on week-end trips or

Corps trips. Is honest in class room, regardless of what he may see others, who are careless of their honor, doing. Realizes that someone is making a sacrifice to give him the opportunity to be at A&M and consequently makes use of his time to the best advantage by conscientious work whether it be his study time or his leisure. He plays hard and studies hard.

To be sure, an Aggie developed other traits and activities as well. He ate spuds (potatoes), blood (ketchup), rocks (ice), cackle (eggs), gun wadding (bread), scabs (post toasties), sawdust (sugar), dope (coffee), worms (spaghetti), and cush (dessert). Aggies had fish (freshmen), horizontal engineers (sleeping students), and bleed meetings (freshman "orientation" by upperclassmen), and lived with an old lady (roommate).

They attended midnight yell practice, saw to it that freshmen polished the bronze statue of Lawrence Sullivan Ross endlessly, and honored their dead with the inspiring "Silver Taps" and monuments. Seniors ended their years at A&M with the unglamorous "Elephant Walk," and then the impressive "Final Review."

Any explanation of an Aggie is inadequate. For greater insight one should read Henderson Shuffler's *Sons...Remember,* John Pasco's *Fish Sergeant,* George Sessions Perry's *Texas A&M,* and numerous other biographies, war memoirs, and reminiscences, many of which will be found in both public and private libraries. But, if you are not an Aggie, you will never truly know what an Aggie is; and the Aggie of the twenties and thirties is now vintage wine.

Former students of Texas A&M now number about 60,000—and even though today's Aggies are not the homogeneous group they were prior to World War II (all male, all Corps, all "Old-Army"), they still constitute the greatest single "fraternity" in the world.

On or about April 21 of each year, former students of Texas A&M meet in the single greatest alumni program known to the world—the Aggie Muster—to honor comrades who have died since the last Muster, and to answer "here" when the name of the fallen comrade is called. And on *any* day of *any* year, when one Aggie sees an Aggie Ring on the finger of someone he meets, an impromptu Aggie Reunion is held on the spot.

Official Class Reunions, held every five years by every graduating class of Texas A&M, are the inspiration of alumni directors all across the country. Most other colleges and universities hold an annual event called "homecoming"—for they could never get enough people together to have a good party, if they held reunions by graduating classes, as the Aggies do.

The five-year reunions, where former students and their spouses meet together to renew acquaintances and keep alive the Spirit of Aggieland, are held in the fall or in the spring on the campus or at some city where the A&M football team is playing. Each year those who are observing the fiftieth anniversary of their graduation are inducted into the Lawrence Sullivan Ross Group and presented "Golden Circle" certificates recognizing them for their devoted interest in Texas A&M.

The Aggies support Texas A&M University and the Association of Former Students in giant, Texas-style—with love, loyalty, and cold, hard cash. They support scholarships, student loan funds, monetary awards for teaching excellence, athletic teams, judging teams, and literally dozens of student programs for today's students. The proudest parents at any Class Reunion are the pair who can boast the most children and grandchildren who are numbered among the Aggie Family.

Today's Texas A&M student body is complex and diverse, including women, graduate students, foreign students, members of many age and ethnic groups—and a lion's share of high-achieving scholars. But, despite this diversity and change, the spirit of the Twelfth Man is alive and well at Aggieland.

Even though today's Aggie is not necessarily a "farmer" or a "red-neck," he (or she) is a part of the loyal and dedicated Texas A&M family. Aggies still "stick together," as can be readily seen at any Muster, or at any Class Reunion, or anywhere former students of Texas A&M get together. The Association of Former Students is a model for the alumni association of other institutions of higher education in the country.

Richard (Buck) Weirus, 1942, Executive Director of the Association of Former Students, loves to tell the story of how he was asked by the Board of Directors of the alumni association of another university in the Southwest Conference: "Buck, please tell us just what it is that makes Texas Aggies take all the prizes at supporting their school? What causes them to generously support every program designed to make a Greater Texas A&M? What do you do to inspire those Aggies?"

To which Weirus smilingly replied, "We don't do anything you folks aren't already doing. We publish an alumni magazine, print a directory, have clubs and hold reunions—just as you do. I'm not sure if you can handle the answer to your question, but here it is: It's in the *quality* of the alumni."

The quality is still there at Texas A&M—and the Spirit of the Twelfth Man is very much alive.

First Coach Did Not Choose To Run; He Quit

A&M survived its first eighteen years without benefit of intercollegiate football, fielding its first team in 1894 and displaying good judgment by choosing a high school team in Galveston for the inaugural opponent. That first season coincided with the outlawing of the flying wedge and the V-trick by those schools that had pioneered the American sport a quarter of a century earlier. Designed to reduce downright brutality, the new rule stipulated that no more than three offensive players would be allowed to group more than five yards behind the line of scrimmage to launch momentum play.

Football was so new in the Southwest that historians failed to log a lot of intriguing information over its advent. Facts are so sparse that the illustrious Kern Tips took note of it in his *Football–Texas Style,* published in 1964. Tips wrote: "Few living then or surviving now would take a solemn oath that the records of all scores and performances—even the names of people—have been handed down accurately and faithfully. In the first instance, the wish was often father to the results as reported; and in the second, an alias afforded considerable flexibility to the happy rovers who played here, there, and yonder from one year to the next."

Frank Dudley Perkins, chiefly responsible for A&M's football debut, nor any of his teammates was available when Tips' football account was conceived, but James B. (Josh) Sterns, who served on the scrub team in 1894 and later became a star, proved to be a self-styled historian. His early recollec-

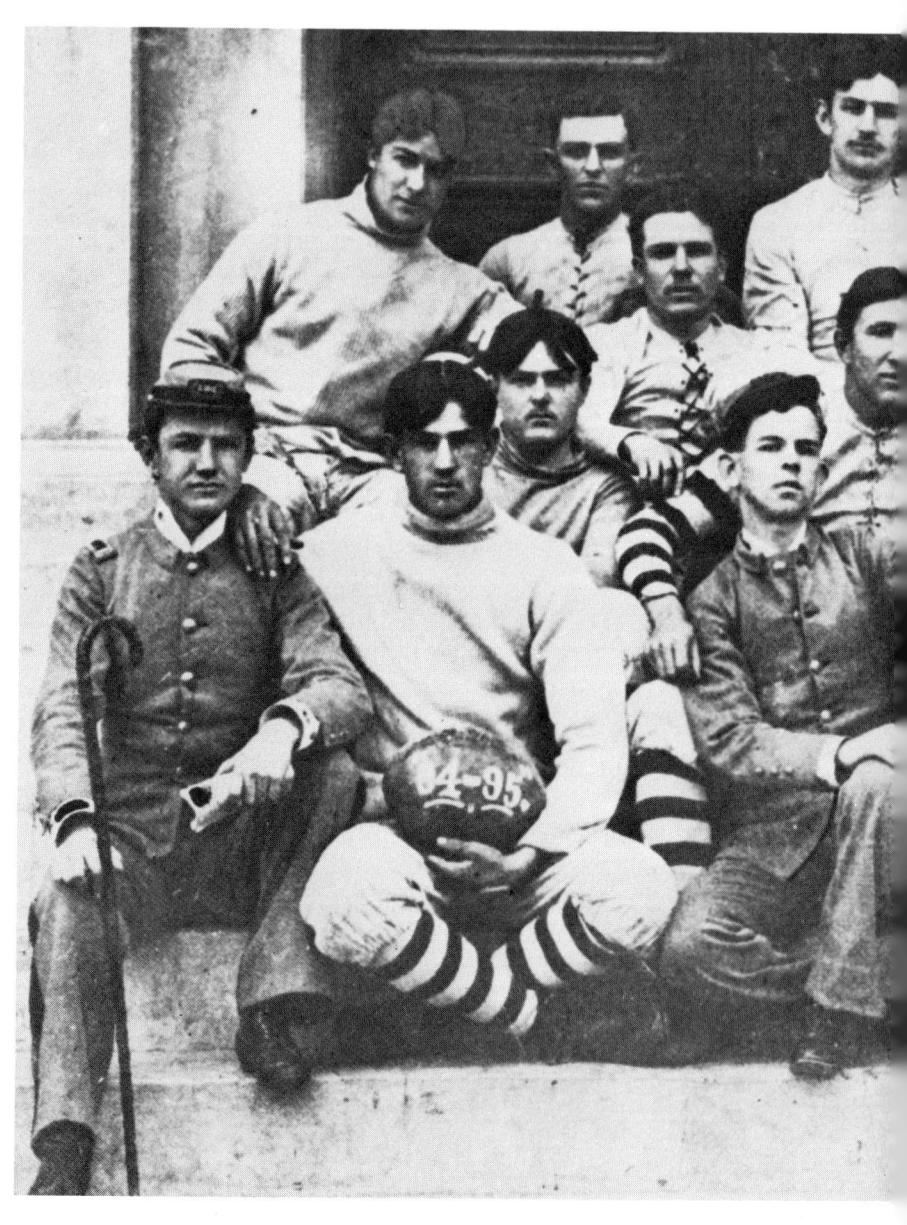

1894 Team: A&M's first
Fifteen players comprised the 1894 Texas A&M football squad that was coached by Frank Dudley Perkins (holding the ball) who played end. The manager was Charles Puryear, lower right. The players, left to right, front row: Harry P. Jordan, Perkins,

F. A. Munro (mascot), Bill Krug, H. T. Chiles. Second row: J. C. McNeill, Hugh McDonald, J. D. McGonagill. Third row: M. B. McMillan, W. G. Mossenburg, Jay Childress, John Burney. Back row: Andy Love, Milton Sims, Russ Burleson, Harry Martin. Arthur P. Watts, the captain, is not shown.

tions were confirmed in an interview by the author four months after he observed his ninety-fifth birthday anniversary in Corpus Christi and just five months before his passing.

"Dudley Perkins was the best athlete I saw during my playing days," Sterns recalls, "and he is due lots of credit for his contributions. In addition to being a good fullback, he served both as manager and coach of the team."

Perkins' teammates on that 1894 team included Arthur Watts (who served as captain), Ed Burgess, Russ Burleson, John Burney, C. Carson, Jay Childress, H. T. Chiles, Hiram Coulter, Bill Krug, Andy Love, Harry Martin, Hugh McDonald, J. D. McGonigill, M. Blaisdale McMillan, J. C. McNeill, W. G. Mossenburg, Captain Frank D. "Cy" Perkins, and M. W. "Mit" Sims. It is significant to note that Perkins was one coach who did not stick around to be fired. He handed the reins in 1896 to Professors A. M. Soule and H. W. South, a couple of volunteer coaches, and concentrated on fullbacking chores in his final two seasons. Soule also served as the school's first athletic director.

Historians in College Station and Austin do not agree on when the first game between A&M and Varsity (*Texas University*) was played, but there is agreement on the outcome. One can understand that it was an event that the Farmers, as they were known in those days, might choose to forget.

Actually, the 38-0 contest opened Texas' second football campaign and closed the Farmers' abbreviated season that had opened with a 14-6 conquest of Galveston High School. Fortunately for A&M, touchdowns were valued at only 4 points and conversions at 2 points each. Varsity's 8 touchdowns and 3 conversions at Austin's suburban Hyde Park would have accounted for 51 points under the current scoring scheme. That would have made that first meeting the most one-sided of their battles. That ignominy belongs instead to the 1898 team that lost, 48-0, a score that benefitted from an increase of the touchdown value to 5 points.

The 1894 meeting was the first intercollegiate football game played in Texas, and the Austin writer reporting the game must have been as inexperienced as the team. He identified the visitors only as "Bryan," a neighboring township of A&M. But he did credit the A&M boys with "showing wonderful pluck in sticking to their colors" and added "had it not been that they

A&M campus as it looked in 1895

were physically unable to cope with the giants of the Varsity team, they would have stood a better showing for scoring."

The only thing A&M won was the opening-game toss. That went for naught, however, since "Bryan" fumbled the kickoff and Varsity needed only two plays to score its first touchdown. W. G. Mossenburg and Milton Simms did receive mention in the "play-by-play" and Arthur Watts, Valdez, and J. D. McGonagill joined Mossenburg as "deserving especial notice for their good work." It was also acknowledged that "Bryan has a good team, nice gentlemen, but they were outclassed as football players."

A&M never generated a scoring threat, but "Bryan's" chagrin must have been diminished by the writer who closed his account with, "One thing that certainly can be said in their favor, and that is they are a thorough set of gentlemen. Their deportment during their stay in the city has been of the best, and we trust to have the team with us again."

In a remarkable documentary of Texas University football seventy-five years later, another Austin writer, Lou Maysel, speculated that, "The defeat apparently was a crushing one for

A&M because it ended its season with this game and did not field a team again until two years later."

He was right about the resumption of football at A&M. The Farmers posted a 2-0-1 record in 1896, winning over Austin College and Houston High School after being held to a scoreless tie by Galveston High School.

TCU, which was to become an unrelenting nemesis three decades later, started its rivalry with A&M in 1897 and scored a 30-6 victory while identified as Add Ran in Waco. This early dominance by TCU was short-lived, however, as A&M won in 1898 and was not to lose in the next nineteen meetings, crowding three victories into the 1903 campaign.

Five collegiate foes appeared on A&M's 1899 schedule, and the Aggies shut out Tulane, 22-0; LSU, 52-0; and Baylor, 33-0, while bowing to Sewanee and Texas, 10-0 and 6-0, respectively. A&M was 1 of 5 that lost to Sewanee over a 6-day span. Sewanee's 21 players forged a 12-0 record for the season that was highlighted by a 3,000 mile trip through Texas, Louisiana, and Mississippi in less than a week. Texas, too, was a victim of the Tennesseans, who brought along their own sipping–drinking–water on a special railway sleeping car.

Meantime, A&M was not venturing any farther away from College Station than San Antonio for the next two seasons.

It was in San Antonio in 1899 that it appeared for a while that the third crack at Varsity might be the charm. Texas managed the only score, however, and when Varsity was awarded possession on the A&M two-yard line after a wild scramble for a free ball, Captain Hal Moseley led his team off the field. The Farmers refused to return, picked up their ball, and went home although twenty-eight minutes of play remained. An *Austin Statesman* writer surmised that "The game, as a whole, demonstrated the fact that A&M is to be a great future rival of the University for football honors."

The Battalion, A&M's campus newspaper, was more concerned in December, 1911, with the immediate past, however, and expressed wrath over the officiating in rhyme:
> "Our players proved they have grit
> And played an honest game
> The referee robbed them 6 to 0
> They held Varsity just the same."

Hal Moseley: Two-season captain and faithful follower

It was in 1900 that A&M and Texas began playing a Thanksgiving Day game, and in that season it was a second meeting. The first had been won by Texas, 5-0, at San Antonio in a morning game limited to twenty-minute halves. The Thanksgiving game was marred by bad weather and was called on account of darkness with two minutes of play remaining, making Texas an 11-0 victor.

Fans apparently were slow in acquiring knowledge of this young sport, and one reader wrote to the *Dallas News* in the fall of 1900 requesting edification. "I know nothing of football," he wrote. "Will you please explain it so that I may clearly understand a game to see it played?" The reply: "Football is not a parlor game of chance, but a contest wherein muscle and ability to butt the adverse player into next week are the principal attributes toward success. It is played on a field 350 feet long and 160 feet wide."

The Farmers were to sink in 1901 to a depth that would not be experienced again until 1948. They dropped two decisions each to Baylor and Texas, after opening with a disputed victory over the Baptists. A&M records that first game with Baylor as a 6-0 triumph, but Baylorites insist it was a 6-6 tie.

Faculty Wins Battle
But Not The War

Over-emphasis, which through the years was to become educators' No. 1 complaint against intercollegiate athletics, was cited by the Texas A&M faculty after the 1901 season, and its concern was manifest in a rule that was passed to prohibit A&M from meeting other Texas educational institutions in intercollegiate competition. The professors could have been disenchanted with a 15-13-2 record for the Farmers' first 7 seasons, but they indicated that their concern was the increasing student preoccupation with sports.

After the students protested vehemently to the president and the Board of Directors, the faculty rescinded its action. The directors respected the faculty's anxiety over the situation, however, and ordered a permanent student-faculty committee to supervise athletics. Thus, the General Athletic Association, to become the Athletic Council in 1906, has been responsible since 1902 for the direction of ticket sales, concessions, the athletic business policy, the recommending of coaches, scheduling of games, and the awarding of letters to participants.

A&M acquired a new coach after the disastrous 1901 campaign, outbidding Ohio State for the services of J. E. Platt of Lafayette College. Coach Platt greeted a nucleus of 1901 veterans, headed by Captain Thomas W. Blake, Bob DeWare, Miles Carpenter, William Beilharz, and E. E. Worthing. Also available was Josh Sterns, a three-year letterman, who realized the value of obtaining a degree and was back on campus after a three-year absence. Sterns had captained the 1897 Farmers, and when an injury in the 1898 game with Austin College cost him so much class attendance, he was not prepared to graduate with the class of 1899. By his own admission, he was dropped from the rolls for what he termed "hell-raising."

Sterns acknowledged that he was the first Aggie to receive seven letters when he returned to the campus: "three in football, one in baseball, one in track, one in hell-raising and one from President Ross telling me to scat."

"Wait'll next year" has been an A&M war cry through the years, and 1902 certainly proved worth waiting for, because success was immediate and constant. Tied by both Trinity and Texas in scoreless games during its first five tests, A&M finished with seven victories and yielded touchdowns only to Baylor and Tulane. The deadlocks with Trinity and Texas were vindicated in successive games at the end of the season, whipping Trinity, then playing out of Waxahachie, 34-0, and Varsity, either 11-0 or 12-0, depending on whose record book you choose. Strangely enough, A&M, in winning and scoring for the first time against Texas, claims the lesser margin.

St. Edward's, TCU, and Baylor were the other victims, the latter twice on successive week-ends. The Farmers were acclaimed the champions of the Southwest, and they, in turn, claimed the championship of the South. After all, Texas' seven-in-a-row supremacy had been broken, and A&M had beaten the team that beat Sewanee, Nashville, Alabama, and Tulane. The Deep South did not concur with this claim.

The game with Varsity was a memorable one for Sterns for a number of reasons. Although a player, he may have become the first scout in Southwest annals when he went to Austin in midseason and scouted the Longhorns, a newly-acquired identity, against Haskell. His scout report to Coach Pratt was simply: "The left side of the Texas line is weak." Sterns was A&M's right end.

The Farmers pounded the left side of the Varsity line with all of the power they could muster and played one of their greatest defensive games ever in whitewashing the hosts. Captain Blake praised all of his teammates, but years later in replaying that memorable contest his recollection went like this: "Josh was one of the most unique characters in the football world that A&M ever produced. He was an earnest, hard-trained player

1902 Southern Champions
This was the first A&M football team to defeat the Texas Longhorns. Players were, left to right, first row: Bill Beilharz, Capt. Tom Blake, Jim Davis, Miles Carpenter. Second row: Josh Sterns, Evan Worthing, Jim Pirie, George Hope. Third row: Ray Ridenhower, Jud Neff, Bob DeWare, Coach James E. Platt, J. W. Benkamin, J. V. Simpson. Not shown are Arthur Bartley, Jim Elder, Stayton Hamner, Shorty Masterson, D. Meyer, L. Miller, Hardy O'Neal, and John Puckett.

and even though he was crippled in one leg or foot, he never went down. The other fellow went down first. He could break the interference like no other man. He would yell: 'Look out Tom, they're coming our way. I'll down 'em and you get 'em.' And we did!"

The *Dallas News* of December 28, 1902, reported A&M's long-awaited conquest thusly:

> "For the first time in the history of the game in Texas the State University went down in defeat before the State Agricultural and Mechanical eleven and it was the first time that team has ever scored against the Varsity. The College boys and their friends are painting the town red tonight, while everything is silent and dark on the campus. The explanation of the unexpected is that College simply had the best team."

Nineteen years later Tom Blake picked up his *Houston Post* and noted that a writer implied that the 1909 A&M eleven was the first to defeat the University. Blake did not vent his spleen on the *Post,* but wrote instead to James Sullivan, business manager of athletics at A&M: "This should be corrected as it is in error. I call your attention to the following facts. The 1902 team was coached by J. E. Platt of Pennsylvania State (earlier identified with Lafayette) and captained by the writer and composed of the following players: Bob DeWare, Jim David, Thomas W. Blake, William Beilharz, Josh Sterns, Miles Carpenter, J. E. Simpson, Asa Neff, E. E. Worthing, Ray Ridenhower, and George Hope.

"I believe in justice to these gentlemen, they should be given credit in the same manner as you have given the other fellows credit, and I am writing this letter in justice to my teammates. The record is that this was the first team which ever scored on the University, was the first team which ever defeated the University and were champions of the Southwest for the year 1902."

The 1903 *Longhorn,* the A&M yearbook that was so named before Varsity decided to label its teams as such, reviewed the 1902 season with plaudits and concluded with this appeal: "Let everyone use all means possible to get new players for the 1903 team, that we may retain our place in football as Champions of the South."

And some people associate recruiting only with the last

half century!

Rivalry with Arkansas and Oklahoma was initiated in 1903, the Farmers breaking even in the interstate battles. Added to its victory over Arkansas were two triumphs over TCU and two conquests of Baylor plus a tie, a parlay over three future SWC foes that A&M was not to achieve again until the national championship year of 1939. Blake repeated as captain in 1903, being the second to double as team chieftain of the Cadets. Hal Moseley was the first (1898 and 1899) followed by Tyree Bell (1912 and 1914) and Monte Moncrief (1944, 1945, and 1946).

Disturbed over a big divergence in player eligibility regulations and playing rules as well, representatives of five Texas colleges met in Waco, March 12, 1904, and formed the Southwest Inter-Collegiate Athletic Association. The colleges were Baylor, Texas A&M, Southwestern, the University of Texas, and Trinity. They were soon joined by Austin College, Fort Worth University, Missouri School of Mines (Rolla), University of Oklahoma, and Washington University (St. Louis). Little enforcement developed out of this organization, and it was replaced in 1909 by the Texas Intercollegiate Athletic Association, which was so large and unwieldy that it could not inspire adequate policing of the membership, nor did it prove as helpful in schedule-making as had been hoped.

Wanted: Final Destination To Resemble College Station

A lady's voice answered when J. B. Sterns' telephone number was dialed in Corpus Christi in a late spring evening in 1973, and she acknowledged, "Yes, I am Mr. Sterns' daughter."

"I realize Mr. Sterns probably is in bed, but I wonder if he would be up to a visit at his convenience sometime tomorrow to talk about Texas A&M football?" the caller asked.

"Papa's in the hospital, and I am going over there shortly to see him. I will check with him and his doctor to see whether he will be feeling up to a visit tomorrow. He will have to be feeling mighty bad to pass up an opportunity to have a visitor who wants to talk about Texas A&M."

Subsequent conversation revealed that the daughter was Mrs. Genevieve Cox, wife of Alex Cox, former track and field captain and Southwest Conference 400-yard dash record holder at The University of Texas. The interviewer (co-author Evans) and Cox were contemporaries in college and had been friends through the years, all of which strengthened the probability of an interview the following morning.

At mid-morning the next day Mrs. Cox called and advised that her father had a good night and that he would be pleased "to sit down and talk" about his playing days at A&M prior to the turn of the century. And sat he did, despite a head cold and a raspy throat that would have been a reasonable excuse for anyone to remain in bed.

"Good to see you," he acknowledged the introduction, then made way for his daughter to sit on the arm of the chair and serve as interpreter. You see, Josh Sterns was virtually deaf after ninety-five years and could tune in few voices other than his daughter's, which has the right pitch and daughterly patience when repetition is necessary.

An apology for the imposition was brushed aside by the man who played his first football almost seventy-nine years earlier with: "Heck, I am glad to have someone to talk to."

"I played rough until some powder puff called my bluff," he recalled when asked for his recollection of the early days.

For the record, there were few who called his bluff, and fewer still of those who dared to call it twice. "My training consisted of running into a brick wall, throwing my body and shoulder into it for a half-an-hour each day." Yet he credits his long life to "letting someone else do the hard work. I chose civil engineering as a vocation and spent most of my life on vacation."

Sterns was born January 15, 1878, in Harris County, "way out in the country, about five miles from the courthouse." He had little schooling at a one-room one-teacher school before his family moved to Houston in 1890, although his father did retain a tutor for him, his brothers and sisters on a part-time basis. As a twelve-year old he was enrolled in the fourth grade at Houston, but he quit school four years later and never made it to high school.

"I wasn't interested in high school," he recalled seventy-nine years later. So, at the age of sixteen he went to College Station, passed the entrance exam, and got himself a job in the laundry. That was the fall of 1894, and A&M was fielding an organized football team for the first time.

"We had to get a written permit from our parents to go out for the team," Sterns remembered. "And what with practicing football after supper and doing too much visiting at other times, I didn't make very good grades."

He did make the grade as a player in 1896, however, as the starting right end and held down the same spot in 1897 while serving as captain.

"In those days we had to do more than just play. We had to raise money for the visiting team to help them defray their expenses. A few days before a team came we would pass the hat through the dormitories and collect enough money to wire it to the teams to cover its transportation expenses. On the day of the game we placed students at the entrance to the college grounds to solicit change from visitors who said they had come to see the game. This was before automobiles, and nearly all of the spectators lived within ten miles and came in buggies.

"The gatekeepers would turn their take over to me. I would pay all of the bills, then after the game expenses had been determined, the net was split with sixty percent going to the winner and forty percent to the loser. I did not have to report to anyone, and some of the guys thought I was using this as a racket to work my way through school."

It was not always a financial success, however, as Sterns grimaced about one of the experiences on the road. "We were told that our transportation would be reimbursed after the game. There was no split after the game, but we were told the money would be paid the following morning. That night they really took us to the cleaners. They stripped our uniforms of our insignia, then told us the next morning they could not pay us because they had to pay off a loan at the bank.

"I am reminded of another unpleasant experience on the road," he interjected. "I don't remember where it was, but someone had put up sheet iron on the fences to keep people from getting a free look at the game. But when we got down near their goal, students or some of their fans started hammering that sheet iron with rocks and sticks. That was before teams huddled for signals. We couldn't hear the signals and couldn't stop the racket."

An injury in the 1897 season forced Sterns to drop from school, and he did not graduate with the Class of 1899, although his Golden Circle certificate identifies him with that class. After three years out of school, he returned in the fall of 1902, played another outstanding season of football, then received his degree in Civil Engineering in June, 1903.

When he advanced to the stage to receive his diploma, the corps gave him a big hand, a demonstration that he probably appreciated as much as the certificate. There is not a single building standing that was there when Sterns played football, but his training tactics of running into brick walls did not bring condemnation to any of them.

Sterns became a highly successful civil engineer upon

graduation. He maintains that he had a hand in laying more than 1,000 miles of railroad track in Texas. One of his first projects was supervision of laying the Missouri Pacific track from Alice to Brownsville in 1903. Later he directed the Santa Fe railway construction in East Texas and insists that he pushed the railroad forward to meet a girl he had heard about but had not seen. That girl, Ethel Stone, who lived in Jasper, was to be his wife for 65 years. He also built sections of railroads for Southern Pacific and for Texas and New Orleans (T and NO) Railways.

At ninety-five he acknowledged a full life yet admitted, "I wasted a lot of years during the depression, when I got trapped in Louisiana and couldn't get back to Texas."

In 1963 Sterns conceived an idea for a project that proved to be a rewarding hobby for him and an incalculable treasure for the Association of Former Students. Shortly after learning that Texas A&M College was to be changed to Texas A&M University, he started the ambitious undertaking of collecting a senior class ring from a graduate of every class from the Class of 1899, the first to wear the famed Aggie ring, through the Class of 1964. He received little encouragement on the idea until 1967, when Thomas H. Clement of Wichita Falls and Thomas W. Griffiths of Dallas, both of the Class of 1900, gave him encouragement. Numerous Aggies contributed a total of $1,500 toward expenses incurred in completing the project.

During a 3-year period Sterns wrote more than 4,000 letters, and with some financial assistance he had collected 54 rings when he turned the project over to the Association for completion. "Most Aggies would rather give you their left leg than part with their ring," Sterns reminded you. Yet included in the collection are the rings of distinguished business men, military heroes, widows, and athletic personalities. Sterns pridefully pointed to such donors as Ernest D. Brockett, Chairman of the Board of the Gulf Oil Corporation; Wilburn T. Askew, Vice President of Sun Oil Company; and Gene Stallings, football star of the 1956 championship football team and later head coach of A&M's next championship team in 1967.

One of the rings was contributed by Mrs. Marion Price Garrison, daughter of W. A. Price, Class of 1905. "We will be

Josh Sterns' Aggie Ring Collection
Admiring the famed Aggie ring collection, now on display at the office of The Association of Former Students, are, left to right: Richard (Buck) Weirus, Executive Director of the organization; Josh Sterns, the pioneer player who conceived the idea of the collection; and Ernest Langford, longtime Texas A&M Archivist.

most happy to donate my father's class ring to this collection. I think Dad would be most pleased to have something of his at A&M. His heart was always at A&M."

The collection was placed in a display case designed and built by the L. G. Balfour Company, which was presented by Martin Hamilton and Willard Clark, Class of 1942. Each ring is mounted on maroon velvet and white satin with the donor's name etched on a gold plate.

Always a good speller and blessed with a good vocabulary, and a good sense of humor, Sterns amused himself in his later years by writing poetry. He estimated that he had composed more than four hundred couplets, most of them about things he loved: his daughter, his two grandsons, and Texas A&M. One that expressed his love for his alma mater:

"When I reach my final destination,
I hope it resembles College Station."

Kyle Field:
Named For Whom?

Kyle Field. Is it named for J. Allen Kyle, M.D., 1890, or Edwin J. Kyle, Ph.D., 1899?

For over a half century that question was argued, but it was not until April 28, 1956, that the Board of Directors of Texas A&M University decided that Kyle Field had been named in honor of Edwin Jackson Kyle, Dean of the College of Agriculture, 1911-1944, and lifelong worker in the interests of athletics at Texas A&M.

That action ended a long and arduous campaign by friends of Dean Kyle to have the Board of Directors decree that Kyle Field had been named for him.

The other side, backing J. Allen Kyle, argued that since he had been a member of the Board of Directors of Texas A&M from 1910-1914, it was most likely that the Board had honored him by naming Kyle Field for him. Yet, there was no record of such action in the minutes of the Board; now, however, there is in the case of Dean E. J. Kyle.

So strong do some of the J. Allen Kyle backers feel on the subject that at least one wrote in to ask that his membership in the T Association be cancelled; that his T card be cancelled and that his name be removed from all letterman mailing lists in the Athletic Department. His request was granted.

But let us look at the whole question.

Most of the early football games were played on the drill field at Texas A&M, where spectators simply stood or sat in carriages around the playing field. Some games were played in

Bryan at the Fair Grounds which was blessed with a grandstand.

On November 10, 1904, the Board of Directors set aside an area of the campus as a permanent athletic field. At that time E. J. Kyle was serving as chairman of the Athletic Council. He first had an area of some agricultural land under his jurisdiction fenced off with a barbed-wire fence, soon to be replaced with a wooden fence. According to Kyle, before he became Dean of the College of Agriculture some lumber was purchased for wooden bleachers to be built on the football field. In addition, the covered grandstand at the Bryan Fair Grounds was purchased. Since the Athletic Department had no money, Kyle gave his personal note to cover the transaction. The stadium provided seating for about five hundred people.

Work on the stadium was completed during the football season. The *Longhorn* for that year depicts the last game played on the drill field and the first on the new field. The editor boasted about the new facility which he said was beyond doubt the best athletic field in the State. "The fence encloses 250,000 square feet, and the bleachers with seating capacity of 500 has been erected."

The athletic field soon became known as Kyle Field, but as time passed considerable confusion existed over the origin of the name. Was it in honor of Edwin Jackson Kyle, Dean of Agriculture between 1911 and 1944, and chairman of the Athletic Council 1904-1911, 1932-34, and 1937-44? Or was it named for Dr. J. Allen Kyle, a member of the Board of Directors 1911-1914? While still unresolved the Board of Directors hopefully closed the question by its action in designating Kyle Field as being named in honor of Dean E. J. Kyle.

The great 1924 winning season started a drive to increase the seating capacity of the stadium. The fund raising fell flat, however, and it was not until 1927 that the university decided to rebuild the stadium. The sale of revenue bonds was to underwrite the cost, and it was these bonds, plus those of the 1929 stadium expansion, that caused Matty Bell and Homer Norton many a headache.

The first expansion of 5 sections of the present stadium was completed in 1927 at a cost of $76,718.84. The second expansion came in 1929 when 16 sections were

Kyle Field as it looked in 1911
Kyle Field as it looks today

finished at a cost of $259,693.68, and it took Homer Norton until 1940 to pay off all of the bonded indebtedness on Kyle Field.

Next expansion was an upper deck at a cost of $346,000. This raised the seating capacity to 35,000, and in 1969 the present structure seating 49,000 was finished at a cost of $1,840,000. Since then an artificial turf and tartan track have been added to the Kyle Field complex.

And lest there be any questions—Kyle Field is named in honor of Edwin J. Kyle, Dean of the College of Agriculture 1911-1944. So the Board of Directors has decreed.

Big Little Man: So Much For So Many So Long

The heavyset, ungainly little guard was so badly bruised he could hardly move when he went to bed that night. Equally as torturing was the fact that he could not sleep.

"Something happened to me while I was awake," he was to recall sixty-nine years later. "I talked to myself and asked: Are you a yellow kid with no guts, no fight?"

Joe Utay had played company football as a freshman along with Charley Richenstein, his high school buddy from Dallas Bryan, and Choc Kelley on a championship team the previous year. Kelley and Richenstein had been invited to try for the Varsity, but the latter would not report unless Joe, too, received a bid.

So, Coach W. E. Bachman invited the 5-7, 190-pound guard. "I was put at one end on the field to return punts, and Charlie DeWare and others were sent down to tackle me and to punish me. I could hardly make it to the dormitory after practice."

The day following his night of torture Utay went back to practice, much to the surprise of his coach who placed him at halfback. Utay was to letter for three seasons, serve as captain in 1907, and play sixty minutes of every game but one.

The LSU game in his junior year is the most vivid and most pleasant in his memory. "We had beaten Tulane, 18-0, in New Orleans and went on up to Baton Rouge on the train. Our special car was put on a siding, and we stayed on it since we did not have enough money to check into a hotel. I remember we

Joe Utay: A pioneer player
Joe Utay: A pioneer bowl man

were given a quarter for breakfast and a dollar for the other two meals."

LSU was defeated, 22-12, as Utay, who had tremendous balance in his ability to run low, Jim Ross, an Indian, and Jim Flenchem, a big fullback, led the charge. Flenchem, incidentally, sent along get-well wishes recently when the eighty-seven year old Utay went into the hospital for a "check-up I had put off for about ten years."

Utay never experienced the joy of being on the winning side against Varsity, but for a few minutes in a second 1907 game he thought his dream had come true after the two teams had played to a scoreless tie in Dallas. Texas had taken the lead by setting up a touchdown through recovery of an A&M fumble of a Longhorn kick, but failed to add the extra point. So when Texas fumbled a punt near its own goal, Charlie DeWare covered for the Aggies, and Louis Hamilton crashed his way across and kicked the extra point to put the Farmers in front, 6-5.

Later, Choc Kelley attempted a pass from his own territory, and Fred Ramsdell, the famed Texas sprinter, picked it off and ran it back forty yards for a touchdown, and the Longhorns prevailed, 11-6.

"How did the players of your era compare with the super stars of today?"

"They were physically stronger than our players of today and had greater stamina. They could play sixty minutes of football, and most of them did, because substitutions generally were made only for the injured. Our players had greater strength in their legs, because they did not have automobiles to ride in. They did a lot more walking. Yet the boys who graduate from high school now may know football better than we did when we graduated from college."

After graduation from A&M, Utay attended Cumberland Law School and finished in 1912. Charley Moran was coaching with great success at A&M and was entering his fourth season in the dual role of athletic director and head coach. Texas had severed its relations with A&M after the 1911 meeting in Houston, and Hal Moseley, representing the school administration, approached Utay relative to taking over the athletic directorship for one year. Moseley had been instrumental in

Moran going to A&M, having played semi-pro ball for him. Utay accepted for one year and one year only and also agreed to coach the freshman football team.

"The only time Charley and I crossed that season was prior to the Baylor game in Dallas on Thanksgiving Day. Ben Dyer had been assigned to the game as referee, but Moran had become upset over the official's work in a prior game and demanded a replacement," Utay recalled. Dyer refereed the game.

Utay and Moseley were not official representatives of A&M in later sessions with L. Theo Bellmont and W. T. Mather of the University of Texas concerning the formation of the Southwest Conference, yet they were interested in helping with the healing process of the relations between the two state schools, a must if the Southwest Conference was to be organized. "One of our highly-secretive sessions with all shades and drapes drawn lasted practically all night in Dr. Mather's home in Austin," Utay acknowledged.

"A&M held out for a home-and-home series, if relations were to be resumed, the first of which had to be played at College Station," Utay pointed out. The two teams had never met at College Station, and the Longhorns were duly warned that it would be a long time before they would win there. They were not to win there until 1923 and were not to score on Kyle Field until the fifth meeting there that same year.

Once the Conference was organized Texas and A&M were scheduled to play on Kyle Field in 1915. "When Hal and I went to College Station for the game, we were warned we would be tarred-and-feathered, because the football squad thought we had sold out Moran. Moran had been dismissed after the 1914 season, but we had assured Texas representatives all along there was no assurance that he would be fired.

"I had been coach of the freshman team that was now the senior team, and Johnny Garrity, the 1915 captain, had been my freshman captain. He finally convinced the players that Hal and I had not been responsible for Moran's dismissal; so there was no tar-and-feathers."

In his *Football–Texas Style* Kern Tips wrote thusly of Utay: "He typifies the breed of men on whom football took a firm and lasting grip, vaccinated them with a virus that has kept

Charles DeWare, Sr.: First of two-generation captains

them dedicated to the game's growth and development. His continuing interest in the Aggies never flagged, but more than that, he exercised an influence on the broad shape of Southwestern football, as an early visionary in the field of the postseason spectacular, as an advocate of the game for the game's sake."

And George White, who wrote sports for the *Dallas Morning News* through most of Utay's involvement in officiating and with postseason attractions reminded: "While others espouse on the great records of coaches and all-America performances of players, some space must be due the little Aggie who has done as much or more for Southwestern football over the years than any other man—a wholly legitimate Texas Sports Hall of Famer overlooked to date."

He has not been overlooked by the National Football Foundation, however. He was named to the National Football Hall of Fame in 1974, the first pioneer player from the Southwest to be recognized.

Utay was one of this section's leading football officials for more than a quarter of a century, 1912-1938, and with Charlie Braun, Lionel Moise, and Burton Rix he organized the Southwest Football Officials Association and served as its president for 19 years. The association now numbers 3,200 members. He refereed for the Conference in intra-conference and intersectional games through the years, and was a perennial in the Arkansas-LSU series at Shreveport for a number of years.

One of his more memorable experiences occurred there while Huey Long was serving as governor of Louisiana. Exhibitionist that he was, Long was serving the LSU team as waterboy on this particular occasion and would communicate with the players. Utay moved in close enough to convince himself that the governor was transmitting instructions to the players; so, he cautioned him to desist. Long ignored him and resumed his conversation with the players.

Tired of warning him, Utay yelled: "You've got sixty seconds to get off this field."

Long thought and hoped he was kidding, but Utay meant it and he marched the governor off the playing field. Later that evening as he sat in his hotel room, Utay reflected on his judgment and was inclined to second-guess himself. About that time his telephone rang, and it was Governor Long calling to apologize and invite him to dinner at the mansion. The two became fast friends thereafter.

Utay's role as promoter of the 1922 Dixie Classic, which was the forerunner of all of the New Year's bowl games in the South, has been mentioned previously. Less than a decade later he promoted three all-star games under the same heading for the Texas Scottish Rite Hospital for Crippled Children. Southwest Conference coaches and players were matched against stars from the Big Six (now the Big Eight) and Big Ten conferences and were directed in order by Ernie Berg (Nebraska), Jimmy Phelan (Indiana), and Bob Zuppke (Illinois). Knute Rockne was scheduled to be one of the coaches in the 1933 game, but his untimely death in a plane crash led to the cancellation of the contest.

Appointed to the A&M Board of Directors in 1935 by Governor James V. Allred, Utay served as chairman of the athletic committee of the board from 1935-41 and promoted scheduling of intersectional games that restored solvency to the athletic department as Homer Norton led the Aggies to national supremacy.

Utay teamed with the late Dan Rogers in fighting against private ownership of the Cotton Bowl Classic and helped to bring it completely under control of the Conference. At eighty-seven he was still active as an attorney and as a member of the Cotton Bowl Athletic Association Board of Directors.

Three In A Row Over Varsity Spiced Uncle Charley's Stay

A&M had compiled a 37-9-4 record over a six-season span under three different coaches when the 1908 calendars were hung. Not a bad record, for it was to compare favorably with the six best strings of Charley Moran (38-8-4) and Dana X. Bible (40-9-3) within a score of seasons. The trend changed sharply, however, in 1908, when H. A. Merriam guided the Cadets to a disheartening 3-5-0 record. It was the first losing season since 1901s 1-4-0.

One other factor in common with the 1901 campaign was the double-setback by Varsity, in Houston, 24-8, and in Austin, 28-12. The Monday game in Houston was a feature attraction of the No-Tsu-Oh (Houston spelled backwards) Carnival in the West End Park.

Texas had grabbed a 14-0 lead by half time when some of its 1,200 students who made the trip paraded on the field with brooms fixed to their shoulders like rifles. A group of Cadets incensed by the inference cleared the fence surrounding the playing field, and a battle that was to become typical of this Carnival was under way.

A&M managed a pair of four-point field goals by Louie Hamilton in the second half, but Texas still added a couple of points to its final margin. The Thanksgiving Day game in Austin started quite auspiciously for the Farmers. They led, 12-0, at half time, counting all of their points on field goals by Hamilton that measured 33, 20, and 47 yards. Varsity took charge in the second half, however, and dominated the game. A&M's cause was lost after the injury of two key players.

Merriam started the 1909 season as head coach, having acquired Moran from the professional Massillon Tigers as his assistant. A&M opened with a victory over Austin College, 17-0, but then was tied by TCU in a scoreless duel.

Later, Caesar (Dutch) Hohn, a sophomore headed for all T.I.A.A. honors at three different positions, had this to say of the impending coaching change in his *Dutchman on the Brazos*: "A clamor went up immediately for his hide. By nightfall the student body had raised enough money to pay off Merriam; he left promptly and Moran was named to replace him."

When a member of the A&M faculty inquired of Moran whether he was teaching his boys to be good losers, the ambitious young coach was quick to counter: "Hell, I didn't come here to lose."

And he stuck by his vow. His Farmers did not lose another game that season, and the decisions that were to warm the hearts of his new followers were a pair of victories over Varsity within the span of a month. Moran proved himself a good "recruiter" from the start. When he arrived at College Station in 1909, he brought along Victor (Choc) Kelley, the Choctaw Indian who had gravitated to the Carlisle Indians after three seasons in the A&M backfield with Joe Utay, and Mike Balenti, who had quarterbacked Pop Warner's Carlisle team in 1908.

The newcomer and the homecomer were to play major roles in A&M's welcomed success, but there were veterans of equal stature in Hamilton, a hero in the two conquests of Texas (one on a ninety-yard run), Scott Moore, Roger Hooker, Bill Parker, J. C. Cretcher, and Hohn, who in successive seasons was to play guard, tackle, and end. Hohn was destined for A&M's Athletic Hall of Fame, as were Tyree Bell, who became a Moran disciple in 1910, and J. W. (Dough) Rollins, who played the first of his three varsity seasons under Moran.

Hohn and Charles DeWare, who preceded him by four seasons, were to be honored in 1969, the Centennial Year of Collegiate Football, on the all-Southwest team for the first half-century of the sport, as tackle and end, respectively. Hamilton; Kelley; Floyd (Jim) Crow, a 1914 tackle; Johnny Pierce, a 1918 center; and Jack Mahan, fullback 1917-1920, were Aggies named to the second team for that fifty year era

Major General James Earl Rudder, World War II hero and president of Texas A&M at the time, presents Hall of Fame plaque to Tyree Bell, the 1912 and 1914 Aggie captain, at the 1965 enshrinement ceremonies. General Rudder was enshrined in 1970, shortly before his death.

(1869-1918).

    Moran had run his string of head-coaching triumphs to 10 in 1910 when Arkansas surprised at Fayetteville in late October. A&M rebounded against TCU but was the underdog going into its annual Monday game with Texas in Houston, because most of the stars of the 1909 battles had departed. The Farmers continued their mastery over Varsity, as Moran increased his string to 3, by a 14-8 score.

    Actually, Moran's only loss to the Longhorns did not come until late in the 1911 season. The Aggies were riding another skein of eight, including conquests of mighty Auburn and Ole

Miss, when they squared off for what was to be Moran's last fling against Texas. Officials of the rival schools had become increasingly aware of the No-Tsu-Oh Carnival attraction that appeared to encourage a hostile atmosphere. They agreed that joint efforts would be made to forestall an outbreak like the one that marred the 1908 meeting. Since such a problem is more likely to develop when the teams are evenly-matched, there seemed less likelihood on this occasion, because A&M was a solid favorite. The Farmers had been unscored on for the season.

Still student spirit was running high on both campuses. A&M, naturally, was expressing delight over Moran's domination of the series, while TU resentment of the turn of the tide was expressed succinctly in this bit of verse:

"To hell, to hell with Charley Moran
And all his dirty crew.
If you don't like the words of this song,
To hell, to hell with you."

A&M threatened early on a 55-yard scamper but was denied touchdown territory by stubborn Longhorn end play. In the second quarter a Varsity punt died on the Farmers' 15-yard line. An A&M back fumbled on a stab at the line, and the ball bounded free toward the Farmers' goal. George (Stud) Barnes, the A&M center, had a shot at it, but Arnold Kirkpatrick, the Texas punter who some insist fouled Barnes in the fight for possession, picked up the ball and stumbled the final yards across the goal with Barnes hanging on to no avail.

That was the only touchdown of the game, and Texas emerged a 6-0 victor on the highly controversial play. There were few incidents among the fans following the game, but the traditional downtown parade following the game was cancelled.

The following day the Athletic Department at Texas A&M received this message from Dr. W. T. Mather, chairman of the University of Texas Athletic Council: "I beg to inform you that the Athletic Council of the University of Texas has decided not to enter in athletic relations with the Agricultural and Mechanical College of Texas for the year 1912."

No reason for the break in relations was cited, but after speculative reports appeared in print Dr. Mather issued this statement:

A scene at the depot in 1911 as students and fans await their returning heroes

"The Athletic Council of the University of Texas greatly deplores the statement of charges in the press purporting to come from semi-official sources. The action taken was based on the belief that in view of the heated state of opinion among students and alumni of both institutions, it was the wisest course to pursue."

Relations were not to be restored until the 1915 calendar year, but A&M was to continue its success under Moran through two of the three subsequent seasons. A&M lost only to Kansas A&M (now State) in 1912, when Bell was serving the first of two seasons as captain. The Farmers had their Kansas counterparts beaten, 10-7, with only two minutes of play remaining. A flat zone pass was attempted from the Farmers' twenty-yard line, and it was intercepted and run back for a score and 13-10 triumph.

Maybe the Farmers would have caught him, if the field had not been reduced in length from 110 yards to 100 yards for that season. The TD value reached 6 that year, and the fourth down was added, both changes of which A&M exploited in counting its all-time scoring record for a single season: 366 points in 9 games.

The 1913 campaign (3-4-2) was Moran's only losing season at A&M. Bell sat out that campaign. After winning their first three tests, the Farmers dropped four in a row without scoring a point, then closed in ties with Baylor (14-14) and LSU (7-7). There was a recovery in 1914, when the only loss was to Haskell, but further along these pages Dough Rollins will recall the sensational LSU game that highlighted the year and later was featured by Robert Ripley's "Believe It or Not."

Gig 'Em! Charley Moran

Among men who have coached college football a decade or more since Rutgers and Princeton inaugurated the sport in 1869, only 15 have compiled a higher winning percentage than Charley Moran posted in his 18 seasons at the helm. Only 5 of those who rank ahead of him have coached any within the last quarter of a century, the quintet being Frank Leahy, General Bob Neyland, Bud Wilkinson, Bob Devaney, and Frank Kush. Neyland played as a scrub under Moran at A&M before going on to stardom at West Point.

Despite that stature, or perhaps because of the manner in which it was achieved, Moran is one of the most controversial coaches in collegiate history. Success followed him wherever he functioned, and the groundwork for his historic coaching career was laid on the hallowed soil of Kyle Field, which was the laboratory on occasion for three other coaches who have been named to the National Football Hall of Fame and for another headed for that acclaim.

The three who have gained the recognition that has eluded Uncle Charley are Dana X. Bible, Matty Bell, and Homer Norton, who served A&M in that order. Paul Bryant is destined for that honor.

It is not the objective in these pages to prove Moran worthy of the honor nor to discredit his credentials. The purpose is to provide an insight into the extraordinary personality through observations, with an emphasis on those who knew him best: the players.

To those who evaluate man's contributions to humanity, Charley Moran has to be a paradox: an idol to those who are convinced he contributed so greatly to them and to their school; an enigma to those who are aware of his great work yet are confused by his interpretation of ethics and his premium on winning.

In his *Football—Texas Style* Kern Tips termed Moran "a catalyst in the chemistry of an oft-remarked tradition of the closely knit fraternity of this military school; this brotherhood was a thing-in-being when he arrived, a more articulate thing when he left."

Whatever he was, he was more than a winning coach. He posted a 38-8-4 record for his 6 seasons at A&M, the best percentage ever achieved there. His overall won-lost-tied record for 18 seasons is 122-33-12, a percentage of .766. He was popular with the players, with the students, and with the alumni, and inspired an extraordinary amount of pride in his players while earning a warm niche in most of their hearts.

Dutch Hohn, who contributed an illustrious career in both football and baseball under the tutelage of Moran and later served him as an assistant coach, appraised his tutor thusly in his *Dutchman on the Brazos*: "Moran was as tough as they come...I've heard of rough-talking coaches who've alienated their athletes. In the old days some of these football coaches were even knocked down on the practice field by irate players, so the stories go. I don't think any of these coaches could have outdone Charley Moran when it came to getting after his players; yet Moran probably was the most popular man on the campus—with the entire Cadet Corps, not just the teams he coached."

Hohn named his only son for the coach, and in writing his book he appeared determined to paint a true picture of Moran, to tell it like it was, yet he reached that point of concern that he might have clouded the picture and wrote: "I hope you do not get a bad impression of my friend Moran as a result of my telling things just as they were; I hope you do not go so far to agree with the people at Texas University who refused to play us until Moran was replaced and in the process all but sent our Athletic Department into bankruptcy. He was tough, he wanted to win—perhaps too much—but he had some good points too."

Charley Moran: Idol to some...enigma to others

Dough Rollins played only his sophomore season under Moran, but he had been in school earlier and had some exposure to the coach and his players. "I want to say this about Coach Moran," Rollins was to reflect on nearly 60 years later. "He believed that if football was properly played, it was a rough game. And if you were going to play a rough game, you had to give 100 percent and had to be in condition to play. In those days you played both ways, and he had the ability to make you want to play that rough game of football.

"Oh, how he worked us. Our average workout consisted of 30 minutes of blocking and tackling every day, then we would scrimmage for about an hour and a half. When we finished scrimmaging, we took 2 or 3 laps around the track.

"Moran brought hard-nosed football to Texas, but he had the biggest heart you ever saw. He took those old country boys and made them love him and football."

The rules concerning eligibility were quite liberal in Moran's time at A&M, and players could come in and play without a great deal of check on their identity. Transfers were frequent and "ringers" occasional because of the laxity in administration of athletics.

In Hohn's *Dutchman on the Brazos* he wrote of two interesting situations: "I think I should record here an earlier venture into progressive football. It was in 1909, when Coach Moran—who had started that season as assistant to Merriam, you know—imported four new teammates of questionable athletic pedigree. But they were fine players. In those days, as I remember, the only requirement for ability to represent a college was that the student must have been attending classes for one day prior to the game in which he played. The Texas colleges were soon to tighten this rule, largely because of the generous use Charley Moran made of its liberal possibilities."

His report of another situation in 1909 in the same book: "The second game with Texas did indeed prove to be closer than the first one, as Moran had feared, and the coach was set to unleash our Tiger, from Massillon, on the Texas team. But just as 'Mr. Ford' was warming up along the sideline, E. J. Kyle, chairman of the A&M Athletic Council, hurried down to Moran and used a few well-chosen words, the exact tenor of which I never knew. I only knew that instead of going into the fray 'Mr. Ford' went to the showers. Needless to say, he left school shortly thereafter. I am not even sure he returned to College Station with the team.

"...The next day Moran's four 'students' who'd played so well against Texas departed the campus, as I recall, and I don't think they returned that year—certainly not for final examinations, anyway."

In December of that year Moran either resigned or the A&M administration failed to renew his contract, dependent on who gives the account. But whatever version you choose, Moran continued to be a hero to many who call College Station home.

The Corps honored him with a full-dress parade the day he left the campus. There was a Charley Moran Day in 1938, and in 1948 the Class of 1913 elected him an honorary member of its class at its thirty-fifth reunion. Still another Charley Moran Day was planned for 1949, but his death altered the observance. Still twenty-five members of teams he coached were guests at the Texas-Texas A&M game, as was his granddaughter Ann. He was named to the A&M Athletic Hall of Fame in 1968.

When he left A&M, Moran returned to professional football, thence to Centre College as an assistant coach in 1918 and moved up to the head job in 1919, and brought his famed Praying Colonels to Dallas to meet A&M in the 1922 Dixie Classic. He moved on to Bucknell for three seasons, thence to Catawba for four more years of college coaching, then devoted full time as an umpire in the National Baseball League, where he worked off season from 1917. He had umpired earlier in the Texas League. He continued in that profession until 1939 and during that span was a contemporary of Ernie Quigley, famed as an official in both baseball and football. Moran umpired in the World Series of 1927, 1929, 1933, and 1938.

Varsity Finally Shows At Kyle Field

Inspired by the guidelines established in the founding of the Southwest Intercollegiate Athletic Conference in December, 1914, at Houston, A&M administrators were determined that proper administration of athletics would be given top priority in finding a replacement for Charley Moran. It was this objective that led to the selection of William L. Driver, who had been head coach and athletic director at Ole Miss the two previous years, and athletic director. A&M had closed out its 1914 season with a victory over Driver's team at Dallas.

Driver did not want the football coaching job and accepted the post of athletic director with the understanding that his plan of reorganization would be implemented. It was his belief that physical education should be as much a part of college athletics as intercollegiate sports and that athletics should be taught in the classroom as well as on the field. He also agreed to serve as head basketball coach.

On Driver's recommendation E. H. (Jigger) Harlan was lured from the University of Pittsburgh staff to serve as head football coach, and D. V. (Tubby) Graves, who had been head coach at Alabama the four previous seasons, was hired as assistant football coach and head baseball coach. Graves and Driver had been teammates at Missouri. Somewhere through the years Graves picked up the nickname, but he chose to be identified by his initials, which is understandable when you realize they stood for Dorset Vandeventer.

Graves later migrated to the University of Washington,

where his stature as athletic director and coach was recognized by naming the baseball field in his honor. Jim Owens, a former assistant coach at A&M, is the head coach there, succeeding Darrell Royal, whose selection at Texas was enhanced by Graves' recommendation to D. X. Bible, his old friend and colleague.

Dough Rollins, one of the veterans left over from the Moran regime, remembers that Harlan had "one of the sharpest football minds I've been around, and he was a great teacher of punting." Harlan had been all-American at Princeton, where he had been a great kicker. At A&M he was to inherit Warren (Rip) Collins, destined to be perhaps the greatest punter in Southwest Conference history.

A&M (5-1) and Texas (6-1) had comparable records going into their 1915 resumption of football relations, yet their performance against Rice, the only common opponent, was poles apart. Just two weeks previous the Aggies had been shut out 7-0 by the team Texas had mauled, 59-0, in its SWC debut. Texas, of course, was an overwhelming favorite, and for the first time in history was to play a football game at Kyle Field. Home-and-home competition had been an A&M requisite on the resurrection of the rivalry, and the game was switched from San Antonio, where Texas hoped it would be played.

Rip Collins' remarkable punting and A&M's fierce, inspired defensive play generally are recognized as the physical factors that proved the oddsmakers wrong, but Rollins thinks a large part of the credit should go to Moran. The controversial coach of the six previous seasons "wrote every player on the squad from his home at Horse Cave, Kentucky, and urged them 'to beat those people from Austin.'"

Rollins recalls that Moran challenged each player with: "If you still love me and think anything of me, then beat Texas." And Rollins thinks the message had a tremendous impact, because "most of our players were so fired up they cried through much of the game in their dogged determination... Texas had a great team and we had an ordinary one. However, Rip Collins' punting exhibition was the greatest I have seen. We kicked a lot on first down, then held Texas and forced a lot of fumbling." And leaders of teams that Texas had refused to play since 1911 also were on hand to prod their successors.

In addition to the power that Collins put into his kicks he had the knack of turning his instep at the instant of contact to propel the ball into a spiral that made it most difficult to field. He punted 23 times that day against the Longhorns, and research statisticians credit him with a 44.6-yard average. Apparently Collins had even more adrenalin pumping than his wild-eyed teammates, because he had something to prove to those in Austin who had not recognized him as a blue chipper and to some who allegedly had maligned him.

Texas lost the ball 12 times on fumbles, a number of them on vain efforts to field Collins' punts. Fumble recoveries set up A&M's first score, a 43-yard field goal by Fanny Coleman, and the game's only touchdown in the third quarter. Captain Johnny Garrity proved himself an outstanding ballhawk and clinched all-Conference end honors despite a lame ankle and cracked ribs. He pounced on one at Texas' 35-yard line in the first period, and when the Longhorn safety fumbled another Collins punt in the third quarter, Garrity picked it up on the Texas 27 and ran it to the 10. Collins carried it across from there and Jim Kendrick added the final point.

Earlier Collins had set up a second field goal by Coleman when he completed a 30-yard pass to the Texas 10. This gave A&M a 6-0 half time lead.

Heroes in addition to those already named included tackles Jim Crow, who was destined for coaching fame at Baylor, and Newt Settegast and guard Nick Braumiller, who was accorded all-Conference honors that season.

Texas won the battle of statistics, gaining 301½ yards to 95½ by the inspired Cadets, but A&M was superior in the air, gaining 76½ overhead while the bewildered Longhorns could complete only 3 of 23 for 14 yards.

The 13-0 upset by Harlan's crowd was to inspire a tradition that was to prevail in 12 of the first 13 meetings of the 2 rivals at Kyle Field. The 1916 A&M annual attempted to tell the magnitude of the memorable conquest in these paragraphs:

"In the life of every individual, every institution, there is one experience, one day that stands out vividly above all other experiences and days in the memory of that person or organization. Certain it is that November 19, 1915, is the day

66

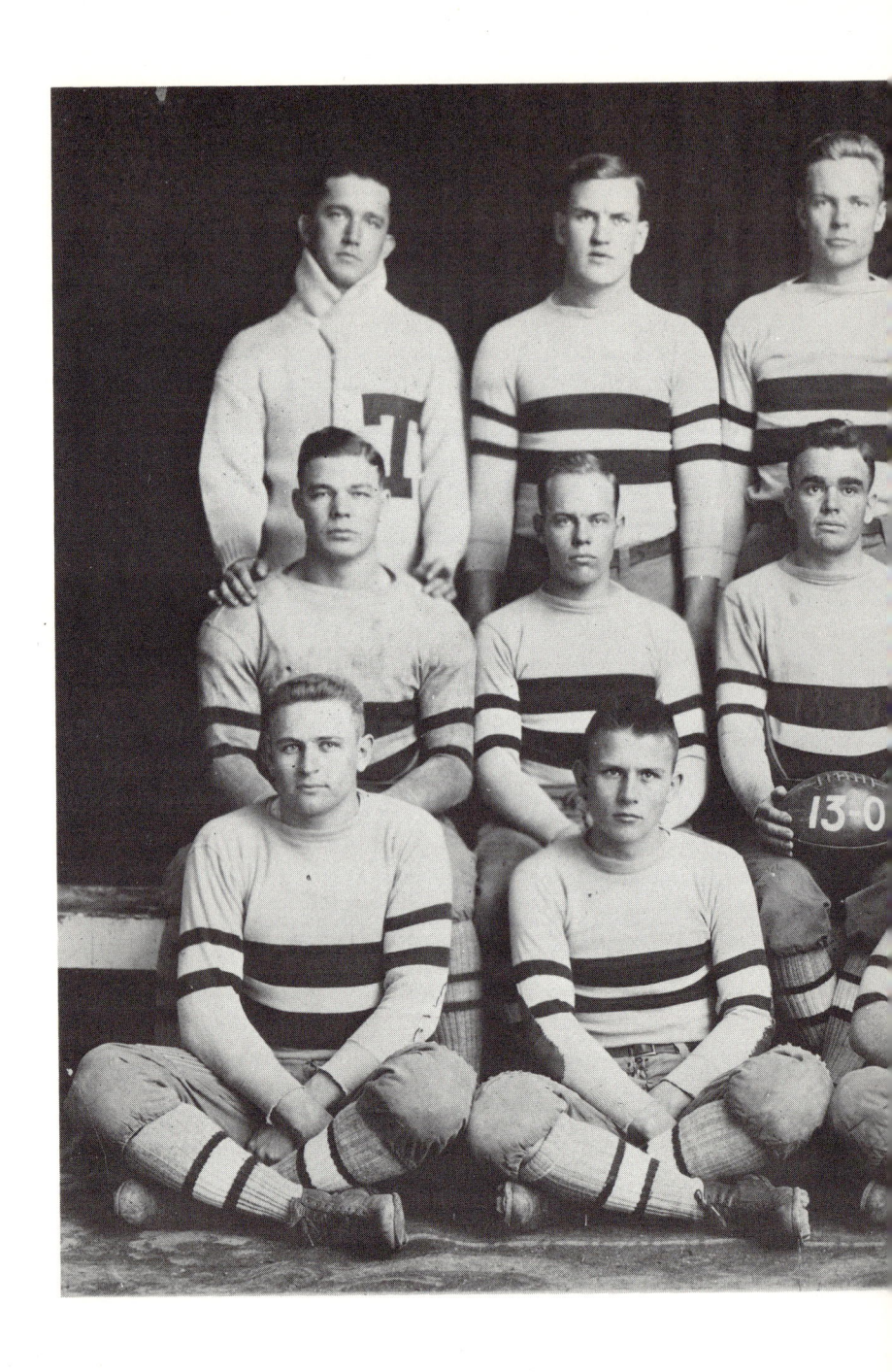

Conference Curtain-Raiser At Kyle Field Memorable: Texas made its first visit to Kyle Field in 1915 in a game that restored relations between the two arch rivals. It also was the first Southwest Conference game played at College Station. A&M scored a shocking 13-0 upset and set a tradition that was to prevail in 12 of the first 13 meetings with Texas on Kyle Field. Aggie lettermen that season were, left to right, first row: W. E. Rylander, Dough Rollins, M. Mitchell, J. M. Kendrick. Second row: Nick Braumiller, D. B. Burns, Captain Johnny Garrity, M. D. Gilfillan, A. C. Eschenburg. Third row: A. C. Bull, manager; M. E. Settegast, J. C. Rogers, F. A. Crow, Rip Collins.

which outranks all other days in minds of cadets and friends of the College. Glad, happy memories run riot, blood flows faster, enthusiasm and loyalty overleap all bounds when they are recalled.

"Certain it is also that our friends, the Enemy, remember it with no less vivid recollections, but certain it is that they taste none of the sweetness which flavors the memories of A&M followers. To them it was a day of defeated hopes, broken pride—and thereby hangs the tale."

Thirteen to nothing was to be a rallying force for the Aggies for years to come, and 13-0 was inscribed wherever it might haunt the followers of the Longhorns. It mattered little that A&M closed its 1915 season the following week in a 7-0 whitewashing by Mississippi State. What really mattered was that a treasured rivalry had been restored and in an atmosphere pleasing to both sides.

Despite the ferocity of battle, the conduct of fans of both teams was on a high plane, a gratifying about-face since the stormy days at the No-Tsu-Oh Carnival games in Houston. Sportsmanship likewise prevailed in the fiery arena, and Garrity, who dared to play though badly injured, and his teammates acknowledged the fact the opposition made no effort to aggravate his injuries.

The Great Score Branded In Bevo's Hide

It commanded little attention in September, 1916, but time was to reveal the addition of Dana X. Bible to the coaching staff by Bill Driver in 1916 a master stroke. While at Ole Miss, Driver had viewed at close range the early and quick development of the young coach at Mississippi College.

Bible's role at A&M was freshman coach, but he remained only half of the season. LSU ran off its head coach in midseason, and an SOS went out to young Bible.

Meanwhile, back at Kyle Field, the Aggies were still blessed with a lot of motivation from the 13-0 conquest of Varsity the previous season. By virtue of a 3-0 victory over Baylor, the Aggies were favorites when they went back to Clark Field in Austin for the first time since a victorious stand in 1909. The overflowing crowd of 15,000 was the biggest that had ever seen a football game in Texas.

Psychology was on the other foot on this occasion, however, with the Longhorns having been haunted by the 13-0 score for a full year. Texas avenged that loss impressively with a 21-7 decision. The outcome scrambled the Conference race to the extent that no team had a just claim to the championship. Four members had lost only a single conference game, and there was no precedent for awarding championships on the basis of winning percentages.

Here are the scores that made it a year without a champion: Texas 21, A&M 7; A&M 3, Baylor 0; Baylor 7, Texas 3; Texas 21, Oklahoma 7.

Bevo's first brand taunted TU fans.

Both Jim Crow and Marion E. (Newt) Settegast were named to the all-Conference teams as tackles, which through the years was to give Settegast an only-one-of-a-kind distinction. He and Marion, Jr., (all-SWC end in 1943) are the only father and son combination ever to gain consensus all-Conference recognition at any member school. Both of the DeWares, Charlie Sr. and Jr., served as captain and made all star teams.

The elder Settegast played under Moran, had a voice in the selection of Bible, and his son played for Homer Norton's Kiddie Korps. Thus, Newt knew intimately three of A&M's four most successful coaches.

"Bible was the finest coach of the three," he recalls, "but I will always have a warm spot in my heart for Charley Moran. He made us play hard, insisted we stay in top condition and chewed out those who didn't. I still remember how he ate us out after Trinity tied us in 1914. But he never encouraged us to play dirty."

Settegast is one old-timer who acknowledges that "the players today are bigger, faster and better than we were." Newt is 6-2 and played at 205. Marion, Jr., made all-SWC as a freshman at 6-3 and 190.

Newt was elected captain of the 1917 team, and when the administration decided to replace Jigger Harlan, Settegast, among others, was asked to make a recommendation to Dr. W. B. Bizzell, the president. "I recommended Bible, who was coming back to the campus after being loaned to LSU in 1916."

But Newt never got to play for Bible. War was declared before the season opened, and he joined the army.

The 1916 Thanksgiving Day meeting between A&M and Texas had been the occasion for Longhorn fans to parade their first Longhorn steer mascot. They decided later that it would be most appropriate to brand the orange-and-white colored animal with the 21-7 score and were making plans to do so as a part of the March 2 observance, the traditional meeting date for TU exes. The word got around, of course, and a group of A&M students decided they would beat the Texas exes to the draw with a branding iron.

Six of them gathered in Waco and drove to Austin for a rendezvous with Abe Bull, who had been student manager of the 1915 A&M team. Bull led them to the mascot's South Austin stall, and they sneaked in, wrestled the animal to the ground, and branded his hide with 13-0, the 1915 game score. Bull's accomplices were Jim Crow and Merlin Mitchell, both of whom played in the two games, Ed Johnson, O. K. Johnson, Carl Braunig, and Hans Rothe.

Legend has it that the name Bevo for the Longhorn mascot was conceived by attempts to alter the brand. The 13 was converted into the letter B, the dash was shaped into the letter E, and V was inserted ahead of the O. Bevo, of course, was the name of a near beer in those days.

In any event Bevo was not much to show after the brand was altered, and it was decided he was not worth his keep. So, Athletic Director L. Theo Bellmont, who had been a Texas leader in restoring relations, decided to have the mascot barbecued. There was a big feed for a gathering of Texas and A&M representatives, including the Aggie branding crew, in Austin, January 20, 1920. Half of the hide was given to each school, A&M being the recipient of the half with the disfigured brand. The head was hung in the UT Athletic Office area, stolen once by SMU students but reclaimed, and in 1943 was reportedly dehorned by A&M students.

Dough Kept Coming Back

When the 15-year-old John Wesley Rollins entered A&M in the fall of 1911, he had never seen a football game. Back at Merit, deep in the heart of the blackest land in Hunt County, Texas, he had attended a three-teacher school and had played a little baseball.

"My dad sent me to A&M with the hope that I would become a doctor," Dough Rollins recalled three score and three years later. "I was to take two years of agriculture, then go to medical school. I had to drop out after the fall semester, however, and go back home to work."

Rollins returned to College Station in 1913 and started playing company football (like intramural) and was well into a second year of it when he caught the eye of Charley Moran. "My roommate and I were playing catch on the edge of the drill field one Saturday morning when Coach Moran and Tyree Bell, who was captain of the A&M team, passed by and watched us for a few minutes.

"Coach Moran told my roommate to back up about 10 yards. 'Can you hit him?' he asked. 'Easy,' I told him, and I did. 'Back up another 10 yards,' Coach said. Finally, when I hit him on the third go-around, Coach said, 'I can use you down on the varsity football field.'

"Coach, I've never played any football except company ball. 'That's fine,' he said. 'I was afraid you were a high school star.' The day before Trinity had tied A&M in a shocking, scoreless upset. I understand he had gotten rid of six or seven players immediately after the game, and he went out to scout the company teams to find replacements."

They had a rule in those days that if the varsity coach asked a company player to come out for the team, he had to report. If he did not, he would not be permitted to play company ball. "So, if I was going to play any more football, it would have to be with the A&M team. He told me to report that afternoon, and worked us from 1 o'clock until dark."

The next opponent was TCU, the following Friday. "Now, here is this country boy who had never played any college football playing three quarters of the game against TCU. I backed up the line on defense and weighed only 155 pounds. I played fullback on offense and threw two touchdown passes with that ole pumpkin football, and we beat them, 40-0. From then on I played in every game on the schedule."

Rollins told us a few pages back about Moran's philosophy and how he inspired his players to condition themselves. "Every morning when the bugle blew first call, the football team reported to the drill field in football shoes and old clothes, and we ran signals up and down the field until breakfast call. And he always managed to have us at the other end of the field; so, we had to sprint from there to the Mess Hall. We were excused from making reveille during the football season.

"We didn't have any such thing as knee and ankle injuries. We walked everywhere we went and we ran a lot. We simply did not have those injuries that are so common today. If you were taken out of a game, you felt like you were disgraced. If taken out, you asked yourself: 'What did I do wrong?' One year I played every minute of every game on the schedule. That was in 1915."

Rollins was playing in only his third game of football when LSU jumped into a 9-7 lead over the Aggies at half time at the State Fair in Dallas. "Coach Moran could get you ready mentally as well as physically," Rollins recalled when he replayed that game. It was Halloween, and Moran must have convinced his players the goblins would get them if they did not turn the game around.

A&M's about-face came with the second half kickoff. "When he lined up to receive the kick," Rollins reminisced, "we put Dudley Everett in the middle. Tyree told us, 'When Everett crosses that LSU goal line, I want everybody to be laying on somebody from LSU.' Everett ran it all the way and the race was on. Everything we tried thereafter turned out right."

That second half performance still ranks as one of the greatest ever by an A&M team. Everett ran for three touchdowns and passed for another and shared the spotlight with Bell, Johnny Garrity, and Rollins, who ran an interception back 65 yards for a score. It was Everett, however, who inspired the most ink. The *Dallas Morning News* writer praised him thusly: "Everett was one of the best who ever played in the backfield of a Texas eleven."

Rollins, destined to gain fame as a football coach at both A&M and East Texas State, credits Moran with "trying to teach me some football" in his baptismal season of 1914. "He made me sit in with the quarterbacks. And later in that LSU game he sent in word for me to move to quarterback. We wound up on the LSU 20-yard line on fourth down, and I did not know what to call. So, I kicked a field goal. Bell was in the game, of course, and he was our regular kicker.

"After the game, Coach asked me why I kicked a field goal with the score one-sided like it was. He wanted to know why I didn't try something else. I told him that I didn't know, that I just grabbed something out of the bag. 'But why did you kick it with Tyree Bell in there?' Coach asked. I got that from the quarterbacks meeting. You told the quarterbacks to give the ball under such circumstances to the man they had the most confidence in, and that's what I did. 'Well, I can't go with that,' Coach said."

Rollins had exposure to both Moran and Dana X. Bible as a player, and he feels indebted to both of them and also to Homer Norton, with whom he worked closely as an assistant coach at A&M for seven seasons. Dough did not play under Bible, who was brought to A&M as a freshman coach in 1916, Rollins' senior season, but "I spent a lot of time with D. X. before he left in midseason to finish the year as head coach at LSU. He was a tutor for the freshmen, especially in math, in addition to coaching. He was a bachelor and lived at the YMCA right across the street from our dormitory. He would stick his head out the window and yell: 'Let's talk a little football.' And over I would go to pick his brain.

J. A. (Dough) Rollins: Player, coach, and administrator

"In later years he was very considerate and gracious to me. He would ask me to come back to the campus and observe practices and games. I spent a week with the team before the 1919 game with Texas. There's never been a finer man than D. X. Bible, a great coach but just as great as an individual. He had an influence on, oh, nobody knows how many youngsters. Everybody who ever played for him wanted to coach like him. Even wanted to talk like him. Bob Berry (Class of 1926) and a lot of his boys smacked their lips just like him when they talked."

Rollins captained the 1916 Aggies and a few months later "my class in 1917 marched out as a body and went to war." For the record, those famed seniors took the oath as second lieutenants under the spreading oaks at Leon Springs in the first Officers Training Camp. Rollins received his B.S. degree in agriculture along with his bars. He advanced to the rank of captain after service in France, Belgium, and Germany.

Eighteen years later he returned to the campus as an assistant coach to Homer Norton in 1935. He was to serve as end coach during that 1939-41 span when the Aggies put together three championships in a row, leading off with the national title in 1939, and to work with Norton again after World War II service. Rollins had attained the rank of colonel in the Infantry.

"Coach Norton has to be the hardest working man I've had anything to do with," Rollins appraises today. "He lived and dreamed football. His life was football. We started the first day of September meeting every night, and we kept meeting every night until Thanksgiving.

"And don't overlook Bill James," he reminded as he recalled a colleague of the Norton staff. "One of the finest gentlemen I ever knew. He never gave up on a boy. Coached more all-Conference guards than anyone who ever coached in the conference. Most of them made it as seniors, and many of them because Bill would not give up on them. A number of years later I attempted to tell him how much I appreciated him. I said, Bill, I am going to tell you something and I mean it from my heart. If I had ever had a boy, I would have wanted him to come under your influence sometime in his life. Everybody who ever worked with Bill was better simply by having known him."

After his coaching career at A&M, Rollins served as Dean of Men and also was Acting Athletic Director when he returned to East Texas State as Athletic Director in 1947. He also served as Dean of Men at East Texas until his retirement in 1963.

Dough was enshrined in A&M's Athletic Hall of Fame in 1970.

Unscored On, Unbeaten Through 25 Games

When the 1916 season closed, D. X. Bible could have had his pick of the head coaching job at either LSU or Texas A&M. Certainly the Tigers of Baton Rouge would have preferred to keep him, for he had coached three victories and two ties during that campaign.

But the 25-year-old Tennessean remembered the great freshman team he had left on the Aggie campus just a few months before. As sophomores, they were ready for stardom during the 1917 season and formed the nucleus of a team that finished the year unbeaten, untied, and unscored on in eight games. Leading that group were Jack Mahan, Roswell (Little Hig) Higginbotham, Tim Griesenbeck, Scotty Alexander, and Kyle Elam.

A 98-0 crush of the University of Dallas came early in the season and the Aggies took victories over LSU (27-0) and Tulane (35-0). With the smashing win over the Green Wave, Bible had his second defeat of Clark Shaughnessy within three seasons.

In those days A&M's keenest rivals were Baylor and Texas. Both provided exciting finishes for the Aggies in 1917, but the unscored-on record stood. A&M led Baylor 7-0 late in the final quarter of the 1917 game at Waco when a Bear receiver caught a long pass and appeared to be in the clear. Only Kyle Elam stood between the Baptists and the goal, and a flying tackle saved the string of shutouts.

Ten days later Texas seemed to have the Aggies held to a

scoreless tie until Higginbotham broke from midfield to the 12-yard line to give A&M new life. But three tries at the line failed to move the ball for a first down, and Rip Collins' fourth down field goal try was wide.

Texas was caught offside, though, and the Aggies were given another chance from the five. Danny McMurrey, a 200-pound tackle summoned for backfield duty in short-yardage situations, needed four thrusts before scoring from a foot away, giving A&M a 7-0 win.

Virtually all of that 1917 championship team went into military service at the end of the season, including Bible who became a pursuit pilot. Tubby Graves took charge of the 1918 team, compiling a 6-1 record and losing only to Texas in Austin.

Bible was back in 1919 and once again was blessed with Jack Mahan as "Mr. Inside" and Little Hig Higginbotham as

1917 Southwest Conference Champions

R. G. Higginbotham circles end for 20 yards in 1917 Rice game as J. B. McKnight and E. S. Wilson clear the way.

"Mr. Outside." Both gained all-Conference recognition along with Scotty Alexander and guard E. S. Wilson. All of the veterans picked up where they had left off before military service and blended well with the new talent acquired in their absence—players like Cap Murrah, C. R. Drake, and G. W. Martin.

Every starter went the full sixty minutes against Baylor in the seventh game, but Higginbotham stole the show. He kicked a field goal from the 30-yard line, then in the final quarter lined up for what appeared to be another attempt from the Baylor 20 while "block that kick" reverberated through the Cotton Palace stands. The kick was a fake, and Higginbotham passed instead to Alexander who shook off four tacklers to cross the goal line and seal a 10-0 decision.

Injuries kept Mahan and Arthur Knickerbocker out of the next game with TCU and claimed G. W. Martin for the remainder of the season. Little Hig had one of his best days against the Frogs, scoring three touchdowns and kicking six of seven points in the 48-0 victory.

A new-record crowd of 8,000 poured into Kyle Field for the Thanksgiving Day meeting with Texas. Higginbotham

1917 Football Staff
Head Coach Dana X. Bible (center); Assistant Coach D. V. (Tubby) Graves (left); and Dr. Blackwell, trainer

crashed through for the game's only touchdown, then after the Longhorns had been turned back at the five-yard-line late in the battle, he punted sixty yards to preserve the triumph. That made it three straight over Texas at Kyle Field, all shutouts.

In the school year of 1919-20, A&M established an intercollegiate football-basketball winning streak that still stands as the longest in history for unbeaten teams in the two sports during the same school year. Ten in football and 19 in basketball gave A&M the mark of 29.

Toward the end of the next season, 1920, it became

Jack Mahan

obvious that time and the odds were bearing down on the unscored-on record. Bugs Morris, now athletic director emeritus of Abilene Christian College, recalls two contests before the final, fateful game, the meeting with Texas.

"We were leading SMU 3-0 in a State Fair game when Jimmy Kitts of SMU attempted a field goal which hit the crossbar and failed to go over. We almost had heart failure waiting for that ball to drop inside."

Later, as A&M played Baylor, which had not scored on the Aggies in four seasons, the streak nearly ended again, though

1919 Southwest Conference Champions

the final score of the game was not that close.

"We held 'em for four downs at the one-yard line," Morris said, "then later in the game Coach (Frank) Bridges unveiled his hidden ball play deep in Baylor Territory. We chased every Baylor player on the field before we found out who had the ball. Jack Mahan finally found it and caught the ball carrier, just before he reached the goal line. If Baylor had pulled that play in our territory, I think the ball carrier could have walked across the goal line."

A&M carried a string of 25 games under Bible without defeat into the meeting with undefeated, untied Texas at Austin. The Aggies had not been scored on during this streak, and the only tarnish was a scoreless day with LSU.

Bible pinned hopes for victory on a strong defense and the punting of Higginbotham, who averaged 49 yards on 10 kicks. Bugs Morris booted a 22-yard field goal to put the Aggies in front, and the Mahan–Higginbotham tandem drove again to the Texas 10 before running out of steam.

The Longhorns began their charge in the second half, outgaining A&M by a decisive margin, but the Aggies stayed ahead through the third quarter, turning Texas back inches from the goal line on the last play of that period. On its next possession Texas moved to a fourth-and-seven situation on the A&M 11. A tackle-eligible pass gave the Longhorns a first down by inches on the Aggie four, and on the next play Texas scored, kicked the point to make it 7-3, and owned its first Southwest Conference football championship.

"You can understand why it was such a bitter defeat," Bible recalls, "and it was compounded by the loss coming so late in the game." Only seven points had been scored against these Aggies for three seasons, but it was little consolation at that hour. "That loss was the hardest to take of my coaching career," Bible acknowledged more than half a century later.

One of Texas' backfield men that day was Kyle (Slippery) Elam, who had been a hero for A&M in the 1917 Baylor game and had lettered also for the Aggies in 1918 before transferring to Texas.

Mahan, one of the heroes in the winning streak, also starred in track and field and was a member of the 1920 United States Olympic team as a javelin thrower. He was inducted into A&M's Athletic Hall of Fame in 1965. Higginbotham was returned to A&M in 1927 by Bible as freshman coach and baseball coach. He continued as baseball coach through the Matty Bell era (1929-33), then joined Bell at SMU as baseball coach from 1935 until he returned to military service in 1942. As a lieutenant commander in the Navy, Little Hig was killed in a plane crash at the Quonset Point, Rhode Island, Navy Base in 1943.

Sight of Centre Orange Had Aggies Seeing Red

The 1922 Dixie Classic between Centre College and the Aggies gave birth to A&M's Twelfth Man tradition, and the dramatic contest left a lasting impact on A&M football.

Ernie Quigley, who refereed the Aggies' 22-14 victory, believed that "the Aggies' victory stamped the brand of football played in the Southwest as equal to that offered anywhere. A&M played on its toes during the entire contest. The 'breaks' went to the Aggies, because they were on deck to take them. Coach Bible is due a great deal of credit for his work in developing the A&M team to such a high point."

Bible's reaction to this team's play was that, "The men went in with the spirit of self-sacrifice, giving up the enjoyments of Christmas week to put themselves in proper condition. They were imbued with the fighting spirit the Aggies always have shown. They did it, and victory is their reward. It may be that Centre had not attained this attitude, and with it conditions might have been different. I am proud of the team's performance."

Charley Moran, who a decade earlier had A&M in the midst of a football renaissance, praised his adversaries. "The Aggies displayed the old fighting spirit, and I am free to state that I had rather be whipped by them than any other eleven." He mentioned some extenuating circumstances, then realizing that could be construed as an alibi, added, "but the Aggies won, and I would not detract from the glory they are due."

Tiny Maxwell, for whom the Maxwell Trophy is named, worked the game as an umpire and as a sportswriter for the *Philadelphia Evening Public Ledger*. In the latter role he reported the contest for a number of papers across the country. "The Aggies would have beaten any team in the country, barring none," he wrote. "...the A&M team played unbeatable football. I can not give too much praise to Coach Bible and members of the team...football critics and fans over the nation can not help but recognize in them one of the greatest football teams ever assembled."

Maxwell, who refereed Centre's stunning upset of Harvard in 1921, was so outspoken in his praise of the Aggies he infuriated the Harvard coach and the Crimson fans who took him to task. He termed Cap Murrah "the greatest lineman I have seen in five years."

W. E. "Cap" Murrah, left; T. F. "Puny" Wilson, right

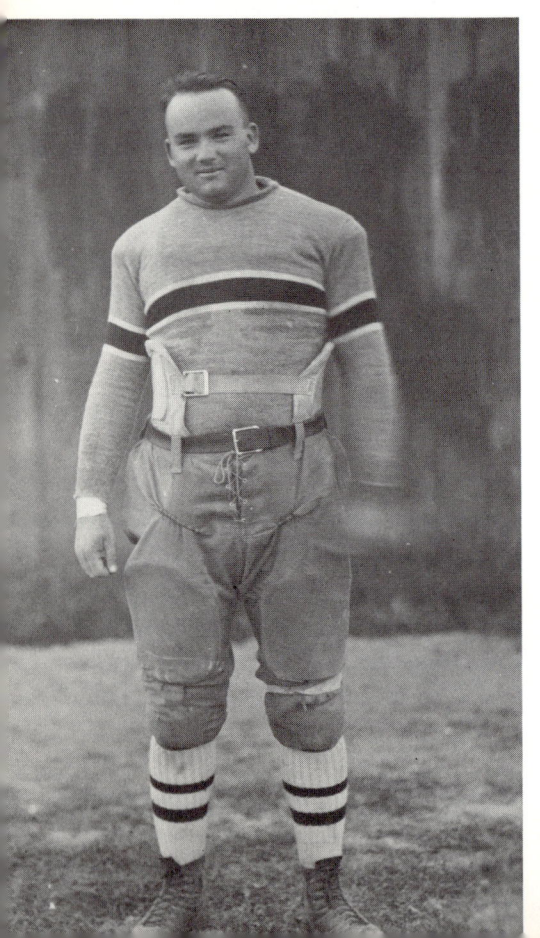

Quigley also praised an individual. At the banquet honoring the victorious Aggies, he said, "If there was to be another all-America team selected, I would head it with Puny Wilson. And right behind him comes Cap Murrah." A natural hit at the banquet, Quigley pointed out, "The reason I know Wilson was there was because he kicked me six times during the game and yelled: 'Get the hell outa my way.'"

Newspapers around the state headlined A&M's triumph appropriately, such as this, in red boxcar type over eight columns:

> AGGIES BEAT CENTRE
> IN MIRACLE CONTEST

Others read:

> Texas A&M Wins National Recognition By Crushing
> Team From Centre College, 22-14, In Classic

Texas Aggie Victory Wins Prestige for Southwest in Football

> Fighting Spirit Born of the Alamo
> Figures in Brilliant Grid Triumph

There were two schools of thought before the game about who should be the favorite.

Horace McCoy of the *Dallas Journal* quoted the odds as four to one against A&M and wrote that A&M was "not even conceded an outside chance to win...advance notices have caused the Texas squad to assume the mien of a lamb led blissfully to a slaughter." And tackle Ted Winn recalls that he received little encouragement at his Dallas home before the game. "My brother kept telling me not to get my hopes up; they're liable to beat you, 40-0."

But some of the pre-game speculation attempted to minimize Centre's role of favorite. Bill Cunningham, a Texas native who had gained sportswriting fame in the East, considered it an inter-urban joust between Dallas and Fort Worth, recognizing Fort Worth as home bailiwick of Centre players and noting that so many of A&M players were from Dallas and the immediate area (Murrah from Plano and Morris from Cedar Hill). Another writer surmised "familiarity with much of the personnel adds to Bible's chances of getting his players ready to play; they won't be stagestruck with Centre's importance for they have met the homebreds before."

Sammy Sanders, who had become A&M's top scoring threat, remembers: "When we came on the field, the Centre players were putting on a great show. The passers were throwing left and right-handed, and the punters were kicking with either leg. Meantime our punter's kicks into the wind were flying back over his head. This added to the pressure on us, and to the onlookers it must have looked like we were outclassed in ability."

When the teams lined up for the kickoff, Red Roberts set

Sam Houston Sanders

Reunion At Cotton Bowl
Dana X. Bible, center, was honored at the 1974 Cotton Bowl Classic and among former players back for a reunion with him were Joel Hunt, left, and Dr. Sam Sanders, former A&M stars.

the ball for a kick down the middle, but Bo McMillin walked over to him and was heard to say: "Kick it toward that little guy in the corner." They re-set the ball, and Roberts directed it right at Sanders. "I was so scared I dropped the ball," Sanders remembers, but "Once under way, the goal posts seemed to be racing toward me."

Buck Buckner, an Aggie back standing on the sidelines on crutches, said, "You could trace Sammy's course by the guys lying on their bellies from the blocks that had been thrown." Sanders returned that opening kickoff 45 yards, then he and Captain Heinie Weir collaborated to get a first down in Centre territory before the Aggies' captain broke his leg and A&M failed in its try to pick up another first down.

T. L. Miller's punt led to a safety when Wilson tackled the receiver behind the goal line. A fumble and a 15-yard penalty

Card section pioneering in 1921 at Aggieland

gave Centre a chance for the lead early in the second quarter, but with two downs to make a foot the Colonels failed. McMillin fumbled on fourth down, and Sanders recovered it inches short of the goal line.

Centre finally took a 7-2 lead early in the third quarter when an A&M fumble was picked up and returned 35 yards to the one. A&M elected to kick off after the touchdown, and Centre fumbled the reception, Murrah recovering at the Colonels 33. An end-around pass play, added for the game, clicked for an Aggie score, with Puny Wilson tossing to end A. J. Evans for the go-ahead points.

The Colonels lost the ball again on a fumble at their 20. Miller raced 10 yards off tackle, and Billy McMillan pushed it to the five. Wilson was called to the backfield and smashed it across for a 16-7 margin. Shortly after, Bo McMillin was rushed fiercely on a pass, and Winn intercepted and ran it back 45 yards to complete the Aggie scoring and clinch the victory.

M. B. Gardner, sports editor of the *Battalion*, thought the fact that the Colonels wore orange jerseys with white stripes may have been a major factor in A&M's success. "They just naturally wore the wrong colors," wrote the young author who saw red when he looked at orange and white, the University of

Texas colors.

The Aggies traveled a rocky road to a 6-1-2 record to become conference champs and host team in this forerunner of the Cotton Bowl. They had to come from behind to beat Baylor, 14-3, with all the points scored in the last quarter by the two backs from Robertson County, Billy McMillan and Sammy Sanders. Sanders' 48-yard punt return put the game on ice, and Bible, who in the words of Harry Pinson, "had sat there as stiff as an Indian chief," tore up his hat in a rare demonstration of excitement.

Rice and Texas were even more troublesome. The Aggies managed ties with both, scoring what was considered a major upset in playing the Longhorns to a scoreless draw. A&M had to overcome loss of the ball by fumble seven times to gain the tie and wound up with a 3-0-2 record in conference play to 1-0-1 by Texas.

Jinx Tucker wrote in the *Waco News-Tribune* that "by holding that powerful team to a scoreless deadlock, A&M brought to Aggieland one of the most impressive moral victories in the history of the gridiron relations between the two schools." The *Battalion* recognized it as a victory with: "The fact that our men did not have to line up under their own goal post after a touchdown is the victory we see in a scoreless tie."

Protecting the tradition of never permitting Texas to score on Kyle Field (in 1915, 1917, 1919, or 1921) was tantamount to victory.

The 1921 game was a "first" in the sphere of communications, being the first account of any sports event reported by wireless, coming before KDKA of Pittsburgh "broadcast" the first prize fight and first baseball game, and a year before WEAF in New York orignated voice broadcasts from football fields.

Progress of the game was known in Austin within moments after the Kyle Field action by an account from two A&M cadets, W. A. (Doc) Tolson and Harry M. Saunders, and B. Lewis Wilson, an electrical engineering graduate, who rigged up a crude but workable telegraph machine to transmit the play-by-play, originated by College Station ham radio station 5 YA, which was to become WTAW later.

Pre-arranged symbols were utilized in the transmission. "TB A 45 Y; T FP 8Y L" was translated to mean "Texas' ball at the 45-yard line; Texas attempts a forward pass but is thrown for an 8-yard loss." Ham radio operators in other parts of the state also picked up the "broadcast," and the Austin American used it as a basis of part of its coverage of the game.

The 1922 season, in which the Aggies went 5-4, could not compare with the previous one, yet it ended with the Texas game in a fashion even more memorable for some of those who had played in the two previous campaigns.

"To me this game proved what a masterful strategist Coach Bible was," Bugs Morris recalls. "Prior to the game we worked out behind closed doors, and just before we left for Austin he told us the story of David and Goliath. I think Coach Bible felt the general public thought the odds against A&M were about the same as against David. I distinctly remember entering Clark

1921 Southwest Conference Champions

Field through an opening in the wooden fence which was made possible by removing a couple of boards. I think the idea was not to be exposed to the fans prior to the game."

Bible also has some fond recollections of this game. A key figure who has sat on both benches in the big upsets of this great rivalry, he thinks the 1922 game one of the most surprising of all. "So often we do not do a good job between halves, but I remember so well the time between halves of that game," he said.

"I remember that I drew a line on the ground, taking the idea, of course, from the Alamo. We did not go to the dressing room in those days. I made a little talk and remember asking those to cross that line who were willing to go back in there and fight in such a way that the memory of the way you play will live and that it will be a pleasant memory for all of us. Bless your heart, they went out there and played in such a manner that it will never be forgotten."

Gill, remembered for only suiting up to become the Twelfth Man the previous January, emerged as one of A&M's heroes in this one. T. L. Miller passed 25 yards to him for the first Aggie touchdown. After Texas tied the score, Puny Wilson handed off to Miller, and he passed to Gill for 25 yards to the four-yard-line. McMillan carried it across from there, and Morris kicked his second extra point for a 14-7 win.

The Glory Years Return In 1925 And 1927

Three seasons passed at College Station without a football championship, and wait-till-next-year talk was thriving when 1925 arrived after the Aggies went 5-3-1 and 7-2-1 in 1923 and 1924. D. X. Bible still had three members of a freshman team of 1922—tackle Bones Irvin, fullback Mule Wilson, and guard Norman Dansby—and a bright spot was an all-letterman backfield of Wilson, all-SWC fullback in 1924, Bob Berry, Taro Kiski, and Joe McGuire.

A young sophomore, Joel Hunt, not so highly regarded at first, wound up contributing heavily to the Aggies' success. "We didn't impress with talent, but we were determined to win," said Irvin, and Hunt added, "It was the most conglomerate group you could imagine. We had 'em fat and short, tall and lean, slow and fast, but Coach Bible molded us into a team."

Victories over Trinity and Southwestern and a 6-6 deadlock with Sewanee set up the first conference game with SMU, a 7-0 triumph for A&M when Wilson made a diving catch of a Hunt pass. Two weeks later, after a 77-0 waltz over Sam Houston, Hunt took over the quarterbacking job in the second half, scored all the points in a 13-0 shutout of Baylor, and began a three-year reign as the Aggies' signal-caller.

A 3-0 loss to TCU, beginning a bad run for the Aggies against the Frogs, and a 17-0 defeat of Rice put A&M at 3-1-0 going into the Thanksgiving Day game with Texas, which was 2-0-1 and heavily favored.

Wilson's touchdown from the three put A&M ahead 7-0 at

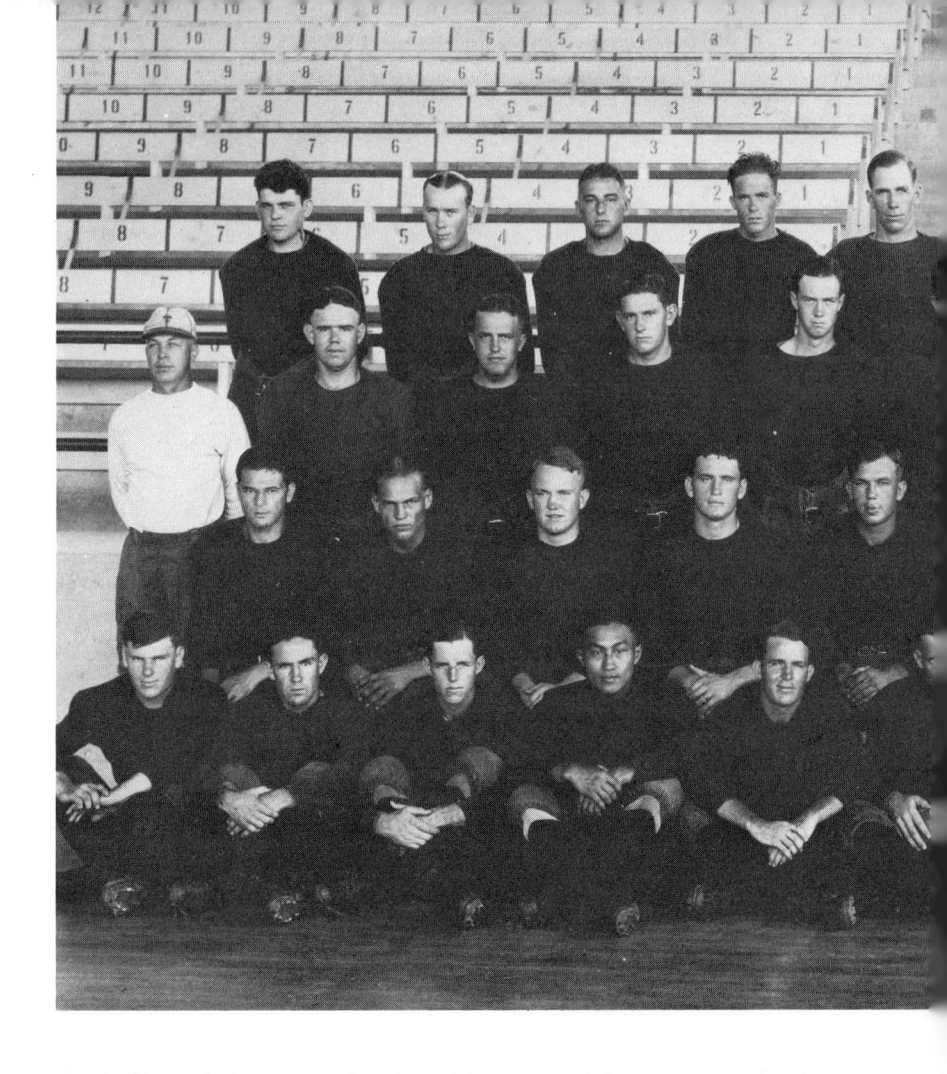

the half, and the game developed into surprising runaway in the second half when the Aggie defense took over. Dansby picked up a Texas fumble and raced back 20 yards for one touchdown, then Siki Sikes played a Longhorn pass perfectly, intercepted on his own eight, and ran it back 92 yards for a touchdown.

General Ike Ashburn, commandant at the time, was doing the play-by-play, and listeners say he got so excited he let loose with a "watch that so-and-so run." The final count was 28-0 and A&M was 7-1-1 and SWC champ.

Little was found to brag about in 1926. But the Aggies did win their first four—all non-conference games—including a 63-0 trouncing of New Mexico that produced a scoring record that still stands. Jelly Woodman scored seven touchdowns and kicked two extra points for a total of 44, the SWC scoring mark

1925 Southwest Conference Champions

for a single game and one more than Syracuse's Jim Brown scored against Colgate thirty years later for the modern-day national record.

In the first conference game SMU—the eventual champion—won 9-7, but the losers registered 29 first downs to 11 for the Mustangs as Hunt accounted for more than 300 yards. A staunch Mustang defense turned the Aggies back four times within the SMU ten, including once in the final quarter when, trailing by two, A&M got a first down on the SMU five, gained two yards in two plays, and gave up the ball on third down on an incomplete pass in the end zone, in those days a touchback.

Jinx (*Waco News-Tribune*) Tucker wrote: "When passing the laurel wreaths for individual glory, you have to begin with the losing team to find the outstanding star. Joel Hunt was one glittering, crashing, dashing sensation from the opening whistle to the final gun. It was Hunt's 52-yard return of the second half kickoff which paved the way for the Aggies' score."

The next game, a 20-9 loss to Baylor, brought a five-year end to relations between the schools. Fighting broke out between halves at the Cotton Palace field in Waco, and Charles M. Sessums, a senior cadet from Dallas, died from injuries suffered.

Of the game, Bible said: "Baylor was determined to win Saturday, and the Aggies were not determined enough to stop them. In football a team can be as good as it wants to, and Baylor wanted to win that game more than A&M did."

The following week the Aggies trailed TCU 10-6 at the half. The TCU players were at one end of the field listening to Coach Matty Bell, as the Aggies sprawled at the other end while Bible spoke. Bell said that Bible was speaking so loud that he and the Frogs stopped to listen. "He made a good talk," said Bell. "So good, in fact, the Aggies came back and tied the final score at 13-all." The final two games ended with a 20-0 whitewash of Rice and a 14-5 loss to Texas for a season count of 5-3-1.

Three straight shutouts opened what proved to be a great 1927 campaign. Then came a 40-6 victory in the conference inaugural with Arkansas. Hunt scored three touchdowns and passed for another. George Cole, now retired athletic director for Arkansas, handled kickoff duties for the Razorbacks, and after Arkansas' touchdown he reportedly asked a teammate whom he should kick it to. Though undocumented the story goes that the teammate pointed and said, "Kick to that number 8." That decision resulted in one of Hunt's touchdowns, a 97-yard return of the kickoff.

TCU provided problems again a week later, and the teams

1927 Southwest Conference Champions

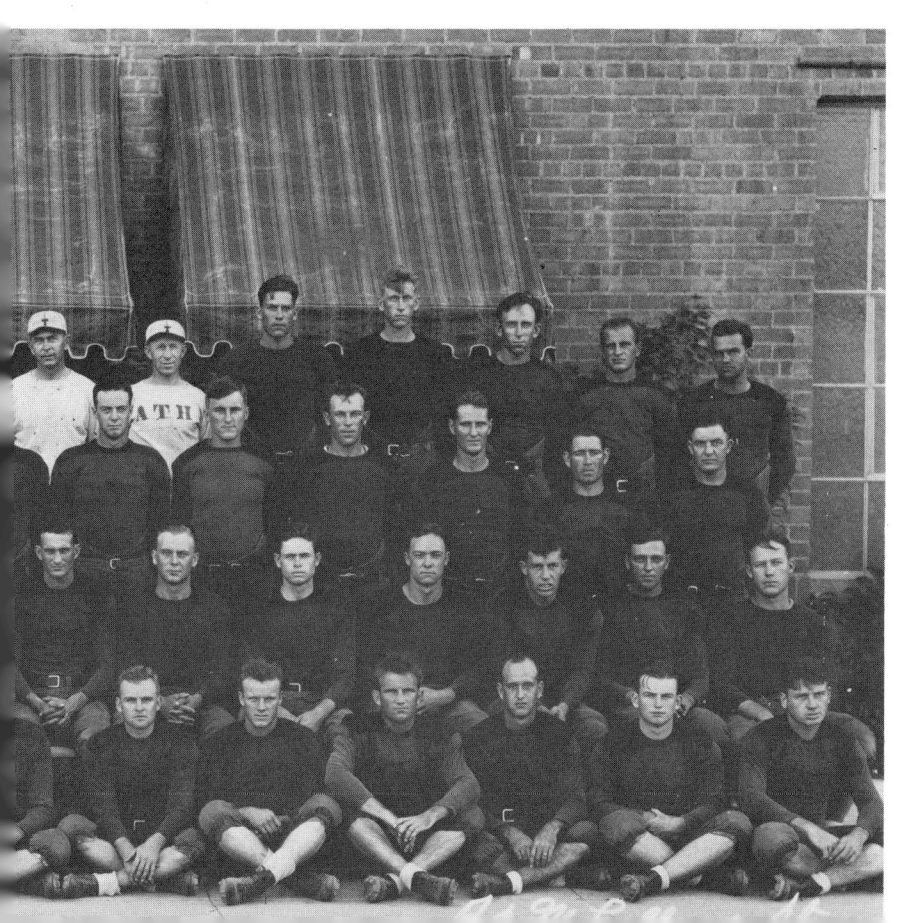

*Razzle Dazzle Pass Clicks For Aggies Against Texas
Herschel Burgess failed to score because of yard-line confusion.*

battled to a scoreless tie. Bible recalls that Rags Matthews had a great day for the Frogs, but he also remembers that "Hunt would forget to call himself when we got the ball down near the goal line. He would call on other backs who couldn't go, then he had to make up for what they had failed to get."

Hunt also remembers: "I didn't run with the ball as much as Mr. Bible wished. From the eight I carried to the four, then I got smart and called on a soph fullback who fumbled and lost five. I carried again and regained the ground, but we still haven't scored."

A 47-6 thrashing of Texas Tech led into the season's highlight, the rubber game between Hunt and SMU's Gerald Mann. SMU was the favorite.

"It was built up to be the outstanding game of the season," Bible recalled. "There was a strong rivalry developing between A&M and SMU and also a great deal of rivalry between the two quarterbacks."

"We had a full year to get ready for this one," Hunt said, thinking of the 1926 loss to the Mustangs. "Looking back on it now I can not single out a single player or performance, because every player performed better than he ever had."

Hunt will not get any argument on that point, especially not from Bible, who beamed as he turned back the pages to the relatively easy 39-13 Aggie win. "Fortunately for us everything went just right. We had spent a good deal of time defending against the forward pass, because all of Ray Morrison's teams could throw the ball. SMU suffered a great many turnovers...A&M intercepted eight passes."

It must have been the greatest of Hunt's many fine performances. He scored three touchdowns, passed for another, averaged 43 yards on eight punts—none of which was returned a step—and intercepted four of Mann's passes. One writer's report of the game pointed to the Mann-Hunt passing combination as the best of the day.

After Rice fell, 14-0, Hunt starred in the 28-7 finale with Texas, completing nine passes, one of them to Pinky Alsobrook for a 22-yard touchdown. He closed his spectacular career by adding two touchdowns, giving him 128 points for the season, still a SWC record.

Herschel Burgess, the fullback, remembers that a play put in for the game clicked almost as planned. It was diagrammed as a Hunt to Sikes pass right over the middle followed by a lateral back to Burgess who arrived at the right spot just as Sikes pulled down the pass. It would have worked except that Burgess slowed down and was tackled a yard short of a touchdown. When Bible asked Burgess why he slowed down, the fullback said, "I thought I was across the goal line." Bible shot back: "Burgess, you do all right until you start thinking, and then you blow it completely." The win made the Aggies 8-0-1 and Southwest Conference kings again.

All-Conference honors went to six players—Hunt, Sikes, guards J. G. (Klepto) Holmes and E. E. Figari, and tackles W. S. Lister and A. C. Sprott—but they all graduated and left Bible a major rebuilding job for 1928 in what turned out to be his final season at A&M.

Three whitewash jobs on non-conference opponents started Bible's last year, but then the Aggies stubbed a toe with a 6-0 loss to Centenary and a duplicate defeat by TCU. Arkansas won 27-12 before a breather with North Texas State gave A&M a 44-0 triumph, followed by a 19-19 match with SMU, and a 19-0 defeat of Rice.

In the final game as underdogs against a Texas team that needed victory to claim its first championship since 1920, the Aggies tried a hidden-ball play in hopes of deceiving the Longhorns. The ball was duly placed firmly in the flexed leg of an Aggie guard, but end Bill Ford of the Longhorns got it before the intended Aggie ball carrier did. Ford lit out for the Aggie goal and Field Scovell, playing the other guard position for the Aggies, took off after him. Ford and Scovell had been high school rivals in Dallas and, perhaps spurred on by this, Field caught Ford before he could reach the goal line.

"Wild Bill, you ought to be ashamed of yourself," he told Ford. "What are all those people going to think of an all-conference end being caught from behind by an old, slow guard?"

As the two of them got to their feet, Ford tried to convince Scovell that "You never would have caught me if I hadn't been dying laughing." Texas won 19-0.

Despite a 5-4-1 1928 record, A&M tried to keep Bible when he announced he was leaving to become head coach at Nebraska. The athletic council offered to meet the Nebraska offer, but Bible felt that A&M could not afford it.

His Name Was Bible — So Was His Word

Texas A&M lost its football coach in 1928 after 11 seasons and 5 championships mainly because the most famous coach in intercollegiate football pegged Dana X. Bible as a winner. Knute Rockne, architect of Notre Dame's great teams of the 1920s, recommended Bible for the head coaching post at Nebraska.

The job was offered to Rockne, who turned it down and said, "I am recommending a man you probably know little about. He is Dana X. Bible at Texas A&M, and I consider him the finest young coach in America. If you can get him, he is your man."

Bible lived up to the recommendation, developing six Big Six championships in eight seasons with the Cornhuskers. In 1946, when Bible ended his career at Texas after 33 seasons as a college coach, only two coaches in football history—Amos Alonzo Stagg and Pop Warner—owned more victories. Today only five have eclipsed his record of 200 triumphs, the most recent being Paul (Bear) Bryant, who also established part of his record as head coach at Texas A&M.

Bible's all-time collegiate record was 200-74-23 (72-19-9 at A&M, 49-15-7 at Nebraska, 63-31-3 at Texas, and 16-9-4 at Mississippi College and LSU). In 29 seasons at A&M, Nebraska, and Texas, he had 14 championships.

In 1951 he was one of the charter electees to the National Football Hall of Fame. He received the Amos Alonzo Stagg Award in 1954, was elected to the Texas Sports Hall of Fame in 1959, the Longhorn Hall of Honor in 1960, the Nebraska

Sports Hall of Fame in 1962, and the Texas A&M Athletic Hall of Fame in 1966.

He is listed in *Who's Who,* is a past president of the American Football Coaches Association, and was a member of the National Collegiate Football Rules Committee for 25 years. Bible and Tuss McLaughry, long-time coach at Brown and Dartmouth, are the only living charter members of the coaches association that was organized in 1922.

At A&M and Texas, Bible opposed two others who served as head coaches at A&M: Matty Bell and Homer Norton.

"Matty always gave us a lot of trouble when he was at TCU and I was at A&M," Bible remembered. "I recommended him strongly as my successor at A&M. When I came back to Texas, he had moved on to SMU. We started meeting again, and we were not to beat Matty until 1941 when we won a fine victory." Bible commanded only an 8-6-2 advantage when their teams played for the last time in 1946.

The Bible-Norton rivalry started in 1928 when Centenary beat A&M and Norton won three of the first four meetings before the tide turned. Uninterrupted domination from 1940-46, when Norton was at A&M and Bible at Texas, gave the latter an 8-3 advantage.

"Homer was such a fine gentleman and commanded a lot of respect," Bible said. "His teams were always sound, well-conditioned and had a jaw-to-jaw, toe-to-toe attitude. Homer often had a surprise for you, but I found he was always generous in defeat and humble in victory."

George White, sports writer in Dallas throughout Bible's career, recalls that "the hackneyed expression 'born leader' tells the true story of his success. Athletics always has been in his blood, and as a participant in all sports at Carson-Newman he earned a reputation for sterling, natural leadership."

Joel Hunt insists, "Mr. Bible did not have to demand respect. You could not keep from respecting him. He was a man who stood above, and you had to look up to him. And you sought him. He was the type of man you could go to and talk about either football or personal matters.

"One of my remembrances of him is that every time we lost a game you could find Coach Bible at the hotel. Everytime we won you couldn't find him. He was big enough to take the

D. X. Bible

criticism or answer questions if we lost.

"He gave me some sound advice when he learned I was going into the coaching profession. He said 'Captain, in dealing with young men, you are going to find that they are nearly all fine boys, but just like in a barrel of apples you will find one over-ripe, maybe even rotten. Now if you have to discipline that boy, or even relieve him of his duties, do it with this in mind: you are helping the rest of the squad.'"

Field Scovell has kept close contact with Bible for nearly half a century. He knew the coach as a taskmaster when there was no financial aid and a coach "did not have to continue with a bunch of guys who did not want to play."

National Football Hall Of Fame Reunion
Three former Texas A&M coaches honored by National Football Hall of Fame join a pair of former colleagues at a reunion of former Southwest Conference coaches in the early 1960s. Left to right, they are Dana X. Bible, Fred Thomsen of Arkansas, Matty Bell, Homer Norton, and TCU's Dutch Meyer, also a Hall of Famer. They won a total of 19 SWC championships: Bible 8, Bell 4, Norton 3, Meyer 3, and Thomsen 1.

Scovell recalls a day after the 1928 loss to Arkansas. "A&M had played poorly, and Coach Bible called the whole crowd together at one end of the field. He told us he was sick of the whole operation and was going to make some changes. He drew a line through the dirt with his foot and said, 'All right, what I am going to do is put those on one side of this line that I am going to keep, and those we do not invite across the line will not be needed any longer.'

"He spent quite a time making a decision on me, and he

looked at me and said, 'Scovell,' and after hesitation that seemed like forever, he added, 'I'll keep you.' He really wasn't convinced, and I knew it.

"He was quite different in those days than during his later years at Texas. He had a short fuse and quite often would explode, throw his cap on the ground, then step on it.

"After the SMU game in 1928, Coach Bible caught me day-dreaming in practice and fired a question at me that I could not answer. 'You obviously are not interested in football,' he said and grabbed me by the neck of the jersey and my pants and marched me right off the field.

"I pouted, of course, quit the squad and all of that, but was in his office early the next morning asking to be reinstated. When practice started, he said, 'Gentlemen, Field and I had a little visit, and he's ready, and I'm ready, and I am sure all the rest of you are, so let's get with it.' He believed in covering things quickly without embarrassing the player.

"Later, when I observed his composure when he was coaching at Texas, it was amazing that he could change his tactics that much."

Dr. Sam H. Sanders will be ever grateful to Bible for advising him to go on to med school in 1922 when good running backs were needed.

"Mr. Bible told us that if we committed a foul against a player, it was an admission that he was a better player than we were," Sanders said. "He would take you out of a ball game if you intentionally fouled. 'Give your all and there shall be no regrets,' he would tell us."

When Nebraska and Texas were paired in the 1974 Cotton Bowl, Bible was invited back to Dallas as an honored guest, since he had coached with great success at each of the participating institutions. Joining him and Mrs. Bible in a memorable reunion were six of his former players, George Sauer and Sam Francis, Nebraska; Joe Parker and Hub Bechtol, Texas; and Sanders and Hunt, Texas A&M.

Gig 'Em! Joel Hunt

Joel Hunt saw Texas A&M play football for the first time as a teen-ager when he paid $2.00 to a concessionaire for apples and peanuts to hawk at an A&M-Baylor game at the Cotton Palace field in Waco.

"I never sold an apple nor a peanut," he recalled more than a half-century later. "I was too fascinated by the game." Hunt recalled that A&M executed an on-side kick and struck for the winning score in the final minutes.

"I made up my mind that day where I wanted to go to college."

Hunt had played in the shadow of Boody Johnson at Waco High School and commanded little attention when he entered A&M. At College Station they were still extolling the feats of Jack Mahan, Little Hig Higginbotham, and Sammy Sanders.

Hunt weighed only 143 as a sophomore and was utilized as a wingback until his triple-threat talent and confidence moved him into a starring role. In mid-October of 1925 he threw a touchdown pass to Mule Wilson for a 7-0 victory over SMU, sending him one up on a rivalry with Gerald Mann that highlighted SWC football in the mid-20s.

Two weeks later quarterback Bob Berry was injured in the first half of the Baylor game with the teams deadlocked in a scoreless tie. "Coach, you didn't name a quarterback," Hunt reminded as the team prepared to take the field for the second half.

"You're it," Bible told him. And Hunt was IT for three

Captain Joel Hunt

seasons, attained all-Conference recognition in each of them, and led A&M to championships as a sophomore and a senior. "Joel turned out better in 1925 than we expected," was D. X. Bible's conservative appraisal years later of Hunt, the sophomore.

All-America recognition was not coming to the stars of the Southwest in Hunt's days, but writers who watched Hunt and teammate Siki Sikes, Rags Matthews of TCU, and Mann of SMU perform in the 1927 East-West Shrine game had their eyes opened. The four Texans were given credit for winning the game 16-6 for the West, and Matthews was named the outstanding player of the game. Hunt was termed "a lost all-America."

The performances of Hunt, Matthews, and Mann were major factors in each of them being named to the National Football Hall of Fame more than four decades later. Dutch Meyer, a Hall of Fame coach for TCU, believes that the play of the four SWC players in the 1927 East-West game brought more recognition to the Conference than anything else up to that time.

Hunt did not play a single down at quarterback in that game. "I know why," he recalls, "because when the coach asked me if I would throw a pass on first down, I said 'yes, sir.'"

"Why?" he asked. "I told him the defense always calls the play. It's not the strength of your offense." Hunt attributes that thinking to "Mr. Bible," and he recalls that "Jerry (Mann) went in there in the second half and threw a pass on first down for a score."

Hunt also has a recollection involving Siki, his old roommate. "I was playing defensive halfback behind Siki, and both of us were getting a kick out of Rags daring the East backs to come his way, as he did in every game.

"I yelled to Siki and told him to tell those all-America so-and-sos to come around his end. Siki turned around and bellered, 'You can go you-know-where. I am going to let well enough alone.' Ole Siki played a great game, too."

"Matthews was truly a great football player, and I admired him," Hunt acknowledged in recalling the ability of the man who gave him his greatest grief on defense. A&M was never able to whip TCU while Rags was at defensive end. "You had to respect his pride, his dedication, and his ability."

TCU's great end likewise held Hunt in awe. Recalling the 13-13 tie with A&M in their junior season, Matthews said, "I had Hunt trapped one time, and you know what he did? He drop-kicked a 43-yard field goal on the dead run."

Hunt hit his peak in the memorable 39-13 win in the showdown battle with SMU in 1927. "It stands out in my memory above any other. It is a game I can always look back to

Gain Stature For Southwest In Shrine Classic
Southwest Conference stars stole the spotlight in the East-West Shrine game following the 1927 football season. They were, left to right, Siki Sikes, Texas A&M end; Gerald Mann, SMU back; Joel Hunt, A&M back; and Rags Matthews, TCU end. Hunt, Mann, and Matthews have been named to National Football Hall of Fame and Texas Sports Hall of Fame.

knowing that the whole squad at A&M was dedicated for that game. Speaking personally, it was the most perfect game I had ever played, offensively and defensively. Naturally it is dear to my heart, and I am very proud of it."

Hunt's record of 128 points scored in a single season is still the Southwest Conference record 47 seasons later. Only eight players in 58 seasons of intercollegiate football had scored that many points in a single season when he did it. He was one of the first five named to A&M's Athletic Hall of Fame (1964), and he was named to the Texas Sports Hall of Fame in 1958.

Of all the accolades accorded Hunt none probably has

Reunion Of Hall Of Famers
Nearly a half century after their heroics in the 1927 East-West Classic, Joel Hunt of Texas A&M, center; Rag Matthews of TCU, left, and Gerald Mann of SMU hold a reunion at a Texas Sports Hall of Fame Dinner. All three are members of the National Football Hall of Fame and the Texas Sports Hall of Fame.

greater credence than that of John Heisman, the Hall of Fame coach for whom the Heisman Trophy was named. Heisman, who observed the best in the East, South, and Southwest for 36 years, closed out his career at Rice, and each of his last three teams went against Hunt. "The best all-around back I've ever seen," he said of Hunt.

Jinx (*Waco News-Tribune*) Tucker was a bit more eloquent

in his appraisal of Hunt in his account of the 1927 SMU-A&M game: "If a statue were erected in Aggieland tonight, or any other night in the near future, intended to personify the flaming spirit of Texas A&M, it would be nothing but a likeness of Joel Hunt, with a football tucked under his arm, his feet lifted as in tremendous motion, and one arm to signify his remarkable stiff arm."

Little wonder that Hunt likewise has a high regard for the late writer. "If I were to say that one man in the Southwest contributed more than any other one person toward the development of athletes, encouraging them, being honest, and writing humane stories about them instead of looking for the goat or the hero, I would name Jinx Tucker. That's how I feel about him."

Looking back on Hunt's play Coach Bible classified him: "exceptional as a runner, as a quick-kicker, and as a faker; he was exceptional at faking a run, a pass, or a kick, and his running skill made him also a threat as a passer; add great defense and leadership to that and you have Hunt, a great all-round back."

From Pink Slip To Rose Bowl

John Madison Bell inherited anything but a warm bed when he moved from TCU to A&M in 1929 to succeed Dana X. Bible, and understandably he could have second-guessed himself. The team of Horned Frogs he left behind to Francis Schmidt won the Southwest Conference championship under the leadership of Howard Grubbs, an all-Conference quarterback who a score of years later became the league's executive secretary and served in that capacity for 23 years.

Bell had been recommended strongly by Bible for the job, and A&M may have decided if you could not beat him, hire him. After losing his first game with A&M while at TCU, Bell claimed two victories and two ties in the next four meetings, and neither of Bible's 1925 or 1927 champions could score against Matty's defenses.

Bell's first production at College Station posted a 5-4-0 record, but Tommy Mills, a Houston lumberman who made the all-SWC backfield, thinks the 1929 Aggie team "should go down as a miracle team of all times, and I am serious. How about this lineup?" he asked as he called off the starters and their below-average weights. No lineman weighed more than 180, and the heaviest backs were Brooks Conover and George Zarafonetis at 170.

Guard Charlie Richter, like Mills and Pinky Alsobrook, had been a sophomore on the 1927 championship team and was named to the 1929 all-SWC team as a 165-pound guard. It was a season of near-misses for the Aggies, the aggregate margin of four losses totaling only 15 points.

Talent became thinner and victories fewer as Bell scraped the bottom of the barrel. "A&M was offering financial assistance only for the few footballers who participated in the program and pillow concessions and the night mail collection," Colonel Frank Anderson recalls. It was not until 1930 that any athlete received financial assistance from the Athletic Department funds. Charlie Cummings, a bluechip tackle from Bryan, was given the job of sweeping out DeWare Field House at a monthly stipend of $25.

Cummings' windfall was short-lived, however, for he became scholastically ineligible at mid-term and had to give up the job. Meantime most of the rival SWC schools were providing campus employment for greater numbers, and the benefits were reflected in the standings. A&M lost all five of its Conference games in 1930, a 2-7 season, but one of its two non-conference triumphs, with Harry Stiteler in the starring role, was over Centenary, the league's No. 1 nemesis. One of the setbacks was to Nebraska, which reflected sharp scheduling by Bible, who knew what he had left behind.

A&M climbed to third-place in 1931 and posted a full-season record of 7-3. One of the big factors was the leadership of Carl Moulden, the captain who gained consensus all-SWC recognition along with end Charley Malone. This team more than doubled the point prediction of the previous season, but defense was its forte. Moulden and his mates yielded only 34 points, only 2 more than the 1927 champions and 3 more than the 1939 national titlists.

"Carl was an outstanding leader," Bell recalled as he looked back on his five seasons at A&M. "He had a burning ambition to do well, and he was such an inspiration that our ball club played like he wanted them to play. Carl did not have size or speed, but he had a great combination of courage, leadership, and desire."

The respect of captain and coach was quite mutual. "Matty Bell was one of the greatest," Moulden reminded. "He put a lot of responsibility on the individual. This was his way of building the man. And he really knew defensive football. He could take seven posts and build a better defense than a lot of coaches could with eleven men."

None of A&M's three conquerors scored more than a single touchdown. Those losses were to champion SMU, runnerup TCU, and Tulane, which wound up in the Rose Bowl.

"We did not have the backfield to generate a lot of offense," Frenchy Domingue, a versatile Aggie back remembered, "so we had to count heavily on the defense." Bell agreed, yet he recalled that Domingue had an exceptional season for a sophomore. "Frenchy lacked size, but he had lots of ability and the desire to play well."

Relations were restored with Baylor in 1931, and the Aggies romped to a 33-7 decision. It was the first meeting of the two teams at College Station since the conference was organized. Nelson Rees, an unheralded newcomer, sparked the victory, and good passing was contributed by Jimmy Aston and Domingue, who later was the hero in the come-from-behind victory over Texas, 7-6. Domingue took charge of the offense when injuries sidelined Aston, who continued to be dogged by ailments during his 1932 captaincy. Aston today is Chairman of the Board of the Republic National Bank of Dallas and a member of A&M's Athletic Hall of Fame.

The conference had three players that season who became college presidents: Earl Rudder of the Aggies, Wilson (Bull) Elkins of Texas, and Willis Tate of SMU. The late Rudder attained the rank of major general and was a World War II Normandy invasion hero. He was president of A&M 1959-1970 and was named to the A&M Athletic Hall of Fame in 1970. Elkins and Tate are currently chief executives at the University of Maryland and SMU, respectively.

A&M barely beat the clock in its lone 1932 conference victory, a 14-7 conquest of Rice. Mere seconds remained in the second quarter when Henry Graves hit R. E. Connelley with a pass at the Rice 10. Ted Spencer called time immediately, but the field judge fired the gun, unaware the clock had been stopped. In the borrowed time Graves passed to Rue Barfield for a touchdown then added the placement. With the score tied in the final quarter, Sully Woodland and John Crow blocked a Rice punt, and the latter, a guard from Milford, scooped up the ball and dashed for the winning score.

Once that season the Aggies played two games in a single

week. They beat Sam Houston, 26-0, under the lights at Huntsville on Monday, motivated undoubtedly by the Bearkats' orange and white uniforms. The following Friday they defeated A&I, 14-0, on touchdown runs of 38 and 47 yards by Domingue. The double duty that week must have taken its toll, because the only scores by the Aggies in the six remaining games were the two against Rice. Yet a defense that was led by Willis Nolan, Cummings, Spencer, and Domingue managed scoreless ties with Baylor and SMU.

Domingue was to become an outstanding referee for the Southwest Conference, and he terminated his career by officiating the 1973 Cotton Bowl Classic between Texas and Alabama.

Ted Spencer sparked A&M to what had the makings of a good season in 1933—four straight victories. Bell's boys bowed to his old TCU team for a fifth straight time, then fell on successive weeks to Centenary and SMU without managing a score.

It was after the whitewashing by SMU that word leaked that Bell was to be fired. "My players heard it," Bell recalls, "and they called a meeting and decided they did not want to play out the season if I was to be fired.

"I found this out and called a meeting. I told them this football business is hazardous, but it is my profession and I want to stay in it. The greatest favor you can do for me is to play good ball games against Rice and Texas in our last two games."

The Aggies thrashed Rice, 27-0. "They went down there real loose and to have some fun," Bell remembered, "and they were going against a team that had upset league-leading Arkansas, 7-6, the previous week." Arkansas would have won the championship except for the use of an ineligible player.

"In the game with Texas our boys got tense, because they were so anxious to beat them. Texas tied us in the final minute with a field goal."

Like Bell, Clyde Littlefield, the Texas coach, was also given a pink slip following that 10-10 stalemate at Kyle Field.

Two seasons later Bell led SMU to the Rose Bowl. Reflecting on this twist of fate Bell pointed out, "I coached some great people at A&M and was associated with a lot of great folks. Those players down there have a great incentive. Gosh, they don't want to let down those students. That student body was the greatest asset we had at A&M. I don't guess there is one in the country that can compare with them for support of a football team."

Reveille:
A Treasured Tradition

A night-time highway accident after a 1931 football game provided Texas A&M with one of its most treasured possessions. A carload of cadets was returning to campus in a Model T Ford. On the highway between Navasota and College Station a small black and white dog appeared suddenly in the path of the car, and the driver was unable to avoid hitting the animal. As soon as the car could be stopped, the passengers rushed to the dog's aid and found her wagging her tail and holding up an injured leg.

The dog obviously was a stray, but no farmhouse was in sight so the students took her back to campus with them and tended her wounded leg. That night—probably in violation of military regulations—the dog slept in an A&M dormitory.

The dog's rescuers tried to come up with a name for their new friend, but Dwight H. McAnally, who as a cadet compiled a history on the animal in 1945, declared that they "decided to sleep on it until the following morning."

McAnally reported that, "When morning came, in the person of the bugler, the pup's sleep was interrupted by the notes of Reveille. She set up such a fuss about this intrusion on her sleep that the problem of a suitable name was solved. Her foster parents simply dubbed her 'Reveille,' and the name stuck."

Dogs were not allowed in campus buildings, but Reveille did not know that and followed her new friends into the student mess hall. A waiter, about to throw her out, was set

Reveille Befriends The Bugler.

upon by Reveille's friends and instead was almost thrown out himself.

According to McAnally, "That day arrangements were made to permit Reveille to eat in the mess hall, and before long she was allowed free run of all of the buildings on the campus, a privilege no other dog has ever enjoyed."

Still quite young, Reveille responded to her new home and friends with a warm personality. She soon learned to recognize the cadet uniform and accepted everyone wearing it as a friend. "She literally adopted the cadets," McAnally related.

And the corps adopted Reveille, especially the Texas Aggie band, of which she soon considered herself a member. She followed them to all of their formations and generally took the lead when they practiced marching on the drill field.

When the band took the field at half time of her first football game, Reveille headed the march and performed as if she were the featured entertainer. She won the hearts of the crowd, just as she had the students, and her performance earned her the title of Official Mascot of Texas A&M.

Her uniform became a maroon and white blanket, with "Tex Aggies" inscribed to be visible on both sides as she performed. Her care became the responsibility of the head yell leader, who saw to it that she appeared in her blanket at all football games and other important occasions. She soon became a familiar sight to football fans wherever the Aggies played, and her first blanket now occupies a place of honor in a trophy case on campus.

Reveille went on most of the corps trips, her feeding and other needs seen to by a freshman. She generally occupied a

Reveille I

whole seat when traveling by train. Conductors balked on occasion, but Reveille always won out because her friends were countless.

Reveille's private life on and around campus was her own. She went when and where she pleased, her only daily duty being meal formation, which she always answered. Otherwise she wandered at will over the 4,000-odd acres of campus. When she got sleepy, she went into the most convenient dorm, found an open door, and hopped into an open bunk for a nap.

"Tradition dictated," McAnally found, "that when she honored any cadet by selecting his bed, he was not to disturb her, but was to find another place for his own repose. If he could not find an empty bed, he slept on the floor."

When a painting of Reveille was unveiled the night before the 1943 Thanksgiving Day game, Dr. Frank C. Bolton paid this tribute to the treasured mascot:

> Reveille is more than an animal. She is a tradition. To many a homesick freshman Reveille represents the dog left at home; that dumb friend that could always be

Reveille III

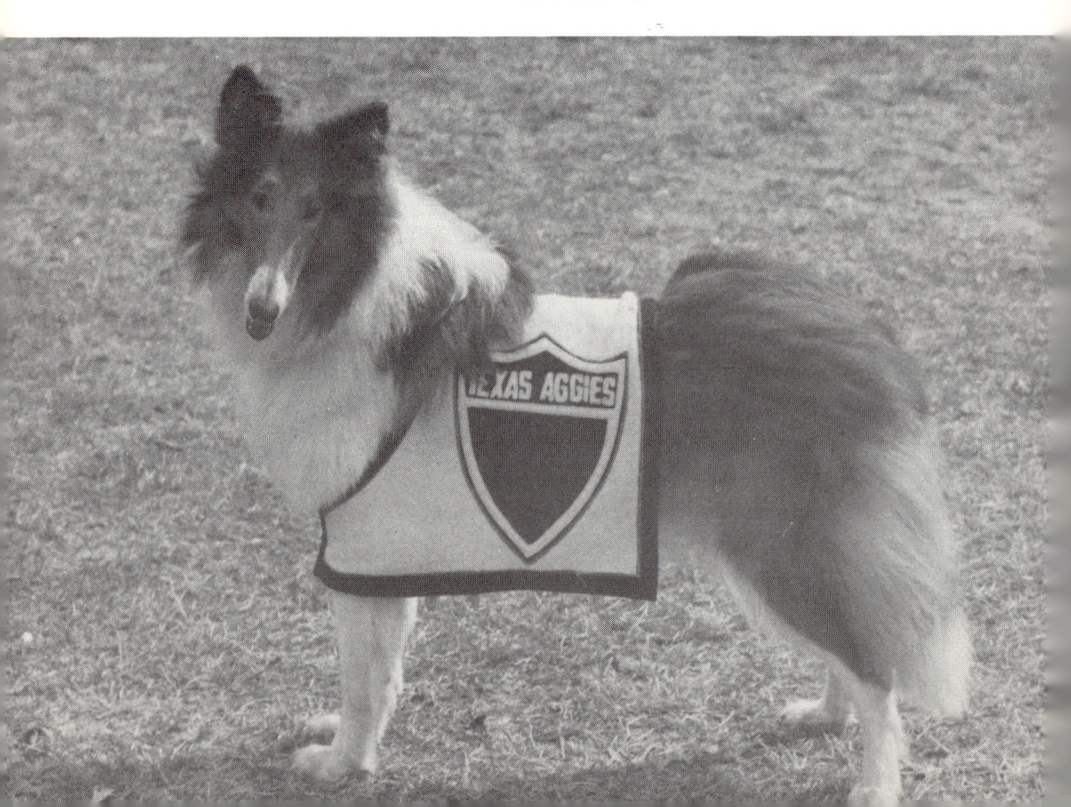

depended on for a wag of the tail and a friendly bark, no matter how dark the clouds or negligent were other friends. Reveille was a tangible, visible connecting link with a carefree boyhood. She has rendered a service that we have chosen to commemorate.

A few weeks later, on January 18, 1944, Reveille died of old age in the A&M Veterinary Hospital. A formal military funeral was given her the following evening in the center of the gridiron on Kyle Field. Reveille now lies at the entrance to Kyle Field, where an appropriate memorial marks her resting place. Reveille II, which served from 1952 until her death in 1966, is also buried there.

Reveille III, a Collie, is the current mascot and has served since 1966 when presented by Mr. and Mrs. Joseph Husa, of Fairbanks, Alaska. Randy and Steve Husa, their sons, were cadets at the time of the presentation.

If Shoe Fits, It'll Take Size 15

When Homer Norton walked into his office at A&M in January, 1934, he discovered that his job was not as rosy as it had looked when it was offered to him over in Shreveport. It took no genius to discover that the Athletic Department was in bad financial trouble, that player material was far from being the best, and that his appointment had not met with the unanimous approval of the former students. There were some exes in the larger cities who felt they should have been consulted before Norton was hired. The first they knew about it was when they read about it in the newspapers.

Norton discovered why he had been named a professor and head of the Department of Physical Education. The legislature appropriates the salaries for faculty but not one penny for the Athletic Department or any of its staff. All assistant coaches also were designated as faculty. All such salaries were supplemented with Athletic Department funds. Gate receipts and income from other sources must carry the whole sports program at all state-supported schools.

Another surprise was the bonded debt of $210,000 standing against Kyle Field and that in 1933 the Department had managed to meet the interest payment only. Norton could see he was going to have trouble in finding the money for the 1934 payment. It must be remembered that this was during the depression, and even cutting the price of tickets to $1.50 could not attract enough people to keep even. They simply did not have the money to spend on football.

Scholarships were the answer to improving the quality of the playing material, but scholarships cost money and that subject hardly had been discussed. Another way to provide the players with financial help was to award them some concession which would provide the money needed. Several could split the program concession sharing the profits from the sales. The selling, of course, was done by other students. Seat cushions, peanuts, and popcorn also provided scholarship aid for others. Dormitory concessions would include candy sales in the residence halls, the sale of Aggie stationery, and the collection of night mail at 10 cents per letter for later dispatching to the two night trains. When a man failed to make enough from his concession, it generally was supplemented by the Athletic Department. Then there also were student labor jobs with duty hours set so as not to interfere with the athlete's program.

Eventually the Southwest Conference came around to setting standards for athlete aid, and that solved a lot of problems for a lot of people. But the problem of unhappy former students was one problem Norton never solved, even when he was leading the Aggies to a national championship and three consecutive championships in the Southwest Conference. Some complained that his teams were not winning by larger scores. Others complained about the ways he coached the team or about any other thing that could cause him worry. Yet he survived the fight for 14 seasons and amassed a winning percentage of .601 for 82 victories, 53 losses, and 9 ties.

Soon after he finished his first spring training session Norton took to the road, appearing at the A&M Clubs throughout the state. He wanted to meet as many Aggies as possible, build a few fences, and set up programs of finding jobs for his players during the Summer. He also was laying the ground for some recruiting help.

One look at the inherited squad convinced Coach Norton that 1934 would not be a good season. He reported on the bleak outlook, and when he got to the Houston, Texas A&M Club he said, "I have told you all about the lack of ability among the players and the financial condition of the department. This coming season doesn't look too good. We will win a few games and for next year I can't raise your hopes by promising any better than we can expect this year. We need scholarships.

"Perhaps by 1936 we can offer more scholarships and get some of the better high school players. However, it will be 1937 before they will be able to play. So in 1937..."

But before he could go any further one of the more rabid exes shouted, "Never mind telling us about 1937, Homer. If you haven't started winning by then you won't be around to worry about it."

In addressing the student body before the 1934 season began, Norton told his usual story about needing quality players and said anyone who wanted to try out for the team would be given a chance. Back in the dormitories some sophomores decided that Roy Young, a 6-6, 250-pound freshman, was big enough to play football; so they ordered him to report.

Young had never played football because his mother was fearful of injury to him. Big Roy knew his mother undoubtedly would protest, but this looked like a chance for him to be another Twelfth Man.

Roswell (Little Hig) Higginbotham, the freshman coach, took one look at the size of Young and decided he could be made into a great tackle, but again there was a problem. That was a down-to-earth problem, for Young wore a size 15 shoe and the supply room had none of that size on hand and had to outfit him in a pair of basketball shoes until he showed he was worth the cost of the shoes that would have to be made to order. Cal Hubbard, the line coach Norton had brought with him from Centenary, was in favor of buying the shoes. Norton, knowing of the cash situation, said he would wait until Young had played in a game and showed promise of being able to make the team as a sophomore.

What Norton saw in the Fish-Allen Academy game and Young's performance in the practice sessions convinced him that Young was a player worth the cost of the dozen pairs of shoes he would need before he graduated.

Just as Homer had warned, the 1934 season was far from a successful one. A&M escaped the cellar only by tieing Arkansas after a 10-7 conquest of Baylor—the Aggies finishing with a 2-7-2 record. And, as prophesied, 1935 was little better with a 3-7-0 finish. Texas was beaten, 20-6, leaving the arch rivals sharing the basement.

In 1935 Norton probably won the recruiting race of the nation when he convinced Dick Todd to enter A&M. Todd had set a national scoring record of 318 points in an 11-game senior season at Crowell, a small West Texas town. Colleges nationwide tried to get him, but the combination of Norton, Lil Dimmitt, the Aggie trainer and chief recruiter, and Bert Pfaff, a Tyler industrialist and strong Aggie alumnus, sold Dick on Aggieland. It was a great day for A&M, and many sensed that this marked the beginning of the Aggie's return to greatness.

Years later in talking about his players, Norton said, "I wanted Dick Todd more than any player I ever tried to recruit."

The player problem was lessening to some degree, but finances became worse. The 1934 season did not produce enough money to meet the interest payment, and banks would not lend the Athletic Department money to pay interest. Joe Utay was called on to use his political influence in Austin to have the legislature pass a bill allowing the school's fiscal department to lend the Athletic Department $30,000. That took care of the bank temporarily, but 1935 was not better financially. The legislature was not in session so that means of getting the money was closed. Accordingly the bank took over the budget. It ran the cash income and outgo.

When the matter of money for scholarships came up the answer was: "You have more than 6,000 boys down there. Certainly you can find 11 who know how to play football." On the matter of equipment, "Can't you get those uniforms cleaned, repaired, and use them again?" On the shoes it was, "Can't you get them repaired at the shoe shop and keep using them?" And still further, "How can you justify the expense of three pairs of shoes per player when you only play ten games a season?" They forgot about the five days a week of practice sessions.

Alumni pressure, two losing seasons, and that money problem put Norton in the Mayo Brothers Clinic for ulcer surgery in 1936. This was only his first trip, but by the time he gave up and allowed the dissident alumni to buy up his contract he had very little of his stomach left.

Before coming to A&M Norton often had sat in the press box scout booth during a game in order to see the plays and spacing of the opponents better. Telephone communications to his bench effected readjustments in the defense quickly. This idea of wire connections to the bench is another of the Norton innovations developed over his career. The dissidents quickly picked on this press box idea and demanded that he get back down to the sidelines where he could slap a boy on the butt as he came off the field. Rather than make an issue of it, Norton did come back down and put an assistant on the other end of the wire.

While recuperating in the Mayo Clinic, Norton did some thinking about how he could apply the overhead view to the day-by-day coaching. The idea of a mobile tower came to him; so when he came back home, he put his idea to work.

He had his groundskeeper get an old Ford chassis and strip everything from it except the frame and wheels. On this he had him build a tower 12 feet above the frame and wheels. It was topped with a seat, small desk, and public address system in order for him to be heard all over the practice field. Being on wheels he could have it moved to any area where he wished to concentrate on the work. It was just one more of the "crazy" Norton ideas.

He asked that no publicity be given to the tower, but anyone coming to the practice field could see it and how it worked. Again the dissidents went after him saying they wanted him to do his coaching from the ground and not up in the air. He withstood this battle until well into the 1938 season when he finally gave up. With reporters on hand and cameramen ready, Norton took an axe and chopped off the legs, letting the tower crash to the practice field.

Years later he told Frank Leahy about his tower. Shortly thereafter the papers carried a picture of Leahy atop his great innovation, the coaching tower. He got the credit, Norton got the static, and had to destroy his. Today many practice fields are equipped with coaching towers.

It was from the elevated view that Norton developed his five-man line. From it he was able to set a series of defense patterns that would apply to almost any offense set up by his opponents. His defenses proved so successful that the mark of allowing only 1.71 yards per play still stands in the national record books since it was set in 1939.

Homer Norton returned from the Mayo Clinic in 1936 to

learn that his Texas A&M football team had been tabbed as favorite to win the Conference championship by the third annual Texas Christian University poll. That forecast of a rise from rags to riches indicated the respect commanded by the talented Dick Todd who was making his varsity debut that fall.

Todd's arrival and the shift of Joe Routt from fullback to guard turned things around for the Aggies at the outset. A&M won its first four tests, the fourth one being an 18-7 conquest of TCU and the most memorable that season for Todd and all of the Aggie followers. When the Horned Frogs arrived at College Station, they were fresh from an 18-14 victory over Arkansas, the eventual 1936 champion.

Homer Norton learned that things that went up had to come down.

"We recognized TCU as the team to beat," Todd recalls, "and, of course, we were motivated by the fact A&M had not beaten TCU since 1924." Seven times over that span A&M had been shut out by the Frogs.

"We changed our offense for that game, running more from the short punt than from the single wing or double wing that we had been using. We ran an option play off the short punt and were lucky enough to beat them. Another recollection I have of that game is the way Ki Aldrich (TCU center) hounded me all day."

Ki hardly nullifed the awesome Aggie backfielder, however. Soon after the opening kickoff Todd raced 51 yards to put the ball into scoring position, then took a lateral from Dick Vitek for the first touchdown. Later in the fourth period Todd scampered 76 yards to the Frog 6, and from there scored on another lateral from Vitek.

Although TCU had the remarkable Sammy Baugh in its lineup and the great passer was to become a teammate and a fast friend in later years, Todd was more impressed by Arkansas than TCU. Arkansas beat the Aggies, 18-0, and made a lasting impression on Todd with its style of play.

"They passed us dizzy in that 1936 game, but the game with them the following year was even more frustrating to me. It was a real hot day in Fayetteville, and we would keep that ball on the ground for seven or eight minutes and finally score. They'd take the ball and start throwing and in three or four plays would have a touchdown." Arkansas won that one, 26-13.

Even by playing 12 games in 1936, three of them coming in an eight-day period, little surplus cash remained for A&M's annual interest payment to the bank.

The "extra" game crowded into the schedule developed while the A&M team was enroute to San Francisco to play the University of San Francisco. University of Utah officials contacted Homer Norton by telegram and asked if he would be willing to help save an Armistice Day celebration planned for Salt Lake City the Tuesday following his game with San Francisco. Utah's intended opponent had cancelled abruptly, and since Texas A&M was to be in the general area it was hoped that Coach Norton would come to the rescue.

Telephone contact back to College Station and to Utah

Dick Todd demonstrates ball-carrying skill against TCU.

approved the game which carried a nice guarantee at little extra expense for the Aggies. Sleeping in their Pullman cars cut out the hotel bills, and, as Norton put it, "We sure needed that money."

The game at San Francisco was an easy one with the Aggies winning, 38-14. They went sightseeing in San Francisco and then on to Salt Lake City and the Tuesday game. Everyone on the traveling squad played in that one which A&M won, 20-7.

The Aggies were back in College Station on Thursday just in time to take off for Beaumont and a Saturday game with Centenary. The tradition Norton had established while at Centenary held, and A&M lost again, 0-3.

Norton's comment on that loss was, "I guess I did too good a job in building up the tradition that the Gents always beat the Aggies." And they generally did, for in the nine games the two teams played, Centenary won six and lost three, with three of the wins for Centenary coming after Norton moved to

A&M. It took his 1939 national championship team to record his one victory over his old school.

A&M gained a share of third-place in the 1936 Conference standings, its highest finish in five years, and an 8-3-1 overall record by whipping Manhattan, 13-6, in its final game.

Joe Routt became the first A&M player to achieve all-America recognition that season, and he repeated in 1937. The classic guard was joined in all-SWC acclaim by teammates Charley DeWare, Jr., center and co-captain, and Roy Young, the big walk-on tackle. Todd was not all-Conference in 1936, but he was a concensus choice the next two seasons and the league's leading ball carrier in 1937 and 1938.

Gig 'Em! Joe Routt

"Joe Routt had the biggest heart and was one of the best fighters I ever saw," Homer Norton observed when he learned that his former all-American guard had been named to the National Football Hall of Fame in 1962.

King Gill, the original Twelfth Man at A&M, recalled that Routt's commanding officer at the time of his battlefront death termed him "the most courageous man I have known."

Joseph Eugene Routt was a captain in the infantry at the time of his death in 1944. He and his men advanced on some German tanks during the Battle of the Bulge, and he was gunned down before the sergeant at his side could warn him of the impending danger. Captain Routt received the Bronze Star posthumously. Some of the bloodiest skirmishes of the European campaign were fought in the area where he was killed. It was said the ground was gained and lost by the Allies and Germans eight times.

When Norton learned of Routt's impending enshrinement into the Hall of Fame, he recalled one of his experiences with his great player. "His mother has told me that this incident may have been the turning point of Joe's life," Norton said.

"Joe was unruly, pugnacious, and hard to handle when he first came to A&M. When we'd go on trips, I'd either have to close my eyes to some of the things he did or go help him out of trouble."

After transferring to A&M from Blinn Junior College in Brenham, Texas, only 10 miles from his home in Chapell Hill,

Joe became scholastically ineligible. At times Norton had as much trouble with him as his professors.

"On this particular day," Norton recalled, "we were playing Centenary at Shreveport, and I pulled Joe from the game. The team went back to the hotel after the game to eat. Joe and I were the last ones to finish. I knew he was mad and was going to whip me, because he was accustomed to having his own way and didn't like being taken out of the game."

There in the deserted hotel dining room, Norton and Routt had their showdown.

"I said, 'Go ahead, Joe, do what you want, but I'm going to run this ball club my way,' I finally got him around to my way of thinking. I talked him out of whipping me, and from then on he was easy to handle."

From that day Routt's attitude toward football improved, as did his scholastic standing. Before he graduated from A&M he made the honor roll.

To a man, Routt's teammates remember his steel-eyed determination. "You talk about a competitor," Dick Todd recalls, "there was no quitting by him. He had so much desire and was so competitive that he would not tolerate others who were not competitive. I was really fortunate to be around Joe as much as I was. I got real close to Joe, because we players had a chance to visit his home frequently, and his dad and mother were so good to all of us."

Routt took football so seriously that at times his teammates dared to play tricks on him. It occurred once in the 1937 season finale with San Francisco University on the West Coast. Writers watching the remarkable Routt play his last regular season college game asked Homer Norton to let Routt carry the ball. Norton had gone up to the press box after the game became one-sided (A&M won, 42-0).

"So, I sent word down to the field," Norton mused later. "The boys were dumfounded when they got the order. They put him in the backfield, and to add to the excitement they decided not to block for him. Those San Francisco boys liked to've killed ole Joe."

H. B. McElroy, co-author of these pages, was sports publicist at A&M at the time and was skeptical of Routt in his early playing days. "He was mean, cantankerous, and opinion-

Joe Routt—A&M's first all-American

ated until Homer straightened him out," McElroy recalls. "But, boy, what a football player he became. The way he played at Houston in the 1937 game, Rice should've lettered him. That Number 43 was in their backfield all afternoon."

Routt went on to captain the West against the East in the

annual Shrine game and won the game's outstanding lineman award.

After winning the heavyweight boxing championship at A&M in his senior year, Routt turned professional and fought his one and only pro bout in Houston. It was a disaster. Joe lost and announced, "If I can't beat this guy, I'm giving up boxing." It was a losing night for Routt, as his ring, watch, team medal, and money were stolen from his dressing room.

Joe was married in 1942 to Marilyn Maddox and fathered two daughters: Marilyn and Rosana. In 1947 Joe's widow married Jim Thomason, her late husband's close friend and also a former Aggie football star.

Enshrined in the National Football Hall of Fame at the same time as Joe were Ben Lee Boynton, a Wacoan and former Williams College star who refereed games in which Joe played, and Cal Hubbard, who was Norton's line coach at A&M before Routt arrived.

The redoubtable Routt was also enshrined posthumously in the Texas Sports Hall of Fame and the Texas A&M University Hall of Fame.

Hitting The Jackpot

Texas A&M's recovery program under Homer Norton moved at a discouraging rate for three seasons, perhaps even more so to him and his staff than to the fans who had not cheered a champion for ten years. It was this staff who agreed that unless A&M was able to go out and recruit on a cash scholarship basis like rival schools, then they might consider going out of the football business and let the bank have a go at it.

They reasoned that it would require 40 scholarships to develop a winner. Through careful screening they came up with a list of the 40 boys in Texas with whom they wanted to produce this team. The only stumbling block was money, and that they surely did not have. It would take at least $25,000 to acquire these players, and the only hope for that kind of cash was a trip back to the bank. Everyone except Norton and Lil Dimmitt insisted that the bank would not loan another $25,000 to A&M when it could not keep current with the interest payments on the indebtedness of $210,000.

Norton had a meeting with the Dallas banker, and as Dimmitt told the story it went like this: Norton, Lil, and Bert Pfaff met in Dallas and headed for the bank. They were welcomed with the obvious observation that they apparently had come in to make a payment. Norton answered, "To the contrary we have come to borrow another $25,000 so we can recruit a team that will win, and in winning will attract a gate that will pay off our debt."

The banker countered, "I am not quite that crazy but am crazy enough to offer to sell you the $1,000 bonds for $400 each."

It was a standoff until Pfaff spoke up and told the banker that as far as he was concerned Norton was going to get the $25,000. "If the bank does not provide it, then I will." Next he intimated that when he got the money for Norton he would withdraw the remainder of his account at the same time.

The banker deliberated a moment, then admitted that Pfaff's stand put things into a different light. He suggested that the three of them go out to lunch while he made contact with his board of directors to determine their attitude. They had explained the entire recruiting plan to him during their pre-noon interview. When they returned from lunch, the banker inquired, "If you get this money, when will you go after these 40 boys?"

"My car is parked across the street," Dimmitt said, "and as soon as I know Homer has the money, I will be on my way to get the first one signed."

"Well," replied the banker, "you're looking at the craziest banker in Texas, but you have the money."

Within the hour Lil had signed Marion (Dookie) Pugh, a quarterback from Fort Worth's North Side High School. By suppertime he had been to Brownwood and had signed Jim Thomason, Tommie Vaughn, and Bill Miller. As he signed a boy he asked him to write to others on the master list and to tell them that if they all joined together at A&M they could win the Southwest Conference championship in their junior year. He reminded them that talent was so sparse many could make the team as sophomores. Nearly every player on the list of 40 had been picked to play in the annual high school all-Star game. It really was a list of "blue chippers," as prospects are classified today.

It would be good to report that all of the 37 who signed to enter A&M reported, but that was hardly a fact. Most of the other Conference schools wanted these same boys, still 23 of the original 37 wound up at A&M. They did better than win that championship Dimmitt had promised. They went on to win the national championship in 1939 undefeated, untied and, as Bill (Rock) Audish, a fullback turned guard, added, "Unaccustomed to the whole damn thing."

Six of the 23 were acclaimed all-Southwest Conference, while John Kimbrough, fullback, and Marshall Robnett, a guard, gained all-America acclaim. Joe Boyd, tackle, also was all-America, but he was a year ahead of those who made the $25,000 loan list.

Eighteen of the 23 were to earn letters, 14 of them 3 times, and all were to win college degrees along with 4 others who joined them on that freshman squad in 1937. Seventy-one percent of the 31 who won freshman numerals graduated.

These Aggies did a lot more than win and graduate. They made that "craziest banker in Texas" the "smartest banker in Texas," for they paid off the mortgage on Kyle Field. They paid off at the rate of $1,000 for each $1,000 and not the $400 the "crazy" banker had offered back in 1937.

The 1937 season with the 5-2-2 record did earn enough money to start paying the bank again. With all-American Joe Routt heading up a great defense and Dick Todd running wild, the gate was good everywhere. Also that great crop of freshmen were achieving an undefeated season. But, unfortunately, the alumni were still restless.

Dean E. J. Kyle, chairman of the Athletic Council, settled one question. He announced that Homer Norton would be the head coach for another five years by an extension of the contract he had signed originally. Some of the exes were even more unhappy, for the real renaissance was still two seasons away.

At the start of the 1938 season only Jim Thomason of the 23 "blue chippers" had won a starting berth, but others were following suit game by game. Substitution regulations at that time provided the reserves little chance of service, for once a player left the field, he could not reenter in that quarter. So, the coach had to consider the score and the position of the ball on the field before he would make any substitutions.

A&M started well in 1938 with lop-sided shutouts of Texas A&I and Tulsa, then fell to Santa Clara and TCU on successive weeks. National-champions-to-be, the Horned Frogs won, 34-6, at Kyle Field with Davey O'Brien leading an aerial barrage while Ki Aldrich was hobbling the Aggie ground attack.

The major dividend for the Aggies in the TCU game was

that John Kimbrough finally logged some playing time. Injuries had prevented Kimbrough from winning a freshman numeral, and he started the 1938 season as an also-ran fullback. Odell (Butch) Herman, with whom he had starred at Abilene, Texas, High School in 1936, was running ahead of Kimbrough and so was Bob Hall until the Baylor game.

By this time Marshall Robnett, a converted fullback, had become a starting guard, and Tommie Vaughn had taken charge at center. Kimbrough was not listed as a probable starter, but his play against TCU and in practice the following week earned him the starting fullback job against the Bears.

The weather, too, may have been a factor in his moving into the starting lineup. It was raining in Waco, and the field appeared too slick for Dick Todd's type of running. It developed that neither Kimbrough nor Todd was hampered by the weather, except that conditions did lead to fumbling.

When Quarterback Cotton Price called on Kimbrough to carry the ball for the first time, he rammed the "Good Ole Baylor Line" for 14 yards. He struck for another good gain to the Baylor 23-yard line, and Todd broke from there to the one-yard line. Kimbrough scored his first varsity touchdown on the next play for a 6-0 lead, but the conversion attempt failed.

Midway of the third quarter the Aggies marched 88 yards in a bid to break a 6-6 deadlock. Todd got a first down at the 10-yard line. Todd put it within inches of the goal on third down, but the Bears forced a fumble by Kimbrough on fourth down and recovered in the end zone for a touchback.

Another Aggie bid was turned back after a 54-yard drive to the 1-foot line in the fourth quarter, and the game ended in a 6-6 draw. It was hardly an evenly-fought game despite Baylor's goal-line stands. The Aggies rushed for 283 yards, with Kimbrough and Todd sharing the honors, while Baylor could gain only 44 aground and only 100 total offense to 316 for the Aggies.

Jinx Tucker, *Waco News-Tribune* writer, was so impressed with the turn of events that he chronicled: "The Baptist faith is the correct religion. Able ministers of other denominations can talk until they are blue in the face to the 15,000 fans who gathered at Municipal Stadium yesterday afternoon and quote all of the passages that they know in the Good Book, but they

John Kimbrough scores his first TD for Aggies against Baylor.

will never convince one of the damp souls present that the Baptists are wrong."

Tucker described A&M's performance as "unleashing the most powerful running game in the history of football at that institution...did everything but sweep the Baylor Bears off the field." Of Kimbrough he became ecstatic with: "Joining hands with Dick Todd and Owen Rogers was a newcomer to the Aggie backfield, just a sophomore substitute in other games. His name is John Kimbrough. He hails from Abilene. He is a substitute no longer. He is the most powerful line smasher in the Southwest Conference."

Felix McKnight, A&M Class of 1932, writing for the *Associated Press,* surmised: "The power that has been simmering at Aggieland apparently is loosed now."

If possible, Kimbrough might have had an even greater day the following week against Arkansas. Harold Ratliff of the *Associated Press* was so impressed with John that he wrote: "Big John Kimbrough, a 210-pound cyclone of a man from the wind-swept Plains country, tore a fighting Arkansas line to shreds here today as the Texas Aggies staged a storybook finish to defeat the scarlet-shirted horde from the Ozarks, 13-7."

A&M was operating from the short punt formation that day, with Kimbrough lined up at tailback about six yards back. "We had a trap play," Dough Rollins remembers, "In which John took a handoff and tore right through the spot the trapped player had vacated." For the record, Kimbrough ran with such punishing power that several of Arkansas' defenders had to be relieved by substitutes.

"Bill Minnock was one of our guards that day and was doing a good job for us physically and psychologically. Things were going so well for us that Bill told the Arkansas player across from him: 'You've been a good boy; so, I'm going to let you in on something. Kimbrough's coming right through here and I'm getting out of here,' as he pulled to set the trap."

At a banquet in Mount Pleasant several years later Rollins was telling of this incident and admitted it might have been embellished since the happening. After the dinner, the Mount Pleasant coach confirmed the incident Rollins had just described by acknowledging "I was that Arkansas guard, and it really happened."

Financially, 1938 was an even better year, for the interest due and that overdue on the stadium indebtedness was paid off along with the $25,000 loan by the Dallas banker. Finally, Norton was in control of his budget.

Gig 'Em! Dick Todd

Dick Todd had a sense of timing when carrying the football that few backfielders in collegiate history could equal. Thus it is ironic and most unfortunate that time ran out on him a year too soon at Texas A&M.

"He would have made the all-America team in a walk had he been on a little better ball club at the time," Homer Norton, his coach, observed many years later. "We just did not have the team for three seasons to back him up."

Winding up his spectacular collegiate career in 1938, Todd just missed the national championship team of 1939. "If he could have been a year later, he would have made everybody's all-American in 1938," says Dough Rollins, who was a member of Norton's staff at the time.

Todd almost made it without the support of a championship team. Prior to the 1938 A&M-SMU game Coach Norton received a telephone call from Grantland Rice requesting some color action pictures be taken of Todd in that game. If A&M won, Todd was to be picked by Rice, the dean of America's sportswriters, for *Collier's* magazine.

The all-America glory was denied Todd when Joe Pasqua, a Mustang tackle, kicked a 46-yard field goal that gave SMU a 10-7 victory. With the loss went Todd's chances for the cherished recognition. Recalling that field goal 36 years later, teammate John Kimbrough said, "I thought surely it was a fake, but once kicked I thought it would never drop." Only one longer field goal had been kicked in the Southwest Conference

Dick Todd—left a year too soon.

prior to that.

Two weeks earlier when A&M outplayed Baylor decisively in a 6-6 tie, Jinx Tucker wrote in the *Waco News-Tribune*: "Dick Todd is the greatest running back in America and never in his most illustrious career was he greater than he was

Saturday afternoon."

An incredible career at Crowell High School in West Texas had made Todd one of the most sought-after players in recruiting history in 1935. He scored a national record total of 318 points in 1934 which gave him a career mark of 664. Todd visited every school in the Southwest Conference, Northwestern, "and a number in the South" during that all-out quest for his commitment.

"I enjoyed all of the visits and met a lot of wonderful people," Todd recalls, "but I did not give too much thought about going anywhere else once I visited A&M. I thought I would feel more at home there. I wasn't used to the big towns. I am proud of A&M and pleased I was privileged to go there."

Todd did not have the supporting cast to continue his fantastic scoring spree in college, but he was all-Conference and the league's leading rusher in both his junior and senior seasons. He was recognized as the No. 1 threat in a broken field, and few foes dared to give him the opportunity to return punts.

Billy Dewell, who was an all-Conference end for SMU in 1938, cited an example of the respect Todd commanded on punt returns. "We had a standing rule that punters would never kick to Dick. In my senior year we kept it away from him with one exception, and he went. Ray Mallouf got off a fine kick, but Dick got hold of it. I was coming in, being especially careful that he didn't pull me in too quickly and get around me. He was baiting me, but I wouldn't go for it. I kept coming in very cautiously. Finally he decided I wasn't going to commit, and he started up the middle.

"I kinda threw a body block across the front of him. I had him, and I could feel his weight up against me. Before I could get my arm around him, he backed away and I sat there and watched him go 58 yards down the middle. To the rest of the ball club coming down, it looked like he had been tackled."

TCU's Sam Baugh, who was a senior when Todd was a sophomore, developed tremendous respect for Dick as a foe and as a teammate. The two of them teamed together with the Washington Redskins in fashioning two division championships after Todd had sparked the Aggies to an 18-7 conquest of TCU in 1936.

After that 1936 season, Baugh was in Houston to receive

the *Houston Post* Award for the most valuable player in the Southwest Conference. That same evening Todd and his teammates were at the Rice Hotel to be feted by Houston's A&M alumni group. When Baugh was accepting his award, he reported that a little earlier he had spotted Todd in the lobby. "I went over and put my arm around him and held him real tight, because I didn't touch him the day we played 'em."

"I always thought Todd was one of the finest runners I ever saw," Baugh said when he presented Todd for enshrinement into the Texas Sports Hall of Fame in 1968. "He was more than that, however, because he was a complete football player, a fine pass receiver, and a heckuva defensive player. He did it all. He could pick the hole well, follow the interference, then cut off it."

"Todd made me nervous for 60 minutes for three years," Dutch Meyer, TCU's retired Hall of Fame coach remembered. "He was one of the great runners this Conference had, as great as the greatest. He just picked his holes and, man, he was gone."

Coach Norton termed his protege "the greatest brokenfield runner I have ever seen. Possibly the next best is Red Grange, and they are just about alike. I think he was in a class by himself in use of the hips. The closest thing I ever saw to him (for hip action) was Jim Thorpe. He had the greatest pair of legs I ever saw, and he had spring like a deer."

Todd was always a star—at Crowell, at A&M, with the Redskins, and in 1943 he was named to the all-Service team while playing for Iowa Pre-Flight, which was truly all-America. After his retirement from pro football in 1949, he held a number of coaching jobs. He was an assistant at A&M and SMU, head coach of the Washington Redskins one year, and at Midwestern University in Wichita Falls for three years. And he also was on Baugh's staff with the New York Titans (now the Jets) in 1960, the inaugural year of the American Football League.

While he was playing at Iowa Pre-Flight it was his good fortune to be coached by Don Faurot, Bud Wilkinson, and Jim Tatum, all of whom developed into legendary college coaches after World War II.

"I feel I have been most fortunate," Todd said as he looked on the past. "I have been privileged to be associated with a great group of people wherever I played or worked. You couldn't believe how wonderful the people have been to me. Every day I am thankful of how fortunate I have been."

All of which gives credence to this appraisal of Dick Todd by Dough Rollins: "He was probably the most popular boy we had while I was at A&M."

Nineteen In A Row

Nineteen-thirty-nine was to become far more than a national championship season for Texas A&M. It was to take its place alongside the Twelfth Man tradition as an inspiration for A&M teams of the future. The players, coaches, and others who had a part in fashioning the success were to be from that year hence a family in itself, bound to each other and to A&M with an everlasting bond.

When the 1939 team holds reunions, which come frequently, the fraternal spirit reaches out for such contemporaries as the student manager, the water boy, the sports writer for the campus newspaper (*The Battalion*), the groundskeeper, the team physician, and the head nurse. On the thirtieth anniversary of their championship an excellent book was published that updated the entire family, including photos of them all, both 1939 and 1969 vintage, and also pictures of wives, children, and grandchildren.

"It was during the latter part of the 1938 season that we realized we could have a winner in 1939," said Marion Pugh, one of the two first-string quarterbacks, as he sat with teammate Dog Dawson, a big end and kickoff expert, to turn back the thirty-five pages of history. A&M had defeated two of the four teams that finished ahead of them in the 1938 standings and had tied one of the others.

"In 1939 when we started two-a-day practices we thought we were going to have a good team, but all of us were sweating out Cotton Price, who had been severely burned in a gasoline fire that summer," John Kimbrough recalled. It was feared that Walemon (Cotton) Price's playing days were finished, but the senior quarterback was familiar with coming through in the clutch. As a sophomore he had subbed into the lineup to kick the extra-point to give A&M a 7-7 tie with TCU, a deadlock that was to cost TCU a share of the 1937 championship. When he came off the field he told Dough Rollins, one of the coaches, "You thought I couldn't make it, didn't you? Well, I knew I could so I never worried about it."

A few days before the opening game with Oklahoma A&M (now State), Coach Homer Norton told the touring sports writers he felt he finally had a team of championship caliber. He had 19 returning lettermen, 5 of whom had lettered twice. Joe Boyd, his 210-pound senior tackle, was one of two consensus all-Conference players who would be returning. Furthermore, there were talented sophomores like halfback Derace Moser, end James Sterling, and tackle Martin Ruby, all destined to become all-Conference players while at A&M.

Still the TCU Pre-Season poll that had picked the eventual champion only once in five years selected A&M for fifth place. TCU was picked to repeat as champion but wound up in sixth place, only a half-game out of the cellar.

The Aggies shut out the Oklahoma Aggies and Centenary to get away to a rolling start. Against Centenary seven of the starters and twelve of the substitutes who played were among that bumper crop of freshmen that Homer Norton, Lil Dimmitt, et al had recruited in 1937.

"When we beat Santa Clara, 7-3, we realized we might go all the way," said Dog Dawson. Santa Clara was a national power in those days and had scored successive Sugar Bowl victories in 1937 and 1938. Its only loss in 1939 was to A&M. The come-from-behind squeaker may have been the making of the A&M team.

A little experimenting with personnel was still going on until the Villanova game, but the lineup was set once the Aggies had trounced the Eastern team that went into the Tyler (Texas) Rose Festival game with 22 straight victories. Herbie Smith and Jim Sterling were the ends; Joe Boyd and Ernie Pannell, the tackles; Marshall Robnett and Charles Henke, the guards; Tommie Vaughn, the center; Cotton Price and Marion Pugh, the

Leaders in 19-game Victory March
Coach Homer Norton, flanked by John Kimbrough (39) and Marshall Robnett (43), two of his all-American players.

quarterbacks; Jim Thomason, the blocking back; Bill Conatser and Derace Moser, the halfbacks; and John Kimbrough, the fullback. Price and Pugh divided time almost equally at quarterback, while Moser and Conatser did likewise at wingback.

"Offensively we jelled in the Villanova game," Pugh reflected. The Reverend Joe Boyd, who was to become an all-American tackle that season, concurred but he also remembered that game for two amusing aspects, both involving Thomason.

As the Reverend Boyd recalls it, "The pre-game tension and emotion prompted Thomason to step up on one of the benches and exhort, 'Fellows, those old boys' granddaddy shot my granddaddy right through the nose. Let's get 'em.' It was so ridiculous to bring the Civil War into a pre-game pep talk that we all rolled off our benches and broke into laughter. It relaxed the team completely."

A&M won, 38-7. Once the game developed into a rout, some heated situations developed. The Reverend Boyd recalls that Thomason became so incensed he kicked one of the Villanova players in the seat in retaliation. "Jimmy Higgins, one of the officials, saw it, threw his flag, and was charging in to declare the penalty. Thomason saw him out of the corner of his eye, tapped the opponent on the shoulder, and when he turned around, Jim said, 'Hey, kick me.' As Jim bent over, that player obliged. He almost made a field goal with Jim serving as the ball. The fouls nullifed each other, and thus Jim was able to stay in the game. That's what I call quick thinking."

TCU was the only conference foe to cross the Aggie goal line that season, but the Aggies' most harassing afternoon was at Kyle Field on Armistice Day (November 11 in that era). It was a rainy day, and SMU, blessed with a great punter in Presto Johnston, had bowed only to Notre Dame, by the thin margin of an extra point, 20-19.

The break both A&M and SMU were seeking came for the Aggies when Johnston fumbled in a failure to get off a punt, and Tommie Vaughn recovered on the SMU 11-yard line in the

Bill James
Builder of Blockers

Jim Thomason
Blocker of Renown

second quarter. The Aggie quarterback did not need a signal from Coach Norton to know what to call from there. He called Kimbrough's signal three times, and the third brought a touchdown.

It was far from time for the Aggies to relax, however. In the final quarter the Mustangs were checked short of the Aggie goal. This left A&M in such a deep hole Bill Conatser was called on to punt out from his own end zone. SMU end Roland Goss, who later became an outstanding game official, blocked the punt, but Conatser proved the better bird dog in the mud and recovered for a safety. The game ended that way, 6-2.

Rice and Texas were shut out in the two final tests, but the stubborn, sophomore-laden Longhorns made it a struggle for a half, and therein lies a story. Since Texas won the game-opening toss, it was A&M's turn to exercise its option at the start of the second half. The choice was to receive the kickoff, which would give A&M a chance to gamble on a hide-out play on the first play from scrimmage.

Earl (Bama) Smith was A&M's fastest back, and he was subbed in at the start of the second half. When Cotton Price brought Longhorn Jack Crain's kickoff back to the Aggies' 30-yard line, Smith hid out near the sideline with fellow-squadmen forming a back-drop to shield him. On the snap to Price, Smith sprinted down the sideline, caught the pass, and made it to the Texas 26-yard line before Gilly Davis of the Longhorns overtook him. Four plays later Price passed to Jim Sterling in the end zone for the tie-breaking score. A 37-yard strike from Price to Herbie Smith set up a second Aggie touchdown by Conatser, and Kimbrough's smash for another gave Rock Audish a chance to make the final count, 20-0.

With Kimbrough leading Southwest Conference scoring and joined by talented ball carriers and receivers, the Aggies impressed offensively on their way to the national championship, but it was on defense that they made their most enduring marks. Their record of holding opponents to the fewest yards per play—1.71—continues as the national collegiate record, while their marks against rushing, passing, and total offense likewise still stand as Southwest Conference season records.

Although the Aggies were No. 1 in the *Associated Press* Poll and accepted as the national champion, the Rose Bowl bid went to No. 2 Tennessee to play No. 3 Southern California. A&M then accepted an invitation to the Sugar Bowl to face No. 5 Tulane and validated its rating with a stirring, come-from-behind 14-13 victory. Meantime, Southern Cal was thumping Tennessee, 14-0. The latter was coached by General Robert Neyland, who had spent a freshman year under Charley Moran at A&M before his appointment to West Point.

There was some speculation over matching A&M and Southern Cal in a mid-January benefit game in Los Angeles for a relief fund for Finland, but the attraction that figured to attract a "million-dollar gate" never materialized.

Turned back midway of the first quarter on the Tulane 2-yard line, the Aggies struck back for the initial Sugar Bowl touchdown on a 2-yard smash by John Kimbrough. Cotton Price made it 7-0. That was the score until the third quarter when Bob Kellogg ran Derace Moser's quick-kick back 76 yards to give the Green Wave a chance to tie the score.

A fumble recovery by Tulane on the A&M 38 gave the Wave a chance to take a 13-7 lead early in the fourth quarter, but the ubiquitous Herbie Smith blocked the conversion attempt. Led by Kimbrough, the Aggies took the subsequent kickoff and powered their way 70 yards in seven plays. The payoff came on a pass from Price to Smith from the Tulane 26 to the 10, and little Herbie lateraled to Kimbrough who carried the remaining 10 yards behind a wave of sharp blocking. Price's conversion sailed squarely through the uprights, and the Aggies had a 14-13 victory and the undisputed national championship.

Kimbrough monopolized the headlines and gained consensus acclaim as the top performer in the Sugar Bowl history to that time, yet he had to share the spotlight with the indomitable Herbie Smith who defied pre-game illness and nausea to bask in the glory. There was also a personal triumph for Smith, because he took home an opponent's helmet as an added trophy.

The Aggie end who weighed only 150 pounds claimed the helmet on a wager made with Tulane's Harry Hays, a halfback who had been Smitty's teammate at San Angelo, Texas, High School. Each had staked his headgear that his team would prove superior.

Smith contributed a number of big plays that were

1939 National Champions

First row (left to right): Herbie Smith, Marland Jeffrey, Ed Robnett, Cotton Price, Marion Pugh, Frank Wood, Bill Henderson, Les Richardson, Joe Rothe. Second row: Mack Browder, Muley White, Charles Henke, Marshall Robnett, Tommie Vaughn, Euel Wesson, Jim Thomason, John Kimbrough, Bud Force, 'Bama Smith. Third row: Cullen Rogers, Bill Conatser, Derace Moser, Odell Herman, Bill Miller, Hugh Boyd, Bill Buchanan, Jim Sterling, Cotton Williams, Bubba Reeves, Martin

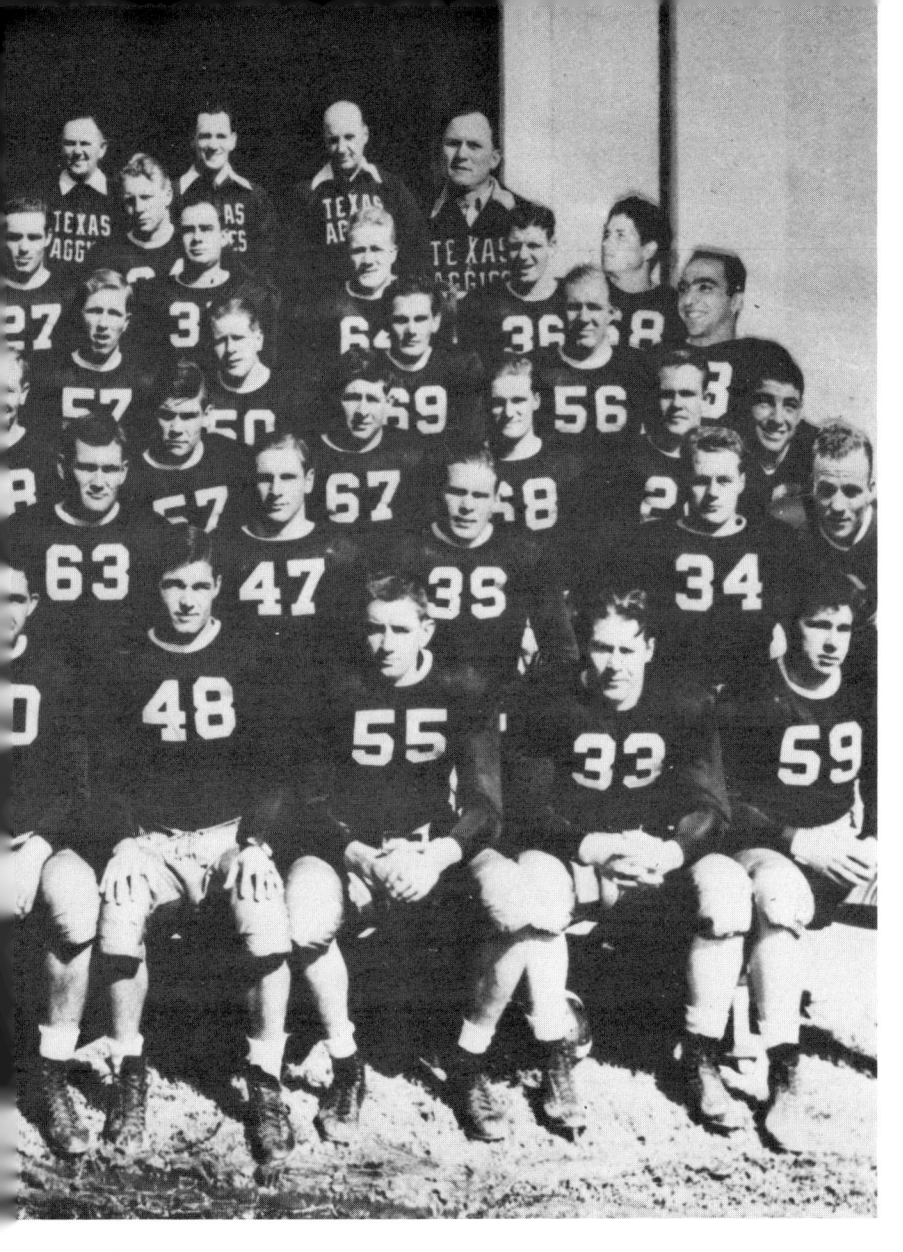

Ruby. Fourth row: Ernie Pannell, Marshall Spivey, Bill Duncan, John Abbott, Zolus Motley, Bill Blessing, Leon Rahn, Harold Cowley, Dog Dawson, Rock Audish. Fifth row: Leonard Joeris, Joe Parish, Howard Shelton, Jo Jo White, Jack Kimbrough, Chip Routt, Carl Geer, Chester Heimann, Joe Boyd, Gus Bates, Willard Clark. Sixth row: Roy Bucek, Henry Hauser, Pinky Williams. Seventh row: Charles Deware, Marty Karow, Bill James, Hub McQuillen, Homer Norton, Lil Dimmitt, Manning Smith, Harry Faulkner, Dough Rollins.

conspicuous to all of the fans, but few realized the remarkable job that he had done blocking and nullifying Harley McCollum, Tulane's all-American tackle. Given belated permission by Dr. Henry Harrison, the team physician, that he could play, Smith subbed in early for Dog Dawson and played the final 59 minutes. After a few offensive plays, Herbie decided that he could take care of McCollum without double-teaming help from teammate Ernie Pannell. He turned to Pannell and said, "Ernie, you go for the linebacker. I can take care of this big SOB all by myself." He did it so thoroughly that McCollum was jerked from the game after logging only 22 minutes.

The tremendous scoreboard success by the 1939 team also proved a financial bonanza for A&M. When the Sugar Bowl pay check arrived, Coach Norton paid off all but $90,000 of the stadium indebtedness plus $30,000 owed to the institution. When the money started coming in for the sale of tickets for the 1940 season, the Kyle Field indebtedness was paid in full.

Norton's personal monetary welfare also took on a good, new look. The Athletic Council tore up his existing contract and gave him a five-year instrument at an annual salary of $10,000. All other members of the Athletic Department were given bonuses in the amount of 10 percent of their annual salaries.

A&M picked up September 28, 1940, where it had left on New Year's Day by defeating Texas A&I at Kyle Field, then ran its string of victories to 19 in a row with only UCLA offering a stern test. The Uclans, who had ranked seventh in the nation the season before, held the Aggies to a 7-0 decision. Jackie Robinson, UCLA's fleet halfback, was injured in the second period and never returned to action. Robinson later became the first Negro to play major league baseball.

The 21-7 conquest of TCU the next week was spiced by the fact that Jim Thomason, who normally served as a street sweeper for John Kimbrough and his talented mates, turned pass receiver with big dividends. Kimbrough passed to him for 14 yards and a touchdown, then Marion Pugh hit him for 35 yards on another scoring aerial.

"Most fans forgot that Thomason could do more than block," Pugh reminded. "Jim could have been one of the best running backs in the conference, but he was so valuable as a blocker he rarely was called to carry the ball."

Pugh believes that the Aggies may have hit their offensive peak for the two great seasons when they whammed Rice, 25-0, for their 19th consecutive victory. That was the day Bill (Jitterbug) Henderson caught eight passes in a row.

"Bug always had the happy approach," Jim Thomason was to observe years later. "He gave it his best, but he could always laugh and break the spell when everybody was getting too serious. He was the best I ever saw at making the hard catches look easy and the easy ones look hard. He used to tell us when we'd get bogged down: 'Throw it to me and I'll unbog us,' and he usually did."

Rice's only other conference loss in 1940 was the 7-6 decision to SMU in the season finale, a victory that enabled it to share the championship with A&M.

Norton had a Rose Bowl bid in his pocket when he took the 1940 Aggies to Austin for the Thanksgiving Day game with Texas. Reflecting on the situation, end Dog Dawson said, "I don't think there was any doubt in anybody's mind that we would win." Kimbrough remembered the circumstances a bit differently. "We were far from overconfident," Kimbrough recalled, "because Marion Pugh was injured and a very doubtful player."

Texas scored in the first 57 seconds, then dug in and turned back repeated A&M threats that developed when Kimbrough ran savagely from a spread formation. Dawson described Texas' whirlwind start by pointing out "They scored almost before the Alma Mater was finished." Texas won 7-0.

Although the Aggies had to share the crown with SMU, it marked the first time in the 26-year history of the Conference that any member had made it to the throne room in successive seasons.

With the Rose Bowl bid lost to Nebraska, and Tennessee booked against Boston College in the Sugar Bowl, the Aggies had the choice of an Orange Bowl or Cotton Bowl invitation. They turned down a trip to Miami and were inclined to turn their backs on Dallas, because some of the seniors preferred participation in the all-Star games that would be more lucrative personally.

Pugh remembered that Dough Rollins made a tremendous

talk to the squad in discussing their obligations and responsibilities to play in Dallas. "I finally got up and had my say, too, because I really wanted to play in the Cotton Bowl. We voted by a slim margin to play." The juniors assured the decision.

Just eight days after announcing a meeting of A&M and Fordham, the Cotton Bowl Classic was sold out, assuring a capacity crowd of 45,507, the largest ever to see a game in the Southwest. It was the first year the Cotton Bowl had been operated by the Cotton Bowl Athletic Assocation in cooperation with the Southwest Conference, assuring the Classic of the Conference champion for years to come.

A&M's 13-12 verdict over Fordham was highlighted by another successful hide-out venture by Earl (Bama) Smith. The swift Aggie attempted the deception on the first play from

'Bama Smith scores on hide-out play in Cotton Bowl.

scrimmage in the second half. Fordham's Rams detected Smith's efforts, however, and he was summoned back to the Aggie huddle and was called upon to carry the ball. After being downed, he headed for the sidelines as if to leave the game.

Then, in full view of the capacity crowd, Smith hid out near the sideline and this time without being detected by the Rams. The Aggies rushed the huddle, and Smith was off with the snap, straight down the sideline. Marion Pugh faded back to his 25-yard line and let go a long, graceful spiral that Smith took in on the Fordham 35, several yards behind Fordham's Len Eshmont. He raced into the end zone to complete the 62-yard scoring play.

A&M was back in the Cotton Bowl the next New Year's

1940 Southwest Conference Champions

1941 Southwest Conference Champions

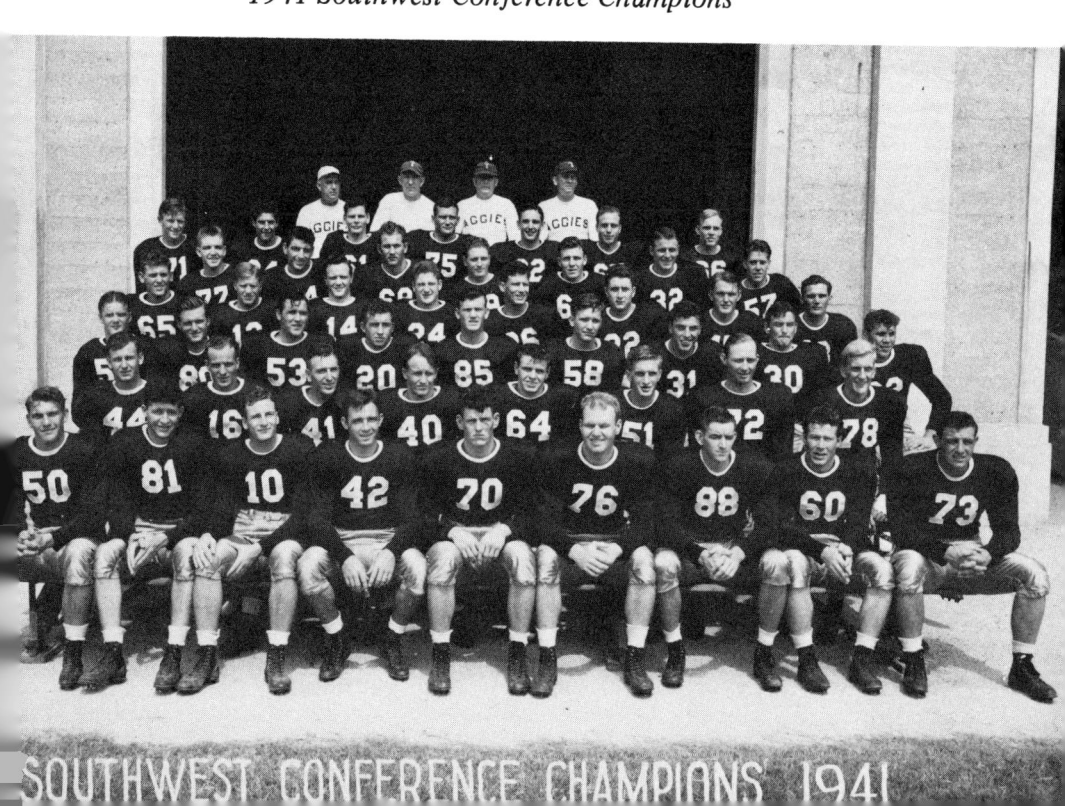

Day despite a 23-0 loss to Texas on Kyle Field, the first loss to the Longhorns there in 18 years. That was the only setback by the Aggies as they finished three successive years with a regular-season record of 27-2-0. All of the regulars from the national championship team had departed except for Jim Sterling and Derace Moser. Both gained consensus all-Conference recognition along with Tackle Martin Ruby and Center Bill Sibley. Moser, who was to sacrifice his life a year later in World War II, led the Conference in passing and total offense and set school career punt return records that still stand.

The Aggies dominated the 1942 Cotton Bowl meeting with Alabama statistically, but their benevolence cost them dearly. They lost the ball six times through fumbles and seven times by pass interceptions. The Crimson Tide made only one first down and netted only 75 yards total offense while A&M was totaling 309. Yet Alabama scored 29 points to only 21 for A&M.

Jake Webster, who had set a Conference record of 29 extra-points from placement in the regular season, added three more on this occasion.

Beset by manpower losses to the service prior to the 1942 season, A&M dropped to fifth in the Conference standings and endured a losing season at 4-5-1. One of the better performances was in Austin on Thanksgiving Day in a game Texas had to win to capture its first championship in 12 years. A 71-yard punt return by Aggie Barney Welch for a touchdown had the score deadlocked at 6-all until the Longhorns counted the winning points in the final 50 seconds for a 12-6 score.

Gig 'Em! John Kimbrough

"Take one part Man O' War, one part Mack truck, one part King Kong.

"Mix well and pour into No. 39 uniform of the Texas Aggies.

"And you know what you've got?

"You have 'Jarring Jawn' Kimbrough, the greatest football player that these 36-year-old eyes have ever lamped."

That was the impression John Kimbrough made on Charles (Pie) Dufour of the *New Orleans States*, who remains one of the most revered newspapermen in that city while serving part-time also as a lecturer at Tulane University.

Kimbrough, of course, had led the Texas Aggies to a 14-13 victory over Tulane in the Sugar Bowl. As a 210-pound junior he had sparked A&M to the first of three Southwest Conference championships in a row as an all-American fullback.

Dufour was not alone in recognizing the role Kimbrough had played in the great victory. Most of the newspapermen and press association writers trumpeted the jarring fullback in their leads. Among them was Arch Ward, then the sports editor of the *Chicago Tribune* and the originator of both the baseball all-Star and College all-Star football games.

Ward, who had seen Tom Harmon, Michigan's great all-American back, during the season, wrote: "Somewhere there may be a better college football player than John Kimbrough, 210-pound fullback for Texas A&M, but you will never be able to convince the 70,000 spectators who today saw him almost single-handedly defeat gallant Tulane, 14-13.

John Kimbrough must have winced when he saw, or else heard, the "single-handed" reference. He knew that one man did not make a team, because he had come up the hard, tedious way at A&M. As a sophomore he had to fight his way from fourth-string designation, and it took him five games to climb into the starting lineup.

Furthermore he remembers the contribution of each and every player on that 1939 championship team. Nearly thirty-five years later he talked about his teammates and said, "You have to start with Herbie Smith. And Jim Thomason was the heart and soul of our football team. He could do it all and was a good man with it. Tommie Vaughn did not get much recognition, but he had the determination and the gift of gab to go with it. You know, he came along with Thomason (both from Brownwood, Texas) just like I came along with Odell Herman."

One by one Kimbrough singled out his teammates, giving each credit for their part in all of the success in a 19-game winning streak in 1939-40.

Kimbrough's great performance probably made the defeat more agonizing for Tulane fans who remembered that at one time the great fullback was ticketed for a Green Wave uniform. Kimbrough had attended summer school there for a short time in 1937 and had planned a medical career. His father had been a physician at hometown Haskell, Texas, and a brother a few years older (Ernest) was interning at Harmann Hospital in Houston at that time. John became disenchanted at Tulane, dropped out, and entered A&M that fall. He had been recruited in a major recovery program Homer Norton had instituted, but he did not take a scholarship at A&M for granted until he and his brother Ernest went to College Station and had a visit with Dough Rollins, a member of Norton's staff.

The youngest of seven children, six of them boys, John was reared by Dr. and Mrs. W. A. Kimbrough. He was talented and big enough to make the Haskell High School squad as a seventh grader, but was ineligible until the following year. As a freshman at that time he was 6-0 and weighed 170. His best season at Haskell was in 1934 when he teamed with his brother Jack to form a great backfield duo. Jack played end when the two of them teamed together at A&M.

John was injured midway of his junior season in high school and transferred to Abilene. He was subjected to a lot of criticism for the move, but his mother came to his defense. "I never would have consented to let him go to Abilene if he hadn't been hurt," she said. "I knew he would be ineligible at Abilene until the next season and would give his shoulder plenty of time to heal. As it was, I was afraid he would try to go ahead and play in Haskell, injured or not."

Kimbrough was not eligible to play at Abilene until midseason of 1936, and Dewey Mayhew's Eagles had been mediocre until John entered the lineup. They had been tied by Lubbock and beaten by the Brownwood team starring Tommy Vaughn and Jim Thomason. Kimbrough teamed with Odell Herman to lead Abilene to the district championship, but the Eagles lost in the quarter-finals to Blair Cherry's Amarillo Sandies, then in the midst of winning three straight state championships.

Kimbrough missed the all-district team by only one vote despite the fact he played in only half the games, but both Thomason and Herman were named to the all-district backfield, and the latter was all-state. Herman also went to Tulane before entering A&M.

John aspired to go to the United States Military Academy, but the offer of an appointment did not come until after his freshman year at A&M. When he left Tulane and decided to attend A&M, he gave up on the idea of becoming a physician because of the added expense of attending medical school.

Backfield talent was so deep that John recalls, "I didn't make the team my freshman year at A&M." Actually, John did not earn a numeral that year, the letter equivalent for freshmen, but mainly because of injuries.

"They tried to make a guard of me my sophomore year, but I couldn't move quick enough. They gave me a mighty bad time then. They wanted a fullback who could move and be elusive, but I wasn't that type."

Of course a lot of big, rugged backs were being converted to guard by Homer Norton and Bill James. A fullback at Klondike (Texas) High School, Marshall Robnett became an all-American guard. Bill (Rock) Audish of nearby Brenham made the same change, while Odell Herman, the all-stater, was converted to center once Kimbrough made the grade in the backfield.

"Although little was heard of John until the Baylor game of his sophomore season," Dick Todd reminds that "he was developing all along and with his size and speed all he needed was the opportunity. Once he got it, he was there to stay." Todd, of course, was A&M's great running back of that 1938 season.

When Kimbrough was acclaimed all-American as a junior in 1939, Coach Norton termed him "the greatest player I've ever had. He can do everything and do it well. He is big, rugged, and can take punishment. He is exceptionally fast for his size, and we use him not only as a line plunger but also on end sweeps.

John Kimbrough "hit hardest when going was tough."

John hits the hardest when the going's tough."

A year later after Kimbrough had been chosen on 31 recognized all-America selections and was named the outstanding athlete of 1940 by Philadelphia writers, Homer Norton surprised football fans by revealing that "John never enjoyed playing football. When he found out how much ability he had, he played because he had to. He played because of pride. I don't think he ever really liked football."

That might explain partially John Kimbrough's designation of his most memorable moment in football. It was not a great run, making all-American, or any of his other achievements. It happened on a later November Saturday when A&M was preparing for its Thanksgiving Day game with Texas in 1939.

"Someone ran out on the practice field and told us that SMU had beaten Baylor, which assured us of the 1939 championship. That was the outstanding thrill I remember."

Kimbrough received his degree in Agricultural Administration in 1941, then after summer camp with the Reserve Officer Training Corps he was commissioned a second lieutenant in the infantry. Before being called to service during World War II he signed a personal services contract with a New York promoter. It was during this interim period that he played one season of football with the New York Yankees and was featured in a movie entitled *The Long Star Ranger.*

After being called to military duty, Kimbrough and a number of his teammates were assigned to an Army all-Star football team to play five games against professional teams. They were coached by Wallace Wade, on leave from his coaching job at Duke University. It was a reunion of one of the 1939 backfield combines of Marion Pugh, Jim Thomason, Bill Conatser, and Kimbrough, and they were joined by Dog Dawson and guard Joe Routt, all-American in 1936 and 1937.

In one of their games they opposed the Washington Redskins that had Dick Todd and Sam Baugh in the lineup. Todd remembers that his old buddy Joe Routt gave him such a bad time that the referee had to put a stop to it.

Kimbrough had aspired to enter pilot training but was under the impression he was too big to qualify. Waddy Young and Don Scott, who had distinguished themselves at Oklahoma and Ohio State, respectively, had become Air Force pilots and were assigned to the Army all-Star football squad. They convinced Kimbrough that he could enter flight training if he got his weight down to 200 pounds. This he did, and he received his wings in 1943 at the Marfa (Texas) Air Force Base. He attained the rank of captain while serving in the Pacific Theater.

After military service John played three seasons of football with the Los Angeles Dons, then was elected to the Texas legislature. He terminated his brief political career after one term in the legislature and has been ranching at Haskell since.

Stopover To West Point

Fielding a team in 1943 presented a major challenge to Homer Norton. World War II service took virtually every veteran player and most of the coaching staff as well. Coaches Dough Rollins, Martin Karow, and Charley DeWare, Jr., went on active duty along with the 1942 seniors and most of the juniors and sophomores.

The exodus of players made a Twelfth Man call a standard procedure at Aggieland during the war years. Norton fielded a team in 1943 that was so young it became known as the Whiz Kids, and as the Beardless Wonders in some references. These youngsters posted a surprising 7-2-1 season record and gained a trip to the Orange Bowl as a reward. They lost in Miami, however, to LSU, 19-14, a team they had defeated earlier, 28-13. Norton, of course, had to be calling on new faces for nearly every game as the season progressed.

Lots of other colleges had Army or Navy training programs, and the men attending were permitted to participate regardless of previous college playing records. Some of the schools in the lower levels that had instituted these programs suddenly became giants. Ironically, Norton's reputation of producing great players also cost him great talent.

Colonel Earl H. (Red) Blaik, then coach at the United States Military Academy, called and asked Coach Norton to send him a list of his best players. Colonel Blaik advised Norton that he could arrange to have the players appointed to West Point or drafted, and once drafted they could receive appointment to the Academy.

In fairness to his players Norton sent along a list including Hank Foldberg, Dewitt Coulter, Goble Bryant, Milt Routt, and Marion Flanagan, three of whom had lettered at A&M. Blaik summoned all of them along with Charley Shira, then Dan Foldberg, and Bill Yeoman after their 1945 season with the Aggies.

Five of those conscripted gained all-America acclaim, and three—Hank Foldberg, Yeoman, and Shira—became head coaches. Hank concluded his coaching career in 1964 after three seasons at A&M, while Shira is full-time athletic director at Mississippi State after serving as both director and head coach. Yeoman has brought the University of Houston to the fore since taking over there in 1962.

Norton had to replace these great players by calling on the student body to come up with more Twelfth Man contributions to supplement those youngsters who stayed briefly before going into service and others who stayed long enough to play out their eligibility. Back Paul Yates and end Clarence Howell gained all-Conference as freshmen in 1944 before being called into service, while Monte Moncrief was a consensus all-SWC tackle for the first of three times.

Freshmen Bob Goode and Preston Smith created a lot of excitement for a young Aggie crew in 1945. The rangy Goode led the league in scoring and gained all-SWC acclaim along with two other newcomers who were to be all-stars each of their four seasons: SMU's Doak Walker and Dick Harris, the Longhorn center. Guard Grant Darnell joined teammates Goode and Moncrief as all-stars.

An unheralded 17-year-old freshman whose name did not appear in the game program squad list had the Aggies on the verge of an upset in the 1945 Thanksgiving Day battle with Cotton Bowl-bound Texas. Gene Johnson, playing only in his second college game, ran 44 yards on his first carry and set up an A&M touchdown. His all-round play was so brilliant Felix McKnight, managing editor of the *Dallas Morning News*, wrote a sidebar on the game extolling Johnson that carried this headline:

Little Guy's Best
Not Quite Enough

Homer Norton, obviously lifted even after a 20-10 loss, told his inspired players: "Never as proud of any team in my life. I've had great teams at A&M, but none ever gave more than you men today. Proud of you."

"When my boys on football scholarships went off to war," Norton was to say later, "They knew they could come back and I would honor those scholarships. I didn't regard them as scholarships to play football; they were scholarships that enabled them to get an education. When they started coming back in 1946, some had families and others had lost their zest for football, but play or no I gave all of them their scholarships because they were entitled to them.

"I knew what I was doing, of course. This used up all of my football scholarships, and I had none left to offer new material to beef up our squad. But it was the right thing to do. Nevertheless it got me in trouble with the alumni."

In 1946 it was suggested that Norton step down as either head coach or athletic director and concentrate on just a single capacity. It appears he made the wrong decision, for his team posted a 4-6-0 record and finished fourth in the Conference standings after impressive shutout victories in the first two league tests. The 1947 record was 3-6-1, and there was a lower drop in the standings.

Following the 1947 season Homer Norton yielded to the dissidents and accepted the offer to pay off the final two years of his contract. The final figure was never released, but since adjustments had to be made to take care of additional income tax and house rent for a two-year period, it was reported to have been a settlement in excess of $30,000.

Appropriately, perhaps, the hide-out play was a factor in Norton's last victory for A&M. Frank Broyles, the highly-successful Arkansas coach, was a 21-year-old assistant at Baylor on this occasion, and he likes to tell the story.

"Early in the week we called in Buddy Crews. He wouldn't start, so his job would be to watch both sidelines on the kickoff and the first play from scrimmage to check for an A&M player hiding out. That taken care of, we forgot all about it. On the first play Stan Hollmig took the snap and turned and passed to Barney Welch streaking down the sidelines. Barney had to lunge for the ball on the 7-yard line, and fall, or else he'd have gone

171

all of the way. Before the play was over we started looking for Crews to find out how it had happened.

"Coach, I didn't see a thing," he said. When we got the films, they showed that the hideout man was standing right by Crews.

A&M won it, 24-0, and kept Baylor in a hole most of the way with uncanny coffin-corner punting by Stan Hollmig.

"It's How You Show Up At Showdown That Counts"

One of the Southwest's—and the nation's—outstanding figures in the development of collegiate football giants almost missed the boat. Using his own words, it is just a "happen so" that Homer Hill Norton became a builder of champions and a National Football Hall of Fame coach.

The first love of the man whose Texas Aggies held the Southwest Conference consecutive winning streak for a quarter of a century was baseball—not football. Although he lettered in all major sports at Birmingham-Southern College, was acclaimed the best all-round athlete in school, and was recognized as one of the best ends in Southern football, Norton's ambition as a youngster was to become a baseball star.

In fact after taking his bachelor's degree in 1916, he signed with a minor league team and played three seasons, progressing so well he was sold to a team in a league of higher classification. He never reported, however. During his off-time from baseball in 1920 he accepted a part-time job as assistant football coach at Centenary. He was line coach under Bo McMillin there in 1922 and was offered the head job when Bo left for Geneva College but turned it down until 1926. In eight seasons with the upstart Centenary Gents he developed three undefeated teams, put together a string of 20 victories once and 14 shutouts in a row on another occasion.

It was his great record and fabulous success against Southwest Conference foes that led to his appointment as Texas A&M coach in 1934. His 1939 and 1940 teams at A&M put together 19 straight victories and championships in those two seasons and again in 1941, enabling him to be the first Conference coach to develop three championships in succession.

Coach Norton is a member of the National Football Hall of Fame, the Texas Sports Hall of Fame, and the Texas A&M University Athletic Hall of Fame.

"He was ahead of his time," John Kimbrough said of his coach when he was presenting him for enshrinement in the Texas Sports Hall of Fame in 1968. "You know, we threw the ball in those championship years. We had two good passers in Cotton Price and Marion Pugh. They threw to wide receivers like they do today. We also used a lot of open blocking like they do now, one-on-one instead of two-on-one. Coach was a real inspirational leader and always considerate. He did not let us run up the score when we could, because he had been on the other end of the stick."

Dick Todd, who was one of Norton's greatest, described his mentor as "a real dedicated person. I don't believe I've ever seen a man who worked any harder. He worked hard, and he expected the boys to work just as hard."

Dough Rollins, a member of Norton's staff except during his wartime leave, had the same impression. "He was the hardest working man I've had anything to do with. He lived and dreamed football. We started nightly meetings the first of September, and we kept meeting every night during the week until Thanksgiving."

Born the son of a Methodist minister, Homer Norton was raised in a strict home. Certain ideals were drilled into him, and he never wavered from them. He believed in the Golden Rule and never played a game to avenge an earlier loss by an unnecessarily big score.

"I am definitely a believer in right," he observed in a 1939 interview. "I think right will prevail. It may take a long time, but it comes as sure as death and taxes. My father (the Reverend John W. Norton) taught me that lesson many years ago. He served in the same job in the Northern Alabama Conference of the Methodist Church for 50 years, and his job was looking after the needs of all of the superannuated ministers in his conference. Right always prevailed for him, and it has for me. That is one creed that I really believe in, and it

Homer Norton had pride in building character.

gives me a lot of personal satisfaction to acknowledge my deep faith in public.

"I'm not ashamed in the least to admit that one of the best and finest things a coach does is to develop character."

Coach Norton believed in a certain type of discipline. Players were expected to carry out their assignment without complaint, and there never was any questioning of authority. Profanity was forbidden by both players and coaches. His rules were observed so thoroughly that only one player was dismissed from his A&M squads because of disobedience.

"Homer Norton coached his players for the greatest things in life," says H. B. McElroy, his long-time publicist at A&M. "Those players have turned out to be high-ranking military officers up to the rank of major general, physicians, bankers, attorneys, accountants, ranchers, educators, insurance men, engineers, and corporation executives. One became a renowned evangelist."

When Norton walked away from Texas A&M, he was heartbroken. He loved the school and only the desire to do the best for the school led him to accept the alumni request for him to quit. He confided at the time to a friend: "They may have ended their side of the contract, but I agreed to coach only at Texas A&M for the past two years, and I will not even consider an offer from any other school."

He entered the motel business in Galveston and later bought one in Rosenberg, but after a few years he returned to College Station to build and operate a popular restaurant across the road from the main entrance to the A&M campus. From his front door he could see the light towers of Kyle Field.

Homer Norton died of a heart attack at his College Station home in May, 1965. The Texas Senate, then in session, passed a resolution praising him for the glory he had brought to Texas A&M and the Lone Star state. Likewise the Board of Directors of Texas A&M University issued a resolution acknowledging the honor, credit, and glory he had brought to the institution.

Dana X. Bible, who had coached at A&M with success before being a contemporary of Norton while coaching at the University of Texas, phrased his regard aptly when he said, "Texas is a better place because Homer Norton lived here."

Norton lived and died by the creed he impressed on his players: "It's how you show up at the showdown that counts." Homer Hill Norton showed up brilliantly.

Played Best Against The Best

When Harry Stiteler succeeded Homer Norton as head coach at Texas A&M, he greeted a bunch of talented freshmen backfielders who were never to bask in championship glory yet were destined to share in some memorable moments. Unfortunately they were not eligible for the 1948 varsity, and they simply did not have enough seasoned help to make a splash as sophomores in 1949.

"Naturally, we had a good recruiting success my first year, for I had been a high school coach through 1945, and I got a lot of help from coaches who were friends," Stiteler reminds.

Among those new recruits were Bob Smith, who was to establish ball-carrying records that would stand for virtually a quarter of a century, Glenn Lippman, Yale Lary, Billy Tidwell, Dick Gardemal, Hugh Meyer, Elo Nohavitza, and James Fowler.

Stiteler, an Aggie quarterback in 1930, had been on Norton's staff in 1947, and he knew the talent well virtually had run dry. "If they had left Coach Norton alone, he would have been back in there winning," Stiteler observed in retrospect. "The man had enough honor about himself to honor the scholarship of every one of those boys who went to service. Some of them could no longer play college football, but he refused to take away their scholarships."

The 1948 Aggies scored two touchdowns in eight of their ten games, but they did not have the defense to stop any of them and failed to win a game. Stiteler recalls that, "We played everybody a good game until we would wear out, and we tied Texas when we did not have any business doing it."

A&M had not defeated Texas in eight successive seasons, which made the 14-14 tie a victory of sorts. Early in the fourth quarter Bob Goode scored a touchdown to tie the score at 7-all, then Texas seemed to clinch victory with another touchdown with less than four minutes remaining. Undaunted, A&M's Burl Baty fired a long, desperate pass from deep in his own territory. One of the Texas defenders got his hands on the ball, but it ricocheted off into the arms of Charley Wright who sped 25 yards to climax a 72-yard scoring play. Herb Turley kicked the tieing point.

Despite the tie Texas was invited to the Orange Bowl and in the face of "third-rate" criticism upset Georgia, 41-28.

The scoreboard improved very little in 1949, when the Aggies managed only one victory and a tie, but Coach Stiteler was encouraged because his talented sophomores never gave up. One of them, Glenn Lippman, vividly remembered his baptism: "I was one of those who was supposed to help lead A&M out of its football doldrums. We started by playing Villanova which was rated even better than the previous year when it beat A&M by three touchdowns. We got walloped, of course, and I guess the thing that embarrassed me the most is that I was never able to find out what the turf was like across the line of scrimmage. I believe I ended up with minus yardage. I knew then we were in for a long season."

After a victory over Texas Tech in the second game, there was only one big moment the rest of the year. "That came," Lippman recalled, "when we tied an SMU team (27-27) that had Kyle Rote and Doak Walker operating in the same backfield."

Lippman had one other recollection of that season: "We were playing Baylor at Kyle Field in the mud and rain. I remember that Baylor was wearing white pants and that Adrian Burk, the quarterback, played the entire game without getting any mud on his pants. Not even a smudge. Needless to say we didn't do a good job of rushing him." Baylor won, 21-0.

Despite all of the ball-carrying talent A&M was picked to finish last in 1950 by those participating in the annual TCU poll. It was understandable. For two straight years the Aggies had been picked sixth and finished seventh each time.

The Aggies made the seers look bad from the beginning, however. They whipped Nevada and Texas Tech and appeared well on the way to a major upset of Oklahoma, which had finished second to Notre Dame in the 1949 ratings and was riding a 22-game winning streak. Big plays by Bob Smith, Billy Tidwell, and Glenn Lippman had A&M in front, 28-20, with less than four minutes to play. Shortly thereafter the Billy Vessels-led Sooners scored, but failed to add the extra point, and A&M led, 28-27.

Victory appeared secure for the Aggies since they had possession near midfield. Oklahoma forced a punt, however, and it carried only to the Oklahoma 31. A&M had been fairly successful in containing OU's awesome split-T ground game, but at this stage Oklahoma was not going to run. There was only 1:46 to play, and they had to make a lot of yardage in a hurry. Four passes carried to the 14-yard line, and Leon Heath scored from there, making Oklahoma a 34-28 victor.

"They ate us alive passing against our defense," Lippman remembered almost a quarter of a century later.

Recalling that an eight-point lead had been wiped out in little more than three minutes, Stiteler said, "It may sound like sour grapes, but I am still not convinced we were not a victim of clock trouble."

Three weeks later the Aggies let another big one get away. Baylor spotted A&M 13 points, but it became Baylor's game after the first 12 minutes. Bob Smith had started the Aggies off on the right foot, racing 66 yards on the first play from scrimmage. Smith suffered a broken nose in the second quarter, and neither he nor Billy Tidwell played in the second half. Glenn Lippman made only one brief appearance in the final periods after being knocked cold.

The Aggies also were plagued by their own mistakes, losing the ball five times on fumbles and three times on interceptions as Larry Isbell passed Baylor to a 27-20 come-from-behind decision.

When the Aggies squared off as decided underdogs in Dallas against SMU, the Mustangs were ranked seventh in the nation. SMU asserted itself early before a full house of 75,000 and drove 57 yards for a score on its first possession. That was only the beginning of the fireworks however, for within the next minute Bob Smith, wearing a grotesque mask to protect the broken nose sustained in the Baylor game, started on a rampage that was not to end until he had set a Southwest Conference rushing record of 297 yards.

The first time he handled the ball Smith took a pitch from Dick Gardemal, and when Billy Tidwell cleared him with a crisp block, he sped 75 yards for a touchdown. Glenn Lippman scored from the 10 in the second quarter after Yale Lary had set the stage with a 64-yard punt return, and A&M stretched the lead to 19-7 on a Gardemal to Tidwell pass after Carl Molberg recovered a Kyle Rote fumble at the SMU 16.

SMU rallied and wiped out the advantage and took a 20-19 lead with the clock showing only 4:12 remaining. Coach Harry Stiteler turned to Smith and said, "Saddle up, you're going in." Smith's reply: "I'm saddled up."

On the first play following the kickoff substitute quarterback Delmer Sikes handed off to Smith at the A&M 26, and he set out on a 74-yard scoring jaunt. He was on his own once he broke into the secondary. He apparently was headed off about the SMU 40, but he faked a lateral at this stage, then shot directly between two defenders to give A&M a 25-20 victory.

Smith's rushing record of 297 yards was to stand for 23 years, and when it was broken on the same Cotton Bowl field, Bob Smith, his wife, and a son were there as spectators to see it. They watched Roosevelt Leaks of Texas rush for 342 yards against SMU on his way to breaking Smith's full-season record of 1,302 by gaining 1,415 in 10 games.

Coach Stiteler was quoted following the 1950 game: "There were two great clubs out there today that wouldn't quit. Time ran out on SMU, that's all. I'm happy for the boys. They're the ones who have been suffering."

Nearly a quarter of a century later Stiteler lauded Bob Smith and Glenn Lippman for their roles in the game. "I've never seen a back who could do what Bob could with a ball. As a pure runner he's the best I've ever seen. As for moves after passing the line of scrimmage, I've never seen one who could hold a light to him."

As for Lippman, who was assigned to a strange role that day, Stiteler observed, "I have worlds of respect for Glenn

Bob Smith as Masked Marvel set rushing record against SMU that stood for 23 years.

Lippman. He could come closer to getting a needed yard than Smith, but in that SMU game he played a role on defense that was equally vital to us. After we took the 25-20 lead, I sent him in at guard on defense with one thing in mind, and that was to stop Rote. The only way they could beat us was with a swing pass."

Lippman remembered, "I recall very vividly the surprise look of the big SMU offensive tackle when he saw this 170-pound midget lining up in front of him. As it turned out on the fourth down play, SMU did indeed throw the ball to Rote near the sideline, and I was able to tackle him and keep him in bounds as the clock ran out."

A fitting climax for the 1950 season was a bid to the Presidential Cup Game in Washington, D. C., December 9. A&M won, 40-20, with Bob Smith setting a good tempo with a 100-yard return of the opening kickoff.

Georgia fumbled on its first play from scrimmage, and Jimmy Fowler recovered for A&M at the Bulldogs' 22. With only two minutes gone Dick Gardemal passed to Glenn Lippman for a second Aggie touchdown. Another Fowler recovery on the A&M 19 set the scene for Smith to break 81 yards for a 20-0 lead. Billy Tidwell added 2 more touchdowns before the intermission, then burst 36 yards to give A&M 40 points before Georgia got on the board.

Smith advanced the ball a total of 306 yards: 158 on 20 rushes, returned kicks 121, caught passes for 22, and completed a pass for 5. Guard Max Greiner and tackle Dwayne Tucker were line stars for the Aggies.

When Harry Stiteler departed the scene after the 1950 season, the coaching position was offered to Barlow (Bones) Irvin, who was athletic director, but he declined. "If Harry had stayed for the 1951 season, I believe we would have won the championship going away," Irvin observed years later.

Ray George took over the coaching reins in 1951 and fashioned a 5-3-2 record yet did not win a Conference game until the season finale. Picked for second place behind Baylor by the handicappers, the Aggies started as if they had been accurately appraised. They won four in a row, starting with a 21-14 conquest of UCLA. They really commanded attention when they knocked off Oklahoma, the defending national champion, 14-7.

"The whole team was pointing for Oklahoma ever since we lost the game we should have won in 1950," Glenn Lippman observed. "We had hoped they would still be undefeated when we played them, however, they had lost in the Sugar Bowl. (Kentucky stopped the streak at 31 games, third longest among major colleges in the last 50 years.)

"It was one of the few times in my career that I could sense before the game that everyone was ready to play. We went out and played probably one of the finest games we had played during the time I was at A&M. We were especially pleased with the way our defense played in that it kept Oklahoma in the hole most of the night."

When the Aggies took the field on Thanksgiving Day, they had lost three conference games and tied two. Texas was still in the running for an Orange Bowl bid by virtue of having beaten

Baylor. Ray George's Aggies settled that situation, however, by upsetting Texas, 22-21, and opening the door for Baylor at Miami. It was A&M's first decision over Texas since the Longhorns started their domination in 1940.

Bob Smith suffered a broken jaw on the opening kickoff, and Lippman subbed in to play the entire game at fullback. He gained 174 yards in what by his own admission was "the best game of my career." A&M scored first, but Texas had taken a 14-7 advantage at half time. The Aggies crammed 15 points into the third quarter on Yale Lary's 68-yard romp, a 31-yard field goal by Darrow Hooper, and a 37-yard pass from Hooper to Lary.

Texas stormed back in the final quarter for a touchdown and narrowed the margin to a single point. Johnny Salyer intercepted a Longhorn pass to thwart one bid, and Texas' June Davis was short with a desperation field goal with only 10 seconds remaining.

Fisticuffs flurried throughout the day, and as the game ended both teams charged with arms and elbows flailing. When it was over the Cadet Corps hoisted the A&M heroes to their shoulders.

One incident very humorous to Lippman and his teammates that day involved Russell Hudeck, a big, jovial reserve tackle who had played very little during his career, mainly because he was "easy going and wasn't mean enough." He subbed into this game and was playing quite well, and when a Texas player took a swing at him Hudeck retaliated by decking the opponent. "Since we had seen Russell on so many occasions when the coaches tried vainly to get him fired up, it was surprising to see him take such an aggressive stand," Lippman recalled.

Tackle Jack Little gained all-American acclaim as a junior in 1951 and was consensus all-Conference along with center Hugh Meyer and Yale Lary, the talented punter who was chosen on the defensive platoon. Lippman, who gained some all-Conference mention, set a school season rushing record of 6.8 yards per carry that still stands.

Quarterback Ray Graves and halfback Don Ellis salvaged some offensive glory by forming a battery that enabled the 1952 Aggies to win 3 games and tie another. Graves led the conference in passing with a 19-completion edge, but he lost the total offense title in the season finale with Texas. Graves' biggest day was in the 31-12 conquest of Arkansas, when he completed 19 of 31 passes for 231 yards and 3 touchdowns. Each of those scoring passes were caught by Ellis, who also had the distinction of leading the conference in kickoff returns and his own team in ball-carrying.

Ellis was switched from receiver to passer in 1953 and was a success at the conversion from the start. He led A&M to a 7-6 victory over Kentucky, then completed 15 of 26 pass attempts in a 14-14 deadlock with Houston. Ellis gained all-Conference recognition and went into the final week as the league's leading passer. His leading receiver was Bennie Sinclair, and another of his targets was Elwood Kettler, destined to be the quarterback the next season.

The 1953 Aggies went into a mid-season showdown with Baylor with a record of four victories and a tie in their first five tests. Baylor likewise was undefeated. Despite 11 completions in 19 attempts by Don Ellis, Baylor emerged a 14-13 victor. The Aggies drove 87 yards in the final quarter and scored on an Ellis pass to Sinclair but failed to kick the conversion attempt that would have tied the score. Connie Magouirk probably had the best performance of his career as he raced 23 yards for the first Aggie touchdown.

A&M's bid for a successful season started caving in the following week against Arkansas, and the Aggies did not win another game.

Junction: A Tale By The Bear

Twelve seasons without a championship was unprecedented at A&M; so, a name coach with a winning record was the objective when the search began for a replacement of Ray George. Oklahoma had its Bud Wilkinson, Michigan State its Biggie Munn, Notre Dame its Frank Leahy, and Georgia Tech its Bobby Dodd. Crowding into the limelight with them was a young coach at Kentucky, who earlier in the 1950s had led his teams to an upset of National Champion Oklahoma in the 1951 Sugar Bowl and a Cotton Bowl conquest of Dutch Meyer's TCU Frogs the following New Year's Day.

Paul William (Bear) Bryant probably could have had any head coaching job that was available after the 1953 season. LSU wanted him to replace Gus Tinsley, and Bear was asked to name his price. He deliberately priced himself out of the job, because he still had not convinced himself he was ready to leave Kentucky. Alabama wanted him also, but Alabama Coach H. D. (Red) Drew had coached him, and Bryant did not want to return to his alma mater at that price.

A&M had contacted Bryant early, but it was not until he closed himself out at LSU that he began serious negotiations with the Aggie administration. He came to terms with A&M in February, 1954, but Kentucky was not going to let him leave. He had a contract that had to be honored, they said, yet they finally released him.

Bryant took A&M sight unseen as far as the campus was concerned, although his Kentucky team had won at Kyle Field in 1952. Thousands of cadets were at Easterwood Airport to greet him on his arrival. He went directly to yell practice at the Grove, and he pulled off his coat, rolled up his sleeves, and gave the Corps some enthusiasm to match theirs. He won the hearts of the Cadets right there. When he registered at the MSC (Memorial Student Center), he paused momentarily when filling out his home address, then penned in College Station, putting Lexington behind him.

Bryant was shocked the first time he gathered his squad together for football practice. He thought if there were 75 players on scholarship there had to be at least 15 football players. He second-guessed himself, however, when he began working with the remnants of a team that had won only one conference game in posting a 4-5-1 record in 1953.

"Two things I remember about that first spring practice under Coach Bryant," Gene Stallings was to recount a score of years later. A freshman at the time and destined to be a head coach at his alma mater, Stallings mentioned, "It was a tough one for No. 1. Another was that we practiced at night. Coach Bryant went to the ROTC authorities in an effort to get us excused from drill in the afternoon, but they refused him. So, we practiced at night."

Coach Bryant posted a list each day of those he was keeping out for practice. "If you were not on that list, you could not participate any more in the spring," Stallings remembered. "Those not listed were not taken off scholarship, however. We freshmen always were down near the bottom of the list. Somehow we made it."

An off-campus, fall training site near Junction, Texas, was suggested by Willie Zapalac, a holdover assistant coach who had played for A&M a decade earlier. Zapalac was familiar with the Junction area that A&M had used for so many other school purposes. Coach Bryant chartered a place for a checking-out mission and was so impressed he started formulating plans for a 10-day stay at Junction.

"When we reported for fall practice," Gene Stallings recalled, "Coach Bryant told us to get a blanket, pillow, and several changes of clothes because we were going on a trip. None of the players had any idea of where we were going. We wound up at the Junction camp. We were out on the field each

Paul Bryant: He knew that Rome was not built in a day, but he was not the foreman on that job!

practice day before the sun came up. Then we would go have breakfast. We would have practice in the afternoon, then a meeting at night. Real soon some of the players began to quit."

Jones Ramsey, who was sports information director at A&M in the Bryant era, believes "the training in Junction made the 1956 team a championship team." Reflecting on all of the players who gave up and went home Ramsey recalls, "I was the only sports publicist in America who could list his entire roster on an 8½ x 11 sheet horizontally."

The manpower situation became so critical after three centers quit the team that Bryant promptly issued a uniform to Troy Summerlin, a 150-pound student manager who had played in high school. Another example of calling on the Twelfth Man for help.

Recognition of the number of players who defected was expressed well by Stallings: "We had planned to stay longer, but we ran out of people. We went out in two buses and came back in one."

Bryant was proud of the sacrifices his troops made at that storied early training camp, but he resented the allegations that likened the player treatment to the Bataan Death March. "It was maligned too much," he recalls with an air of futility. With the Junction boys Bryant accomplished his purpose. He established a standard of toughness Aggies to this day and those of the future know they have to meet.

Bryant's methods of coaching and recruiting were under constant fire, and all agreed that he was a strict disciplinarian. He was accused of being overly harsh and of driving away good players, but those who stayed idolized him.

Actually this off-campus pre-season training was not a first for A&M. Charley Moran took two of his squads to Seabrook and La Porte for comparable periods of training. The 1911 training camp was perhaps even more remote than the one 43 years later at Junction.

In his *Dutchman on the Brazos* Dutch Hohn told of a trip to Morgan's Point to get ice for the camp. He and his companion left La Porte at midnight and were lost in the bay for six hours on the return trip. When they got back to camp at noon the following day, they had only 100 of the 300 pounds of ice they had bought at Morgan's Point.

When Mickey Herskowitz of the *Houston Post* returned from Junction, Sports Editor Clark Nealon challenged him with: "Mickey, there's got to be dissension up there with all of those people quitting." Mickey's first day as a full-time *Post* employee had been his first day at Junction.

A bit awed, perhaps terrified, at facing Bryant with a question about dissension, Herskowitz prevailed on Ramsey to broach the coach with the provocative question. So Ramsey opened the interview with, "Coach, Mickey doesn't want to ask you, but his boss insists that he ask you whether there is dissension on the squad."

"Mickey, I don't think there is any dissension on this team," Bryant answered, "but if there is, I am going to cause it." Mickey wrote a good story on that pitch and was to write hundreds more good ones about the Aggies.

A&M scored first in its opening game with Texas Tech in the 1954 season but ran out of gas and Tech won, 41-9. "After the game," Stallings remembered it as if it were yesterday, "Coach Bryant told us all to go to the dorm and get to bed and turn out the lights. He told us we did not deserve to have any dates. He said 'Texas Tech played well and they deserve to have some dates.' So, that's what we did."

The Aggies won only once that season, a 6-0 conquest of Georgia. We took only 27 people over there," Bryant recalled 20 years later. "That 1954 A&M team might be the greatest bunch of folks we ever dealt with. I have a lot of respect for that football team, and I am not so sure that they didn't have more guts and the ability to fight back than a lot of teams blessed with more talent. They hung in there week after week."

That 1954 team is one of the more memorable ones produced at A&M. The team spawned in the Junction hill country retreat inspired a saga that yields only to the Twelfth Man among Aggie legends.

By mid-season the Aggies had lost five of the first six, and the media and fans were hounding both Jones Ramsey and Coach Bryant for explanations. Bryant sat down with his publicist and reminded him, "Jones, when you are winning, everybody is for you. When you are losing, everybody is against you. Well, we have been losing and everybody is asking 'How is your team doing?' They don't want to know how their team is doing. I just

Texas A&M achieved only one victory in 1954, but this touchdown run by QB Elwood Kettler (12) against Rice gave him the scoring championship for conference play. All 22 players and the 4 game officials are pictured.

want those people to know it is my team now and I am going to accept them, but if anybody ever fails to put out 150 percent every Saturday they're going to be disassociated with this outfit."

"I called Harold Ratliff (*Associated Press* sports editor in Dallas at the time), and he was delighted with those comments and sent them all over the country," Ramsey remembered. "Hundreds of telegrams came the following day from the fair-weather followers, which was the reaction coach wanted."

Arkansas was coming up that week, and Ramsey recalled that during the 1954 Southwest Conference Press Tour Bryant had told the writers, "Arkansas will be a surprise winner of the Conference." The writers were picking Rice or Texas and ranking Arkansas down near the bottom with A&M. Bryant was right.

"Arkansas came to College Station with a 3-0 record in the Conference, and we had 'em tied, 7-7, with only a few minutes left in the first half," Ramsey recalled. "Coach Bryant sent Bennie Sinclair in to tell Elwood Kettler not to pass. There was a pass, however, and Arkansas intercepted, scored a touchdown, and won the game, 14-7."

Bryant left no stones unturned in his determination to convince his undermanned squad it could win. SMU was the next opponent, and Elmer Smith went to Bryant a few days before the game and told him of a scripture passage that might be helpful in lifting the Aggies' confidence. "It was a scripture about moving a mountain through faith," Bryant remembered. "Mary Harmon and I contacted all of the coaches by telephone about midnight and told them to meet us at the athletes' dormitory at 1 a.m. The players must have thought the old man had lost his mind. I quoted the scripture (St. Matthew, 17th chapter, 20th verse) and said, 'Good night' and walked out."

SMU, runner-up to Arkansas, had to fight for its life to prevail, 6-3.

In 1954 one of the freshman players chalked this message on one of the blackboards in the squad meeting room:

Conference championship in 1956
National championship in 1957

Ramsey tabbed that talented freshman crowd as the "Team of Tomorrow." And the freshman with the chalk proved to be a good prophet. His prophecy for 1956 came true, and after the victory over SMU in 1957, the Aggies were ranked No. 1 in the nation with only two games to go.

Except for the probation that was imposed for recruiting violations in 1954 the Aggies undoubtedly would have made successive bowl appearances following the 1955, 1956, and 1957 seasons.

Bryant was optimistic over the prospects in 1955, because he knew a lot more of the potential of his talented sophomores than did the media which picked the Aggies to finish in the cellar again. Among those sophomores were John David Crow, Charley Krueger, Kenneth Hall, Loyd Taylor, James Wright, Bobby Marks, Roddy Osborne, and Bobby Joe Conrad.

The curtain-raiser for that season was against UCLA in Los

Coach Bear Bryant huddles with key figures of his recovery program on 1955 Press Day. Standing, left to right: Tackle Charley Krueger, End Bobby Marks, Tackle Jack Powell, Center Lloyd Hale. Kneeling, left to right of Bryant: Guard Dennis Goehring, Tackle Jim Stanley, and End Gene Stallings. Powell, Hale, Goehring, and Stallings were among the Junction "survivors."

Angeles, and Red Sanders' Bruins were all set to defend their national championship. Early in the week Bryant was quoted as saying, "We're going out there in a big, four-motored plane. If we lose, we're coming back in a Greyhound bus."

UCLA won, 21-0, and Mel Durslag of the *Los Angeles Examiner* was well aware of the odds when he asked: "Bear, you didn't really expect to beat 'em, did you?"

"You silly cluck, why in hell do you think I came out here?" he bellowed.

Years later Bryant classified that loss as "a big disappointment for us and our followers, but that licking made our football team, because after that we were tough." Just how tough is indicated by the fact the Aggies were not to lose another game until the season finale with a Texas team that was inspired to wipe out a season of disappointments.

Along the way the Aggies had some trouble, however, like the day they squeezed by TCU, 19-16. That was quite a significant victory for it was A&M's first conference triumph since TCU was beaten two years before. At the conclusion of that stormy battle Referee Cliff Shaw joined Paul Bryant and Abe Martin, the two head coaches, in midfield and observed: "Gentlemen, that was the hardest-hitting, cleanest football game I've ever worked."

Arkansas proved an even greater menace a fortnight later by playing the Aggies to a 7-7 deadlock in the Ozarks. John David Crow, who was a sensational sophomore that season remembers that game vividly: "We were miserable. Everything went wrong. At halftime our dressing room was like a tomb, and Coach Bryant walked in and stood there for a minute looking around.

"Then he said, 'All you riff-raff get out of here. Everybody get out but me.' That's what he said, and there was the maddest scramble you ever saw. Coaches, trainers, old grads, and players stumbling over each other trying to get to the door.

"Finally Coach Bryant saw what was happening and called the players back. Shoot, we thought he meant us, too. After everybody left he just prowled around the room. He'd call a player's name, pick him out, shake him, and tell him what he did wrong.

"He called 'Crow!' and he shook me. Why? A couple of us had been laughing on the bus going to the game. He put the fear in everybody that day, the players and the coaches."

Two weeks later the Aggies turned apparent defeat into one of their greatest of all come-from-behind victories. The poorest Rice team since the lean war years solemnly had collected for its one great effort of 1955 and was rewarded with a 12-0 lead with 8:09 remaining. Four minutes later Loyd Taylor took a pitch-out at right end and raced 58 yards to the Rice 3-yard line behind Jack Pardee's clearing block. Taylor scored from the 2, then narrowed Rice's lead to 12-7 with a placement as the clock showed 3:18 to play.

Jess Neely alerted his Owls about an on-side kick, but it worked, nevertheless. Pardee placed the kick perfectly, and Stallings covered it on the Rice 43. Suddenly A&M was on fire. Jim Wright lofted a bullseye pass to Taylor, on the Rice 5. Taylor scored and added the placement with 2:32 left. He had scored 14 points in 46 seconds, and A&M was in front, 14-12.

Shortly thereafter Pardee intercepted a King Hill pass and ran it back 37 yards to the Rice 8. Don Watson scored from there with 1:09 remaining, the Aggies having scored all of their points in two minutes and nine seconds. The rally ended a trend of 10 successive Rice victories, and as one observer put it, "terminated a Rice winning streak of 10 years and 56 minutes."

"Rice outplayed us and deserved to win," Bryant offered in the strained humility that was destined to become a trademark with him. "We were very, very lucky. But let's not forget Loyd Taylor. He's a back no one seems to notice but does a fine job each week."

The game ball was given to Bill (Jitterbug) Henderson, then dying of multiple sclerosis. Fifteen years before Henderson had caught eight straight passes as A&M beat Rice for a 19th straight victory. Herskowitz, a young reporter whose pulse was controlled by A&M success and failures, was trapped in the elevator while all of this was in the making at the 1955 Rice game and did not know the Aggies had won until he reached the dressing room.

Willie Zapalac was in Austin scouting Texas against TCU and shared a press box radio with Rice's Red Bale, who was scouting TCU. The Austin game ended first, and Zapalac headed for his automobile to catch the remainder on his car radio. His wife, Dorothy, was in Houston for the game, and prior arrangements had been made for a rendezvous there in event the Aggies won. He was unable to pick up the broadcast, because the game had ended by the time he reached his car. Knowing Rice had led, 12-0, he headed for College Station, but he picked up Morris Frank's score program from the Rice press box, and on hearing that A&M had won he changed his course and headed for Houston.

A&M went into the Texas game needing only a tie with the Longhorns to be assured of a share of the championship. If they had achieved it, the honor would have been incomplete, because Southwest Conference faculty representatives had put A&M on probation at their May meeting, which denied them bowl game participation. The Aggies were heavily favored since Texas went into the game with a 4-5 record for the season.

A&M scored first, driving 80 yards just before the intermission. Jim Wright's 34-yard pass to John David Crow carried to the Texas 1, and the Aggies scored with 1:45 to play. The conversion attempt was missed, and Texas took charge from that point. The Longhorns went ahead, 7-6, with only 10 seconds left in the first half.

A&M made only one first down in the second half, as Texas' defense hobbled talented Aggie backfielders. The Aggies' total offense aside from the scoring drive was only 17 yards, and Texas won, 21-6.

Gig 'Em! Jack Pardee

The recruiting and keeping of a rare football player can require much effort. In the case of Jack Pardee it ranged from a malt shop in Christoval, Texas, to an oval office in Washington, D. C.

Assistant Coach Willie Zapalac succeeded at the malt shop, getting from Pardee a commitment to play football for Texas A&M. President Richard Nixon failed in the White House's oval office twenty years later in his effort to talk Pardee out of a pending retirement as a player for the Washington Redskins.

Zapalac's assignment in 1953 was to scout two players on the San Angelo High School team. The school was to play on Friday night, and Zapalac arrived about noon in order to have time to do some checking on the prospects. In the course of his conversations someone mentioned a big fullback playing on a six-man team in Christoval that afternoon.

Zapalac drove the 17 miles to Christoval on a mission which he thought was to satisfy his curiosity more than anything else. What he saw so convinced him of Pardee's ability that he invited him to the malt shop and offered him a scholarship before rival recruiters could stumble onto this gem he had found.

Pardee was not an instant success at A&M. In fact he did not really blossom until his senior season of 1956 when, as tri-captain with Gene Stallings and Lloyd Hale, he helped the Aggies to an undefeated season and the Southwest Conference championship.

Pardee, a 6-2, 212-pound fullback, gained all-conference and all-America recognition that season and was named academic all-America. He received the *Houston Post* award given annually to the most valuable player in the conference.

A few seasons after Pardee's departure Zapalac was talking to a reporter about some promising Aggie sophomores. "You can't tell when a boy is going to develop," Zapalac said. "One day he isn't a football player. The next day he is.

"I remember Jack Pardee in his sophomore year. Jack wasn't much of a player then. Bear (Bryant) had about given up on him. He didn't think Pardee was a fighter. He had just been an arm tackler, a bear hugger. He hadn't really hit anybody.

"That spring our baseball team went to Austin for our final game. We'd just clinched the conference title, and the corps had been given a holiday. Almost everybody went over, including the football team.

"That day a dozen fights must have broken out at the game, but the big one was between Pardee and Buck Lansford (Texas tackle and 1954 co-captain). They fought all over the stands. Who won? We thought Pardee did. But anyway, after that fight we knew Pardee had instinct."

The late Smoky Harper said later, in reference to the incident: "I've always thought that if Pardee hadn't had that fight he wouldn't have made us a football player. I know I came back home that night and went to Bryant and told him to quit worrying about Pardee."

"I don't know what it was," Zapalac recalls, "but suddenly Pardee was a football player."

Pardee's work for the American Cancer Society led to his presence in the White House oval office in April, 1973, to receive the society's Courage Award from Mrs. Nixon in recognition of his winning battle against cancer in 1964.

As the presentation was made, the President stepped forward and said: "You are a great athlete and a great leader of men. Your example is a great inspiration to all of us. I wonder what the Redskins will do without you. I hope I can get you to change your mind."

Today Pardee travels around the country to appear for the society. Not only did he overcome melanoma, a cancerous mole on his arm which required eleven hours of surgery to remove,

Jack Pardee

but he returned to play eight more seasons of football. He had played seven with the Los Angeles Rams prior to the surgery.

Pardee did not feel that he had a good season in 1964 and decided to take a position on the new Gene Stallings coaching staff at A&M. "I planned all along to enter coaching, and this looked like a good opportunity," he said.

After one season as an assistant coach, Jack decided he was in shape physically to return to playing. "That year out of pro football taught me the value of an off-season conditioning program," he said. "I reported to Los Angeles in 1966 in the finest shape I've ever been, and I've tried to maintain that level since. I still play handball or paddleball every day."

After returning to the pros, Pardee continued to work with A&M in recruiting and spring training through 1969, while gaining recognition as an all-pro linebacker for the Rams and Redskins. After one season as a full-time coach for Washington, Pardee became head coach of the Orlando, Florida, team in the World Football League.

Looking back on his playing days at A&M, Pardee said, "I kinda remember seasons or teams more than unusual incidents or big plays. A team that holds a dear spot in my heart is that 1954 team that had a real poor record (1-9). We played a lot of close games, though, and I believe that team formed the backbone and foundation for the 1956 championship season.

"Playing for Coach Bryant was an experience I treasure. He took that 1954 team that finished at the bottom and built it into an undefeated team when we were seniors. To see it all turn around was a tremendous feeling. We (the Junction group) built something together instead of inheriting it or having somebody give it to us. For that we will always be grateful to Coach Bryant.

"We eight seniors on that championship club formed a mighty close relationship dating back to our freshman year." Then Pardee named the other seven, where they were residing and what they were doing professionally. Bound together as one family much like that of the 1921 and 1939 championship Aggie crowds, they are guard Dennis Goehring, center Lloyd Hale, end Bobby Drake Keith, tackle Bobby Lockett, guard Dee Powell, end Gene Stallings, halfback Don Watson, and Pardee.

In the dressing room after the bruising 1956 battle with

Baylor, Hale summed up the awe that Pardee commanded with his teammates. Pardee did not start because of injury, but Bryant admitted, "I was afraid he would whip me if I didn't put him in the game." That was when Hale broke in and said, "When that big devil (pointing to Pardee) came in, it gave all of us a lift."

Bear Bryant reflected years later that "one thing in particular stands out about Jack Pardee. He practiced with as much enthusiasm and desire as he played on Saturday. I can still see him anxiously twitching his shoulder pads, a nervous action that indicated he wanted to hit somebody."

"Went According To Prayer"

Handicappers figured the 1956 Southwest Conference football race would end with TCU and Texas A&M ranking 1-2 in that order, just as they had stood at the end of the 1955 campaign. This, of course, was to set the stage for one of the most spectacular games ever played in the Southwest.

There was a lot to transpire prior to the TCU-A&M showdown, however. TCU put together one-sided triumphs over Kansas, Arkansas, and Alabama, in that order, and ranked fourth in the nation when it arrived at Kyle Field. A&M's course had been a bit more rocky, as the Aggies put down Villanova, edged LSU, 9-6, then were held to a 14-14 deadlock by the University of Houston.

"We drove 94 yards from our own 5-yard line to the Houston 1-yard line in the final 4 minutes, then I second-guessed myself with time left for only one play," Coach Paul Bryant remembered it 18 years later as if it were yesterday. The score was knotted at 14-all.

"I sent Don Watson in with the tee with the thought of Loyd Taylor trying a field goal, but I called him back, figuring that with (Jack) Pardee and (John David) Crow in there we ought to get a yard. We didn't score, of course, and it would have been a cinch field goal for Taylor."

TCU was established an eight-point favorite the week following A&M's draw with the Cougars. The Horned Frogs also were rankled by a 19-16 Aggie upset that had put the only blot on their 1955 record. A sellout crowd of 42,000 fans jammed

Kyle Field, and the impudent Aggies responded by driving to the TCU 25 on their first possession. That was to be the only threat by the Aggies, however, until the final quarter, as they fought against frequent TCU raids and a roaring rainstorm that was to reach hurricane proportions.

The wind that bent Kyle Field tower lights to an alarming degree and the torrential rain drove half of the spectators under the stands, but few of them left the premises. The Cadet Corps stayed in the stands and wildly cheered each Aggie goal line stand.

Chuck Curtis, the TCU quarterback, completed the first six passes he threw before the rains came, and amid the lightning and under skies almost black as night the Horned Frogs bombarded the Aggie goal time and again. Every time the Aggies held it seemed that a fumble gave the visitors another chance.

TCU's frustration was wrought by fruitless drives to the A&M 38, 2, 6-inch line, 16, 23, and 13. In the eerie mid-afternoon darkness the Horned Frogs once moved to a first down on the A&M 2. TCU's Jim Swink went across, but a teammate was offside, then on fourth down the Frogs lost the ball on a fumble at the Aggie 5. The ball was fumbled right back to the Frogs on the A&M 8, then with 5 plays, one of them a bonus by an offside penalty against A&M, TCU could not get across. So it was a stormy, muddy scoreless first half. Angry TCU fans were convinced that Jim Swink had scored at least one touchdown in the 5-play series from the Aggie 8.

The weather improved in the third quarter, and TCU continued to remain on the attack. It was near the end of the period when the game's first score finally went on the board. An Aggie fumble gave the Frogs a chance to go from the A&M 30. Six plays covered the distance, the touchdown coming on an 11-yard pass. The kick failed, and TCU led 6-0 going into the final quarter. A blocked Aggie punt set up another TCU threat, and the Frogs appeared headed for a clinching score when the lights came on again for A&M.

Don Watson, who had been the hero in the 1955 game, intercepted a first-down TCU pass from the A&M 19 in the end zone, and the Aggies started a game-winning drive from their 20.

"The sun came out about this time," Coach Bryant recalls. "We had an ole option play that I borrowed from Bud Wilkinson. It's really a quick flip, run or pass, and we put it to steady use."

The results were fruitful and in big chunks. John David Crow struck for 21, then Watson broke for 37 all the way to the TCU 20. Crow pushed it to the TCU 8, and from there it was third-and-goal and A&M had not tried a pass all day. Roddy Osborne took the snap and headed to his left, then pitched out to Watson who flipped it to Crow on the goal line. Taylor's placement made it 7-6 with 9 minutes to play, and TCU was to make only one first down in a vain effort to overtake the Aggies.

When it was all over, the dressing room writers descended on Paul Bryant and asked the inevitable question: "Bear, did it go according to plan?"

"No," replied the coach grimly, "it went according to prayer."

Bryant then told the writers "There's never been a team with more guts," then he asked to be excused with, "Now I want to get home and get out of these wet clothes. I don't want to die if I can help it, although this would be a good time."

Years later in reflection Bryant recalled, "One of the nicest visits I ever had in my life came after that TCU game. My son Paul, who was about 8, and I walked all the way across the campus and all of the way home, which gave me time to soak it all in. It was *so* good. That year we had a truly great football team. In our conference games we scored the first time we had the ball in the second half in every game but one, and that's pretty convincing."

The 1956 Aggies' second big test came just a week after the squeaker over TCU, when they traveled to Waco. "The thing up at Baylor was a real blood-letting," Coach Bryant recalled as he termed it "the bloodiest, meanest, and toughest game I've ever seen. I remember that (Jack) Pardee was hurt, but he didn't know it. I didn't start him, and tried to avoid getting close to him. He was staring me right in the face, and I was afraid he might slap me any minute. I finally put him in and he played his usual great game."

Pardee also figured in a controversial play. En route to the winning touchdown, Pardee fumbled as he made a first down at

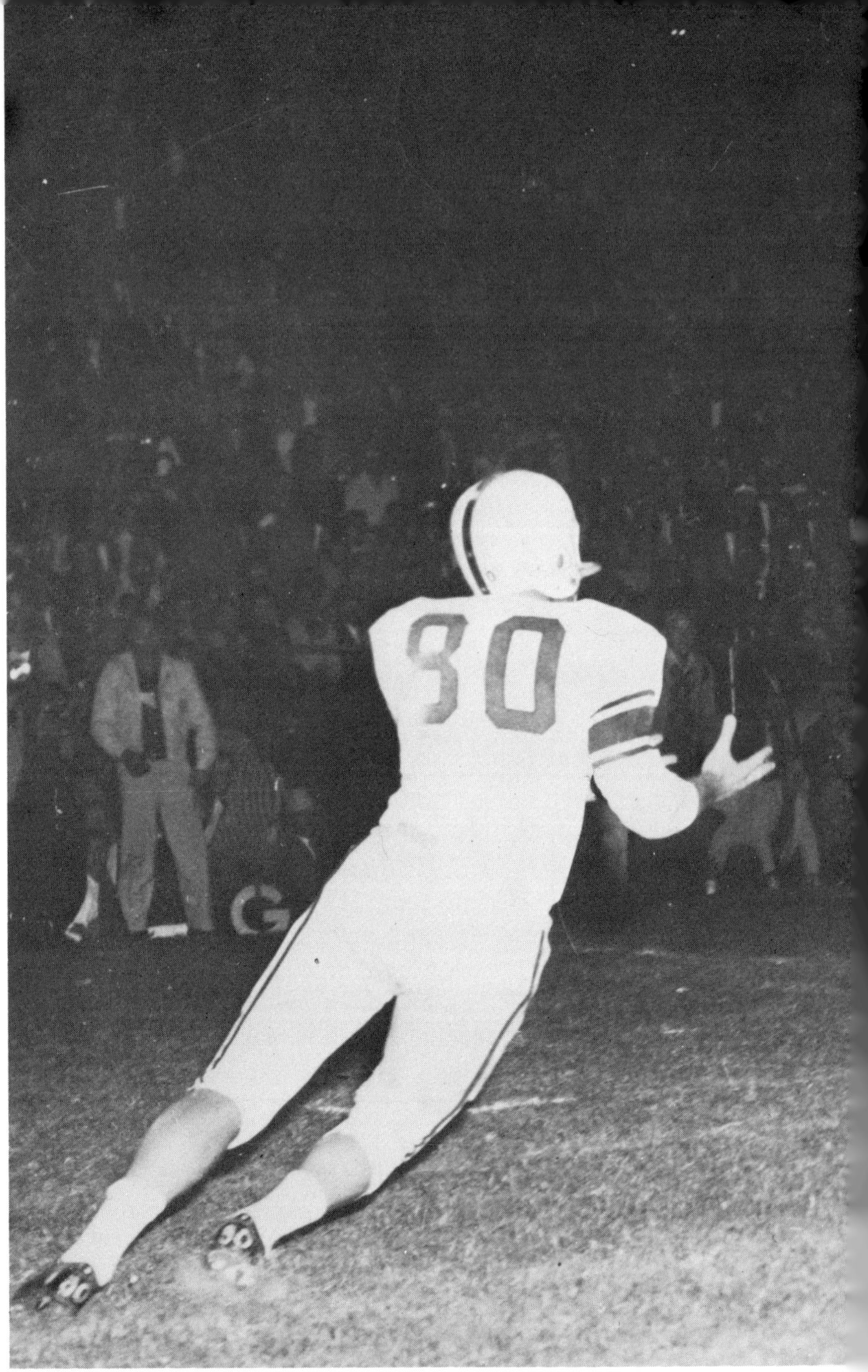

Sophomore John Tracey awaits a touchdown pass from John David Crow in the 19-13 conquest of Baylor in 1956.

the Baylor 26, and the Bears recovered. The official ruled that the ball was dead before the fumble, keeping A&M's 63-yard come-from-behind march alive. To this day you will not find a Baylor fan who will agree with the call nor an Aggie fan who will disagree.

The call was made by the late I. B. Hale, who had been an all-America tackle at TCU in 1938. Years later Hale called it "the toughest call I ever made." In his version of the play Hale remembered, "It was a terrific tackle; the runner was hit so hard he bounced into the air and turned completely over. He came down upside down, landing on his back...I ruled the ball dead, for when a player lands on his back like that the ball is whistled dead immediately."

"We got two great plays on that winning drive," Coach Bryant remembered. "On one of them Roddy Osborne started an option to the left, but we blocked for a counter back the other way. He was so quick, he just cut back and made four or five yards. On fourth down and with all of the marbles riding on it, Crow said 'give me that cockeyed ball, and I'll put it behind there.' And they did, and he put it behind there for about six yards." And A&M owned a 19-13 victory.

Jones Ramsey, who was sports publicist for A&M at the time, recalls, "Roddy Osborne hit Don Watson on a long pass for one of the touchdowns against Baylor after teammates had argued with him in the huddle that he could not throw the ball that far."

Coach Bryant's post-game observation: "Baylor, we think, had a fine football team. We were fortunate to win, and I don't think I've ever been any prouder. Not even last week. It seemed we had to pull uphill all the way. That's what I like about this club more than anything—the way they come back. From where I sat it looked like one of the finest football games I've ever seen."

The Southwest Conference had lifted its probation of the Aggies at its May meeting in Fayetteville, Arkansas, and there was hope that the National Collegiate Athletic Association might do likewise in time for the Aggies to get into post-season play.

The NCAA Council met November 13, 1956, to consider lifting the probation against A&M, but it refused to do so. A&M

was represented at the hearing by Dr. David Morgan, president; Dr. Chris Groneman, chairman of the Athletic Council; Dr. Phillip Goode, member of the Athletic Council; and Dr. M. D. Harrington, chancellor of the Texas A&M System.

Rival Southwest Conference coaches deplored the NCAA Council's action. "Our feeling regarding the probation was expressed by our Conference some time ago," observed Ed Price of Texas. "As a bowl participant A&M would have been a terrific attraction and a worthy opponent for any team in the United States."

"The ruling stymies a top bowl team," said TCU's Abe Martin. "The Aggies would have made a fine representative of the Southwest Conference in either the Cotton Bowl or the Sugar Bowl."

The ruling opened the door for two of A&M's October victims to represent the Conference in post-season play. As the eventual runner-up, TCU served as host team and defeated Syracuse in the Cotton Bowl. Baylor went to the Sugar Bowl and upset Tennessee, ranked No. 2 nationally.

After the rugged test with Baylor, A&M was not extended again until Thanksgiving Day. The Aggies had never managed a victory in 16 previous trips to Memorial Stadium, but on this occasion they were heavily favored, for the host Longhorns had achieved only one victory.

"We were about five touchdowns better than Texas," Paul Bryant observed years later, "yet I recall we were leading by only one touchdown as late as the fourth quarter. Texas was driving, but Lloyd Hale intercepted for us, and we added an insurance touchdown real late with Texas making a stubborn goal line stand."

Jones Ramsey, who was to defect to Texas four years later, recalled, "I was impressed with how much the Longhorns played over their heads. A&M was really never in danger of losing, but Aggies who respected the tradition lived in fear until the end."

Coach Bryant was given an unscheduled shower bath by his players after the game. Thoroughly drenched and thoroughly happy, Bryant said, "Man, I feel better than I have in three months," as a bystander handed him a towel. The he asked for the attention of his happy warriors. "My limited vocabulary won't permit me to tell you how proud I am of you. Act like a champion. Have a good time, and I'll see you next week."

The Aggies had won their first championship since 1941 and owned their first undefeated season since the national championship season of 1939. It was a fitting climax for Bryant's rebuilding job that had brought A&M from mediocrity to a national power in a brief span of three seasons.

"In 1957 I thought we were going to have an even better team than the one in 1956," Bryant was to observe years later as he turned the pages of history. "We lost three key players in the summer, and I did a lousy job in not making some changes in positions. We should have put John Crow at fullback so we could have run the option both ways, Roddy Osborne at left halfback, Bobby Joe Conrad at quarterback, and Richard Gay

*1956 Southwest
Conference Champions*

at center.

"This is all hind sight, of course. I talked about it all that summer but got talked out of it. I don't think it would ever have been close if we had made those changes. In addition to Conrad, who could have played anywhere, we would have had Jimmy Wright and Charles Milstead at quarterback."

The 1957 Aggies thundered along with consistent success and ran their string of games without a loss to 18 before the tide turned. The defense of the conference championship started favorably with successive shutouts of TCU and Baylor that had been so troublesome in 1956, and the first big scare did not come until the Aggies invaded the Ozarks, November 2.

With only 1:20 to play in the game, A&M held a 7-6 lead and had possession of the ball on the Arkansas 12. Coach Bryant knew quarterback Roddy Osborne would run out the clock, but he sent in a substitute nevertheless to instruct the quarterback to stay on the ground and play possession ball.

Osborne called a run-and-pass option with John Crow set as the flanker, but he did not intend to pass until he saw Crow open at the goal line. So, he passed, and Don Horton of the Razorbacks moved in to intercept and race 64 yards to the A&M 27 before Osborne overtook him.

The tension mounted as Arkansas passed to the Aggie 15, where Crow made a saving tackle. Then on the final play of the game Crow intercepted to preserve the victory.

Paul Bryant observed after the game that, "Horton was just running for a touchdown, but that Osborne was running for his life." A number of years later he was to recall, "Crow made two of the greatest defensive plays I've ever seen in my life."

Roddy Osborne was probably one of the most maligned successful football players to perform in the Southwest Conference. Mickey Herskowitz, who followed the Aggies for the *Houston Post* throughout the Paul Bryant era, defended Osborne with some interesting observations:

"Roddy is the unlikeliest star of an unlikely football team. They say Osborne does nothing well, but he does everything well enough to beat you. In 20 games he directed the Aggies to 17 victories and a tie, and few quarterbacks can match that.

"He had the uncanny knack of turning bad plays into good ones. One teammate observed: 'He's the only quarterback I know who can miss a handoff to the fullback and gain 13 yards.'

"The crew-cut youngster from Gainesville (Texas) showed up unexpectedly as a prospect on a film that Phil Cutchin (an assistant A&M coach at the time) was grading. Osborne earned his first letter as a fullback.

"The careers of John David Crow and Charley Krueger have been more illustrious, but Osborne's is the more remarkable, because only the Aggies wanted him."

A&M was ranked No. 1 in the nation when it went to Houston to play Rice, November 16. The morning of the game the *Houston Post* carried a story speculating that Bryant would be going to Alabama in 1958.

"The story was premature at the time," Bryant said. "Jack

Gallagher (*Post* sportswriter) called me the night before the game regarding a remark that Dr. (Frank) Rose (then president of the University of Alabama) had made. Dr. Rose had said he was going to get a coach with certain qualifications, all of which pointed to me.

"I can not accept the blame for the effect that story might have had on my ball club in the Rice game, but I do accept the blame for not attempting a field goal that eventually could have been the winning margin. But Rice richly deserved the victory. I was real proud of our boys. Just mark it down as the difference in coaching and preparation."

Rice won, 7-6, and went on to the conference championship when A&M fell to Texas on Thanksgiving Day, 9-7.

"Texas should have beaten us worse than they did, and would have if Crow had not knocked down a lot of passes," Coach Bryant said. "The field goal beat us, but actually it was the great quick-kick that broke our back."

Texas' Walter Fondren quick-kicked 62 yards to the A&M 4 early in the game, and Texas got the ball back on the Aggie 33 and moved from there in 8 plays for the game's first touchdown. A field goal had built the lead to 9-0 when the Aggies managed their only touchdown on a 67-yard drive that featured a Roddy Osborne to John David Crow pass for 57 yards.

Regarding the successive losses and observations that A&M appeared to be tired, John David Crow said, "We played only fifteen men, but there are a lot of teams that play that few. I think if we had been tired, it would have showed earlier. Rice made us respect their passing, then ran the ball down our throats, but they did not whip us as bad physically as Texas. Texas was bigger, faster, and better. We had two weeks to get ready for them. If you're tired I think it will show up before eight games. I don't know what caused us to lose those two, but I don't think we were tired."

The successive losses by one and two points by the Aggies had changed the post-season bowl picture drastically. Rice became the host team in the Cotton Bowl; Texas went to the Sugar Bowl; and the Aggies lost, 3-0, to Tennessee in the Gator Bowl.

On Thanksgiving night Paul Bryant announced to a

television audience that he had accepted the head coaching position at Alabama, his alma mater. "Mama has called me," was the way he put it.

Thus his stopover to an eventual dynasty at Alabama was a renaissance for A&M that produced 25 victories and 2 ties against 14 defeats over a 4-season span. During that period he had developed 9 consensus all-Conference performers, 3 all-America players (Jack Pardee, Charles Krueger, and John David Crow) and a Heisman Trophy winner (Crow). An automatic choice as a National Football Hall of Fame coach once he is no longer an active mentor, Bryant ranks third in all-time coaching victories. Only Amos Alonzo Stagg and Glenn (Pop) Warner have won more, and they coached 57 and 44 seasons, respectively.

Gig 'Em! John David Crow

Texas A&M had just cleared its second major hurdle en route to an undefeated season and its first Southwest Conference championship in 15 years, and a sportswriter asked Bear Bryant for an observation on the performance of John David Crow in the game just concluded.

"I think he was magnificent," he said, then smiled. "Wait, that's a pretty big adjective. Maybe I should have said he played a good game."

That was typical of Bryant, who normally saved the plaudits for his players until they concluded their careers. He had said, however, when Crow was a freshman that "John David can be great, if he wants to pay the price."

No one ever questioned John David's willingness and determination to pay the price, and shortly after he had played his last game in an Aggie uniform, Coach Bryant observed: "John David is the greatest athlete who ever lived, for my money. He had a burning desire for the team to win."

Shortly before, Crow had been presented the 1957 Heisman Trophy in New York City before an audience of 1,000 at the Downtown Athletic Club. John David had received an overwhelming majority vote of the 1,267 registered writers, nearly doubling the runner-up in the balloting. During the balloting Bryant had been quoted as saying: "If John David doesn't get it, they ought to quit giving it."

In accepting the award Crow said, "The Number 1 person knows how much I thank Him. I'll be looking back on this occasion as long as I live, and I hope to set an example for other high school boys who will one day receive the support I have here tonight."

Then as he ran his hand down the handsome black and gold trophy, he said, "It all seems like a dream, and I want to sit down before I make a racket that might wake me up."

"This is a great occasion for Texas A&M," Dr. M. T. Harrington, then president of the institution, assured the New York audience. In answer to those who had described Crow as a hard-nosed football player, President Harrington reminded, "We're also hard-nosed academically at A&M. John David had slightly less than a B average and barely missed qualifying for Who's Who in American Colleges and Universities."

An all-American in his senior season, Crow also received the Washington Touchdown Club Award, the Walter Camp trophy, and was named the *United Press International* Back of the Year.

John David went to A&M in 1954 from Springhill, Louisiana, which he admitted was "so far back in the woods they have to pipe in sunshine." He credits Elmer Smith, then an assistant coach for Bear Bryant, with having the greatest influence on his decision. Smith had coached John David's brother, Raymond, at an Arkansas college before joining the A&M staff. Crow also credited Bryant's philosophy and personality as being major factors.

Smith thought the credit belonged to Bryant, although he acknowledged the first contact and said that he had a motel room in Springhill for three months. "John David got so disgusted with me hanging around so much he said, 'Coach, I don't know whether I'll be able to finish high school or not.'"

It should be recognized that in 1967 when Elmer Smith was enshrined into the Arkansas Sports Hall of Fame, both Bryant and Crow were present to join in the tribute. During the reunion John David turned to a writer and said, "It's been 10 years since I played for him (Bryant), but right now, if he told me to run through that wall over there, I'm sure I'd give it a try."

John David went on to an illustrious career in professional football and made the all-pro team before embarking on a coaching career that started with three seasons of apprentice-

John David Crow attained highest honor available for collegiate footballers, the Heisman Memorial Trophy in 1957 season.

ship under Coach Bryant at the University of Alabama. With all of his success as a player at all levels one wonders which of the moments stand out greatest in his memory.

"When I think of football," Crow said with no hesitation at all, "I think of Coach Bryant."

Like, how?

"We were playing SMU in my sophomore year, and I was supposed to catch the ball on punts. They kicked to us on our 40. When I got tackled, I was back on our 10. I tried to get around the wave and lost 30 yards.

"We ran a couple of plays and kicked, and then we got the ball back. On first down I was supposed to go around end, and I thought I could give ground and get around the corner man. I didn't make it and lost about five yards. When I got to my feet, I saw Bill Dendy trotting on to the field. He was my substitute.

"I thought, 'Uh-oh, here's where I catch it.' As I came off I didn't even look at Coach Bryant. I kept my head down and headed for the opposite end of the bench, as far from him as I could get. I was scared to death and knew what was coming.

"I sat on the bench, and I never looked up. I kept looking at the ground, and all of a sudden I saw Coach Bryant's shoes. I kinda braced myself, and he put a hand on my knee. I looked up then, and he pointed out toward the field. All he said was 'John, our goal is THATAWAY!'"

A score of years after enrolling at A&M, John David reflects on his days there with, "I was really fortunate to go to a school with rich traditions and a high regard for discipline. I think that was one big reason that I was able to be as successful there as I was.

"The great thing about A&M is the people associated with it. Anybody will back a winner, but it takes mighty good people to stick with a team year in and year out whether it's a winner or not.

"I have been away a long time, and I really miss the association. I went to the Aggie muster out here (San Diego, California) this year, and the experience reaffirmed how proud I am to have gone to school there."

Gig 'Em! Charley Krueger

People who knew Charley Krueger when he left Caldwell, Texas, to play football at Texas A&M, 20 miles away, probably did not expect him to become an all-America, yet were not surprised as they watched his development.

It must have been quite a jolt, however, to learn nearly a score of years later that this same hometown boy who had ventured a long way from home had become a devotee of the opera, of symphonic music, and of fly-fishing.

Incongruous as it may seem to old acquaintances, those interests really have not changed the indestructible football player with a reputation for quiet, fierce play on the field and a mild disposition off it. After nearly a quarter of a century as a player, Krueger retired from professional football after the 1973 season and now has time to devote to his hobbies while involved in real estate development in the San Francisco Bay area.

"I attend the opera occasionally," Krueger admits. "I particularly enjoy French and Italian operas." Charley is married to the former Kris Adler, whose father is general director of the San Francisco Opera.

Krueger credits Bear Bryant with teaching him strict, fundamental football, and he is forever grateful. "I played for a high school team with a poor record. I still think I was lucky to get a scholarship to A&M, though Rice and Houston did show an interest in me. I was a sleeper and had no real track record."

At one time in his A&M career, however, Krueger became

Charley Krueger

so disenchanted with Bryant's discipline that he wrote his coach a letter explaining that he was transferring to Texas A&I. This was in the summer after his 1954 freshman year, and he walked off his job in Houston and accompanied a member of the A&I coaching staff to Kingsville, Texas.

The unheralded Krueger spent much of his time as a freshman on the sixth team, which might have been a big reason for his decision to leave. Dennis Goehring, a good friend and teammate, went to see Krueger and convinced him that Coach Bryant, despite an apparent disinterest, valued him highly and wanted him to return. Krueger told Goehring that he was afraid to go back and face Bryant.

Anyone familiar with the unbending Bryant and with the stern manner in which he coached his football team in those days could sympathize with Krueger. Yet it is a measure of Charley that he returned to A&M, and asked Bryant to forget the letter and permit him to return to the squad. Krueger started every varsity game for three seasons and achieved all-America recognition as a tackle in both 1956 and 1957.

In the spring after his sophomore season Krueger was given an indelible reminder of what Coach Bryant expects of his players in practice. The white-jerseyed first team was playing the scrubs in the fourth quarter of an intra-squad game and was trailing. Unhappy with what he was seeing, Bryant snatched the official timepiece away from one of the volunteer officials and said, "From now on I'm keeping time. I'll tell you when the quarter is over."

"That quarter must have lasted 40 minutes," Krueger recalls, "and we still got beat. We knew we were in for it. Coach Bryant sent the red team (the reserves) in, but he took the first team over to the practice field and scrimmaged us some more.

"I was supposed to make a talk that night at a football banquet in Caldwell, and Pat James (one of the assistant coaches) was to go with me. I knew we'd be late, but I wasn't about to say anything. For a moment I thought about letting down all those people, but I didn't think about it long. All I wanted to do was survive.

"Pat didn't want to say anything either. You know Coach Bryant's assistant coaches feared him as much as the players. But finally we had only about 20 minutes to make it (Caldwell is 20 miles away), so Pat coughed, cleared his throat, and told Coach we had to go to this banquet.

"I took off. I was so happy and relieved, but half way across the field I heard Coach Bryant yell at me: 'And, Krueger, when you get there tell them how (expletive) you are.'"

Krueger played at 6-4 and about 230, and was exceptionally quick, mean, and smart. In his senior season the Aggies were going against Missouri, whose new Frank Broyles coaching staff included Jerry Claiborne, a former assistant at A&M.

During a squad meeting the night before the game Coach Bryant turned to Krueger and asked, "Charley, how does Coach Claiborne like to start a game?"

"By running at the other team's strength," answered Charley.

"Then where will the first play come?"

"At me."

Mickey Herskowitz, of the *Houston Post,* wrote: "It was simply a direct answer to a direct question, no self-tribute intended or imagined. The next day Missouri's first play from scrimmage sent a halfback on the power smash off tackle. Krueger played off two blockers and tossed the runner for a loss."

Bryant seldom lavished praise on the players from whom he expected the most, and Krueger had to wait for the practice period prior to the Gator Bowl meeting with Tennessee for Bryant's evaluation of him. Bryant decided to excuse some of his players from contact drills the week of the game for one reason or another. He picked them out during practice, singling out the chosen few as he moved through the ranks. When he came to Krueger, "I know he'll hit," and waved him off.

Krueger is proud that he was a member of the 1958 College all-Stars who upset the NFL Champion Detroit Lions, 35-19. One of the outstanding players for the all-Stars was Bobby Joe Conrad, who had been his teammate at A&M. Conrad kicked four field goals and went on to stardom in professional football also.

Charley Krueger was one of the tackles named to the 50-year all-Southwest team (1919-1968) during the observance of the College Football Centennial in 1969. He was joined on the all-star selection by backs Joel Hunt and John Kimbrough, who preceded him by many years at A&M.

The small town boy who made good was chosen for the Texas A&M University Athletic Hall of Fame in 1972. On the occasion of his enshrinement, when a game with Green Bay prevented his attendance, Krueger asked Clarence Jamail to accept the cherished award for him. It was at this time that he chatted with Jack Gallagher of the *Houston Post* and acknowledged: "I owe A&M a lot. I got my military commission from

A&M, and I stayed in the reserves 10 years after graduation."

Though the Aggie lifestyle may be more relaxed than in Krueger's undergraduate days, the basic values remain the same. Of this change Krueger observed: "Time changes and people change, but I guess A&M is like every other place. If you work hard and persevere, you'll make it. Maybe the Aggies are proud squares. Maybe they are somewhat conservative. I can't give them any advice, except that I believe in hard work, and there's not a damned thing wrong with that."

Charley's younger brother, Rolf, was a two-time consensus choice for the all-Southwest Conference team as a defensive tackle and was a member of the 1967 championship team that whipped Alabama in the 1968 Cotton Bowl Classic, 20-16. Young Krueger also went on to stardom in professional football.

The Big One Got Away

Finding a replacement for Paul Bryant developed into a stormy, seven-week search that zoomed in on Red Sanders of UCLA, Duffy Daugherty of Michigan State, Frank Leahy, who had been out of the coaching scene for four years after leaving Notre Dame, and Ed Erdelatz of the United States Naval Academy, in that order. Reports of dissension among the A&M Board of Directors and the situation in general prompted Texas Governor Price Daniel to initiate an investigation, a report on which was pending when the selection was finally made.

Jim Myers' appointment and acceptance came 11 days after he had withdrawn from consideration in the face of known opposition by the Board. Myers was to be the fifth to serve A&M as head coach over a 12-year period, but only the ninth since Charley Moran left after the 1914 season, 43 campaigns previously.

What really won Myers to Texas A&M was a telegraphic appeal bearing nearly 2,000 names and a mission to Ames, Iowa, by two members of the Twelfth Man, Gary Rollins, sports editor of *The Battalion* of Houston, and Cadet Colonel Jon Hagler of La Grange.

Myers' reaction to the students' appeal: "A week ago I didn't have a chance, then a couple of days ago I got this message from the Aggie student body who asked me to take the job. They were so persistent I couldn't turn them down."

Myers greeted 17 lettermen, but only five of them had achieved two letters. When Bryant departed, 14 lettermen were lost with him and 10 of them had three awards. This, of course, was in the double-duty days when substitutions were rare; so, Myers commanded very little experienced talent for the 1958 season.

Fortunately, however, he inherited an exceptionally, talented quarterback in Charley Milstead, and an outstanding pass receiver in John Tracey. The two were destined to all-Conference recognition as one of the league's foremost batteries. Milstead lost the 1958 SWC passing championship to Baylor's Buddy Humphrey and the total offense to the same player by 59 yards, as the two of them ranked third and fourth nationally, respectively.

Charley Milstead gained all-SWC recognition for Aggies in 1958, co-captain in 1959.

The Aggies opened their 1958 season in the Cotton Bowl against Texas Tech and bowed, 15-14. Both teams exploited the new two-point conversion rule, but A&M had missed an extra-point from placement after its first touchdown.

After ranking No. 1 in the nation in mid-November of 1957, A&M had a losing streak of five in a row when the tide turned with successive victories over Missouri and Maryland in October, 1958. Gordon LeBoeuf and Don Smith joined Milstead in big plays, as the Aggies came from behind twice to nip Maryland, 14-10.

That set the stage for the Conference campaign, but after losing only three league tests over a three-season span the Aggies were dropped to a tie for fifth place. They did achieve two conference victories, however. The Aggies wiped out a 20-point deficit in the Baylor game on the passing and running of Milstead, who engineered two last-quarter touchdowns for a 33-27 decision. The game-winning play was a 63-yard scoring strike to Luther Hall. Earlier in the game Milstead had broken on a 77-yard scamper.

Revenge was achieved against title-defending Rice, and the Aggies' 28-21 victory denied the Owls a share of the championship. Rice had beaten A&M, 7-6, the season before which prevented successive championships by the Aggies and a trip to the Cotton Bowl. Although slightly injured, Charley Milstead scored two touchdowns, passed for another, and kicked four extra points. LeBoeuf ran a Rice punt back fifty-five yards for the clincher, with tackle Ken Beck throwing the clearing block at the Rice five.

Randy Sims booted a 31-yard field goal to give the Aggies a 9-7 upset victory over Michigan State in the second game of the 1959 season, and the Aggies had won three in a row when they headed into the Conference campaign. After being extolled in the third straight victory, a 28-6 threshing of the Houston Cougars, Milstead accepted the accolades with: "It's easy to quarterback this team. They do the blocking and tackling, and you just follow after them."

A&M was not to win a conference game, but four of their losses were by a margin of only five points or less. Two of the tri-champions—Arkansas and Texas—had trouble gaining that much edge, especially the Longhorns. The Aggies carried a 10-0 advantage over Texas into the intermission, getting away to a spectacular start when Robert Sanders carried the opening kickoff back 58 yards to set the stage for the first score. Randy Sims' 52-yard field goal that stood as a Conference record for 7 years came just as the first half closed.

Limited on a single first down in the first half, Texas went into the lead, 14-10, in the second half. Charley Milstead met that challenge by passing A&M back in front, 17-14, midway of the final quarter. Texas then salvaged a 20-17 decision with a passing barrage of its own.

The No. 1 task in rebuilding for 1960 was finding a replacement for Milstead at quarterback, and this was to become a perennial problem. The only source of encouragement was the sophomore talent, and Willie Zapalac, assistant coach, termed the sophomore linemen as the "best prospects we've had since I've been here," and his first-hand knowledge dated back to 1953.

Coach Jim Myers was a bit more cautious: "It's been my experience that linemen need a while to develop. They are fine prospects with great potential, but they haven't played a down yet."

The Aggies achieved a 14-14 tie as Texas Tech made its debut as a football playing member of the Conference, and they were to play two other deadlocks in the league, fourteen-all with TCU and a scoreless tie with SMU. The lone victory was a 14-0 decision over Trinity.

Despite the disappointments of 1960 and the fact that eleven seniors had never played in a winning Conference game, the outlook was brighter for 1961. Hopes were lifted at the start, as the Aggies battled highly-ranked Houston to a 7-7 tie in the season inaugural. Texas Tech was trounced, 38-7, and the following week A&M achieved its biggest victory margin since 1944 by walloping Trinity, 55-0.

Features of the revitalized offense were a trio of impressive fullbacks and an aerial attack that utilized four passers in the Tech game. John Erickson, Ronnie Brice, Jim Linnsteadter, and Jim Keller took turns in completing twelve of fifteen against the Red Raiders.

Baylor and SMU were defeated, 23-0 and 25-12, as the Aggies climbed to fourth place in the standings with a 3-4-0 record. Coach Jim Myers was so impressed with the fullback play after the Baylor victory he observed: "I thought all three of our fullbacks played well, especially (Sam) Byer, (Lee Roy) Caffey, and (Jerry) Rogers." Dave Campbell of the *Waco News-Tribune* rationalized that, "In the people's minds the Cadets seem to have a fullback named Byercaffeyrogers."

Hal Lahar, head coach of the Houston Cougars who were tied by the Aggies, recalled: "They had fine fullbacks, but (Jerry) Hopkins made their power game go." Hopkins was named all-Conference center, an honor that was to come his way again in 1962, while Byer had been the all-SWC fullback as a sophomore in 1960.

Buddy Joe Eilers received the A. W. Waldrop Award as the best A&M lineman for both the 1960 and 1961 seasons, another tribute to a contribution by the Twelfth Man. The youngster from Hallettsville, Texas, played freshman football at A&M without a scholarship. "I just decided I was going to play football, and I stayed with it until I did. Oh, I got discouraged at times and got mighty tired of standing out there and holding the tackling dummy."

Hank Foldberg, who played one season at A&M in 1942 before becoming an all-America end at West Point, returned to his alma mater in 1962 as successor to Jim Myers as head coach. Hank faced the same quarterback problem that had plagued Jim Myers after Charley Milstead played his last down in 1959. The new coach was to divide quarterbacking between John Erickson, Jim Keller, Jim Willenborg, and Danny McIlhany, which prompted one writer to observe: "A&M has more field generals than Cadet colonels."

Mike Clark's kicking toe was to author most of the season's success, but Danny McIlhany's kickoff return against Texas Tech had to be the most spectacular and the most exciting. Only 19 seconds of play remained when Tech appeared to have assured itself a victory with a field goal for a 3-0 advantage.

Second-guessers had a field day when Tech chose to go for distance instead of resorting to a squib-kick that would have been harder to handle and less likely to be returned. McIlhany took the kickoff in his own end zone and raced the length of the field for a touchdown. The Twelfth Man enthusiasm reached such a height that most of the students poured out of the stands to carry their heroes off the field. The disruption cost the Aggies 15 yards by penalty and Clark had to kick the conversion from the 25-yard line.

McIlhany's runback broke a school record of 97 yards that Joel Hunt had set 35 seasons earlier against Arkansas. One of the fans who might have enjoyed it the most missed the thrill because he was on his way down to the ground aboard the press box elevator. That was Jim Butler, then a student assistant in the Athletic Department and today the assistant sports information director.

The first of Mike Clark's seven field goals that season was for 31 yards against Houston, and it kept A&M in the lead for 57 minutes. He booted two in the 6-3 conquest of Baylor, the winning one coming with 1:09 remaining. He added two more against SMU for a come-from-behind 12-7 victory in the last half.

The seventh one against Rice was to little avail, but he kicked one against Texas in a nationally-televised game that enabled the Aggies to prevail at halftime, 3-0. The Aggies utilized tactics similar to those Texas had employed in upsetting A&M five seasons earlier to storm the Longhorn goal repeatedly in the first half. Texas came from behind to win, 13-3, and register its first undefeated season in 39 years.

"We were close to being a good football team," Coach Foldberg said in retrospect. "We would have been, if our passing game had just been average, but it wasn't even that. It was a combination of poor protection, poor throwing, and poor receiving."

At one time or another in the next spring training the Aggie coach tried 11 different candidates at quarterback. Jim Keller took charge, and he sparked the Aggies to victories over Houston and Rice and a 14-14 tie with TCU. He was joined by Budgie Ford, Jim Linnstaedter, George Hargett, Bill Ward, Tommy Meeks, Travis Reagan, and Bob Lee in the telling blows for this scoreboard success, but the biggest accomplishment of the season may have been the near-miss.

That big one got away, of course, but the Aggies were on the threshold of a monumental upset that came within one minute and nineteen seconds of realization before a national television audience on Thanksgiving Day. If the upset had materialized, it would have atoned for the loss of a game and a national championship that A&M had lost in Austin 23 seasons previously.

The Longhorns were undefeated and ranked No. 1 in the nation when they invaded Kyle Field. A&M was not intimidated and was undaunted by the fact the Longhorns jumped into a 3-0 lead on their first possession. Jim Keller passed to Travis Reagan for 54 yards and an A&M touchdown early in the second quarter to give the Aggies a 7-3 advantage at halftime. In the third quarter Ronnie Moore recovered a Texas fumble at the A&M 44, and in 8 plays the Aggies held a 13-3 lead. The payoff came on a 29-yard pass from Keller to George Hargett.

Texas narrowed the gap to 13-9 early in the fourth quarter, but twice in the final four minutes the Aggies muffed opportunities to preserve victory. John Brotherton had the first opportunity when he intercepted a Tommy Wade pass, but in his anxiety to lateral it off to a teammate he fumbled, and Texas recovered at the A&M 45. With 2:24 remaining and Texas on the A&M 20, Wade attempted to hit George Sauer in the end zone, but the ball fell into Jim Willenborg's hands, and it was ruled that the Aggie did not have possession when he fell across the end line. Hargett came close to picking off Wade's next pass, but three plays later the Longhorns scored to salvage a 15-13 victory.

A&M started the 1964 season by playing LSU to a standstill at Baton Rouge, the Tigers gaining victory by blocking an A&M punt in the end zone for the deciding play in a 9-6 contest. The Aggies were to achieve only one victory over the full campaign, a 23-0 decision over SMU, but four of the contests were decided by five points or less, three of them conference games.

Hank Foldberg disliked players being singled out for recognition, because he thought football was a team sport. This philosophy prompted him to project different players into the leadership role. It was Danny McIlhany at the throttle in the LSU game and again in the battle with Texas Tech when he outgunned Tech's Tom Wilson. McIlhany completed 12 of 25 passes for 184 yards, one of them to Lawson Howard for a touchdown.

Jim Willenborg intercepted two passes in the 1963 game with Texas and picked off a third that might have assured an Aggie upset if he had controlled the ball before falling over the end-zone line.

Eddie McKaughan took over as the big gun against TCU, and he sparked the Aggies to a 16-6 lead over Baylor going into the final quarter. His passing contributed to two scoring drives, and he had a 39-yard run in the march to a field goal. Baylor scored twice in the final period to emerge a 20-16 victor.

In the triumph over SMU McKaughan led the Aggies to a 9-0 lead in the first three quarters, then Charles La Grange and McIlhany took turns at throwing touchdown passes. La Grange hit Billy Uzell for 17 yards, then McIlhany found John Poss for 10 more and a touchdown.

Texas Special's Longest Run

"Make Something Happen" was Gene Stallings' philosophy the day he returned to his alma mater as head coach in 1965, just nine years after he had played his senior season for Texas A&M on a Southwest Conference championship team. All of those intervening seasons had been spent as an assistant to Paul Bryant, who had tutored him throughout his varsity career at Aggieland.

Only 30 years old, Stallings had been tabbed by Bryant as "the top young college coaching prospect in America." Much of Bear Bryant had rubbed off on young Stallings in the eleven years of exposure, and it showed in his speech and mannerisms as well as his philosophy. Stallings immediately surrounded himself with young assistant coaches, four of whom—Jack Pardee, Loyd Taylor, Dee Powell, and Don Watson—had played with him on the 1956 championship team.

The energetic Stallings and his eager assistants swarmed the Southwest on a whirlwind recruiting campaign that reaped 63 signatures to letters-of-intent, a commitment to attend Texas A&M. These youngsters were to be the nucleus of the rejuvenation of a winning tradition for the Aggies. Recruiters zoomed in on competitors that year and in seasons to follow, because Stallings emphasized, "I want the competitors, because that's who you win with. Size is relatively unimportant."

The squad Gene Stallings inherited had enjoyed little winning experience. The seniors had played in only three victories, the juniors one, and the sophomores had not won a game as freshmen the previous year.

This was not to be a get-rich-quick experience, but from the opening game it was obvious the Aggies were determined to "Make Something Happen." LSU, which had been ranked No. 7 in the nation in 1964, whipped the Aggies 10-0, in the inaugural, but its only touchdown came on a blocked punt covered in the end zone. Among those the Aggies impressed that night was a high school senior from Lafayette, Louisiana, who had driven over to Baton Rouge to see the game. Ross Brupbacher was to gain all-Conference recognition at A&M four years later.

The Aggies won two of their first four tests. One of the losses was the spectacular 20-16 loss to Texas Tech that Will Grimsley of the *Associated Press* listed as one of the top eight Southwest Conference games (1935-1965, inclusive) in his book entitled *The Greatest Moments in the Southwest Conference.* A&M was a participant in four of those eight games.

A&M scored twice in the third quarter on successive possessions to come from behind to beat Georgia Tech, 14-10, in the season's second game. Quarterback Harry Ledbetter scored the first touchdown after leading his mates on a 77-yard drive in 14 plays. He passed to Lloyd Curington for 26 yards for the go-ahead score that climaxed a 73-yard drive in 7 plays. Two weeks later Ledbetter teamed with Bill Sallee and field goal kicker Glynn Lindsey in leading the way over Houston's Cougars, 10-7.

A Ledbetter to Curington pass for three yards and a subsequent field goal by Lindsey gave A&M a surprising 10-0 advantage over Texas Tech in Lubbock. The lead changed hands three times in the stormy fourth quarter, however, with Harry Ledbetter dueling Tech's Tom Wilson in a sharp passing battle. After losing the lead on a Wilson to Mike Leinert pass, the Aggies regained the advantage on their next possession. Ledbetter hit Dude McLean for 38, then speared Jim Stabler for 41 to put the Aggies back in front, 16-13, with only 1:38 to play.

Wilson pulled the game out of the fire for the 20-16 Tech victory on a 49-yard aerial that was caught by Jerry Shipley and lateraled off to Donnie Anderson for the final 37 yards. Wilson and Anderson carried Texas Tech to a share of the runner-up position in the Conference race and a bid to the Gator Bowl against Georgia Tech.

The Aggies bounced back from three straight shutouts later in the season to score a 14-13 come-from-behind victory over Rice. Eddie McKaughan quarterbacked A&M's two scoring drives. He passed 32 yards to Stabler for one and to John Poss for the other on a 19-yarder.

The biggest surprise of Stallings' rookie season as coach was still to come. Texas had lost four of its last five games, yet still reigned as slight favorite in the season finale with the Aggies. Neither team threatened in the first quarter, and there was nothing ominous about A&M's position early in the second quarter with a second-down-and-nine situation on its own 9-yard line.

"We had not made a first down up to this point," Coach Stallings remembered in a post-mortem years later.

Then lightning struck. Harry Ledbetter bounced a lateral out to Jim Kauffman, who was not normally used on offense. Kauffman feigned an air of disgust as though it were an incompleted pass, all of which froze the onrushing Longhorn defender momentarily. Meantime, Dude McLean had slipped beyond the startled Texas secondary, and was in the clear when Kauffman threw him a forward pass. The completion was good for 91 yards and a touchdown. The Kauffman to McLean pass still ranks as the longest scoring aerial in Southwest Conference history. It became known as "The Texas Special."

"That play was significant for more than just being unusual," Stallings reminds. "That particular play turned everything around for a while."

After that sensational touchdown, A&M kicked off and got the ball right back on an interception. Bubber Collins went 13 yards for a second touchdown, and by half time the Aggies had increased their margin to 17-0 on a 22-yard field goal by Glynn Lindsey.

Texas scored one touchdown in the third quarter and two more in the fourth for a 21-17 victory. Both of the Longhorns' final two tallies were made by Jim Helms, whose father (Jake) had joined Stallings' staff for the 1965 season.

Lloyd Gregory, a former Houston newspaperman whose blood runs orange, observed of the trick play after the game, "I'd rather be beaten by the Aggies than be fooled by them."

Gregory teamed with Coach Stallings on a weekly television show.

The 1966 Aggies managed a 7-7 tie with LSU, and they started their conference campaign by thrashing Texas Tech and TCU, 35-14 and 35-7, respectively. Those two teams had shared runnerup honors to Arkansas the previous year.

Sophomore Edd Hargett entrenched himself as the starting quarterback before the opening game, and he passed for two touchdowns and scored a third in the games with Tech and TCU. Tommy Maxwell and Bob Long were the primary targets in those games, and they were joined as standout receivers as the season progressed by Larry Lee, Wendell Housley, Tom Buckman, and Ronnie Lindsey.

Glynn Lindsey, a senior field-goal kicker, teamed with Hargett and Maxwell to give the Aggies a 17-0 lead over Baylor in Waco, then the Aggie defenders held off Terry Southall and his Bruin mates to gain a 17-13 victory. The 3-0 record in conference play had the Aggies sharing the lead with SMU, the eventual champion, when they lined up against Arkansas the following week.

"We were off to a good start until we ran into Arkansas," Gene Stallings recalled. "We had their quarterback trapped once, but he got out of trouble by throwing the ball left-handed instead of with his right. After that they could do no wrong, and we could do little right. They wound up beating us 34-0, and we lost three of our last four games."

Afterwards the Aggies jumped to a 14-0 lead over SMU, but the Mustangs maintained the league leadership by breaking a 14-14 deadlock in the final quarter on an 83-yard punt return by Jerry Levias. A&M edged Rice, 7-6, the following week, as Wendell Housley scored after a Hargett to Maxwell pass had set the scene. Lindsey's conversion was the difference, as Rice failed on a two-point conversion attempt after its fourth-quarter touchdown.

Texas led all the way after getting a touchdown on its first possession, but Lloyd Curington ended his A&M career with two big plays. He took a handoff from Bob Long on a criss-cross of a kickoff return and raced 67 yards before he was hauled down on the Texas 23. A&M scored its first touchdown on a deliberate drive from that point and got its second when

5-8 Charlie Riggs hit Curington with a 17-yard scoring pass in the final minutes.

Tackle Maurice (Mo) Moorman and guard Gary Kovar were consensus all-Conference selections as they teamed with other offensive linemen in providing good protection for Edd Hargett, the passer, and in leading a convoy for Wendell Housley, whose net rushing of 548 yards was A&M's highest total since all-American John David Crow carried for 562 in 1957.

Gene Stallings displayed a memento of that 1966 season on his desk the following year. It was the helmet that had been worn by Robert Cortez, the linebacker from San Benito. "The color of every team we played in 1966 is on that helmet. Whenever I am feeling low, I look at that helmet, and I know where I can find a contact football player, and I start feeling better."

Robert Cortez: His helmet became a keepsake.

Beat The Clock
And The Teacher

Bumper stickers and decals for sundry uses proclaimed in 1967, "The Aggies Are Back." *Texas Football* magazine labeled 1967 as "The Year Not To Pick A Fight With The Aggies."

Bill Beall, then an assistant coach at LSU who had scouted the Aggies in their spring game, predicted, "They're going to be the surprise team in this part of the country next fall." Louis Cox, veteran sports writer for the *Dallas Times Herald,* gained some sort of distinction by being the only sportswriter in the *Texas Football* poll to pick A&M to win the Southwest Conference championship.

Something went wrong in the very first game of the season. Title-defending SMU upset the Aggies in a nationally-televised game on Kyle Field. SMU's Mustangs sounded a warning on their first possession by marching for a field goal after Jerry Levias returned the opening kickoff 46 yards.

Wendell Housley scored from 10 yards out to give the Aggies a 7-3 advantage at the end of the first quarter, but the lead was to change three more times before time ran out and the scoreboard read: SMU 20, A&M 17. SMU led at the intermission, 10-7, but Charlie Riggs' 22-yard field goal pulled the Aggies back even going into the final quarter.

SMU regained the lead five plays into the final period, 13-10, on a 25-yard field goal by Dennis Partee. Late in the quarter the Aggies started an 83-yard drive that, when culminated, had them in front, 17-13, with only 36 seconds of play remaining.

It was far from an ordinary drive. It survived a bit of derring-do when the Aggies faced a fourth-and-seven situation on their own 20-yard line. Steve O'Neal lined up in deep punt formation, but the snap went instead to quarterback Edd Hargett who passed to Tommy Maxwell for a first down. Hargett passes to Maxwell, Jimmy Adams, and Ross Brupbacher carried the Aggies to the SMU 29, from where the sharp-eyed quarterback hit his favorite receiver, Bob Long, for a touchdown.

It appeared to be a hopeless situation for the Mustangs, because Mike Livingston, their starting quarterback was injured, and 5-4 Ines Perez was his relief. Jerry Levias returned the short kickoff 24 yards to the SMU 42, where he stepped out of bounds to stop the clock. In little more than half a minute Perez completed four of five passes, the last for the winning touchdown, 20-17 SMU. There was only enough time for the subsequent kickoff, which Brupbacher returned only 2 yards.

A&M was to lose its next three games, and some of the gagsters disparingly had inserted the word "Way" into the bumper-sticker slogan to make it read: The Aggies Are Way

Wendell Housley

Back.

Bill Hobbs, en route to becoming an all-American linebacker that season, recalled how the Twelfth Man demonstrated its support at a time when it was needed the most. "The night before we left for the game with Texas Tech the students held a pep rally in front of our dorm. It was pouring down rain, and they kept it up for an hour. An hour in the rain for a losing team. You respond to that."

In the game just two years previously at Lubbock, Texas Tech had salvaged victory in the final minute as the lead changed hands three times in the last quarter. The 1967 game had the appearance of a replay, except it was to produce more scoring and a more dramatic finish.

Neither team got on the scoreboard in the first quarter, but each scored in the three subsequent periods. The lead switched once each in the second and third quarters and three times in the frantic fourth quarter, which started with Tech holding a 17-14 advantage.

A&M regained the lead at 21-17 early in the period on an Edd Hargett toss to Larry Stegent for 13 yards and a subsequent conversion by Charlie Riggs. Late in the quarter

Bill Hobbs *Bob Long*

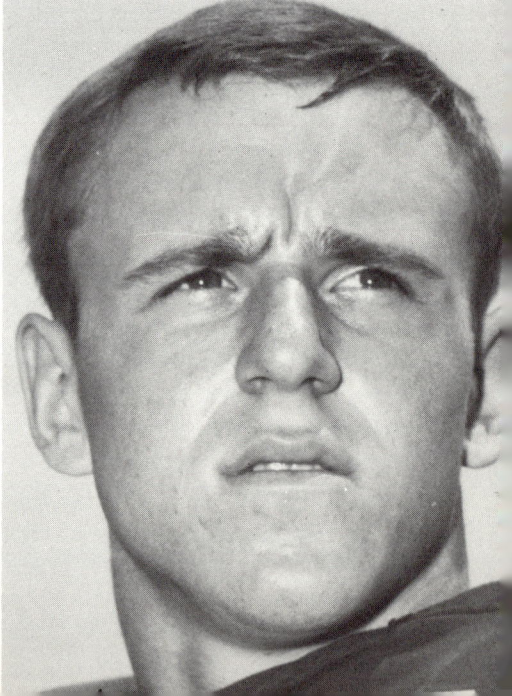

Larry Stegent breaks loose from a Texas Tech tackler to score one of the Aggies' touchdowns in the 28-24 thriller in 1967.

Tech was operating from its own 18-yard line, but two 15-yard penalties against the Aggies gave the Red Raiders field position on their own 48. Quarterback John Scovell took them in from there in 7 plays, and Tech was back in front, 24-21, with only 53 seconds to play.

After Ross Brupbacher covered Tech's short kickoff on his own 41, the Aggies were to crowd 6 plays into less than a minute. Hargett hit Stegent for 19, but the Aggies lost 5 by penalty that nullified a first down. It was fourth-and-fifteen on the Tech 45, with 11 seconds remaining when Hargett found white-shirted Bob Long in a crowd of Red Raiders on the Tech 15. Long's catch was incredible.

As time ran out, Hargett rolled to his left to throw, but all receivers were covered. He then headed for the red flag at the right hand corner and scored to give Tech a 28-24 victory and the turning point of the season.

"It was an exceptional finish," Gene Stallings remembered in an understated summation. "Except for two reasons, one of which was my stupidity that got us in a predicament. We had them deep in their territory and threw them for a loss but were penalized for holding. That gave them a first down, then I got penalized 15 more, and that gave them field position to fire a go-ahead drive."

Thereafter Arkansas offered the only serious challenge to the Aggies prior to the season finale with Texas. The Aggies had to score three times in the final quarter to overcome Arkansas, 33-21, for their fourth victory in a row that pulled them to 4-4 for the first eight games. Hargett passed to Wendell Housley and Tommy Maxwell for two of the three fourth-quarter scores, and Larry Stegent scored the other.

Texas and Texas Tech were still challenging A&M for the

1967 Southwest Conference Champions

championship and the trip to the Cotton Bowl when the Aggies hosted the Longhorns on Thanksgiving Day. A&M answered all of the questions by edging the Longhorns, 10-7, when Hargett and Bob Long collaborated on an 80-yard scoring play. This fourth-quarter clincher came on the second play from scrimmage after Texas had moved in front, 7-3.

"Probably the biggest thrill that season was looking up to watch time run out as we beat Texas, 10-7," Stallings recalled. "Buster Adami had made a great interception to end Texas' final threat."

Receiver Bob Long, who had the knack of pulling in home run receptions, recalled how Coach Stallings held the team together after the four-loss beginning. He told us, "SMU is not going to win it. So anybody who wins it has got to beat us."

A&M owned its first conference championship in eleven seasons and was headed to the Cotton Bowl for the first time in

26 years. The opponent was to be Alabama, which had beaten the Aggies in the 1942 Cotton Bowl Classic, 29-21, while making only a single first down. The 1968 meeting packed far more drama, however, for it matched Gene Stallings (the pupil) and Paul Bryant (the teacher). Bryant had coached the 1956 A&M champions that Stallings had served as a tri-captain. The 1956 Aggies were on NCAA probation and ineligible for bowl participation.

Alabama drew first blood, but A&M gained a 13-10 half time lead on Edd Hargett passes to Larry Stegent and Tommy Maxwell, then fashioned a 20-16 upset when Wendell Housley romped 20 yards for a third touchdown, shaking off seven would-be tacklers in one of the Bowl's best demonstrations of bruising power.

Hargett and Bob Long were consensus all-SWC performers on the offensive platoon, while end Grady Allen, tackle Rolf Krueger, and linebacker Bill Hobbs achieved like accolades on the defense. Hargett rewrote the school game and season records for forward passing and was joined the following season by buddy Bob Long in rewriting the career marks for most of the aerial catagories.

The return of all but five of the players who fashioned the seven-game winning streak by the 1967 team prompted the seers on the 1968 Southwest Conference Press Tour to pick the Aggies to win a second straight championship. It looked like a good prediction when the Aggies jumped into a 12-0 lead over LSU in the season inaugural. LSU rallied to win by one point, 13-12, but when the Aggies whipped Tulane, 35-3, the forecast took on added credence.

A&M was to win only two other games, however (27-7 over TCU and 24-14 over Rice), despite consistent marksmanship by Edd Hargett on his forward passes. The senior quarterback threw touchdown aerials in nine of the ten games played, and on five occasions he was credited with two or more. Barney Harris led the Aggies in receptions with 49, but for a second straight season Bob Long pulled in eight scoring tosses to wind up with a school career record of 19.

Hargett was the only Aggie to gain consensus all-Conference recognition on the offensive platoon, but end Mike DeNiro, Rolf Krueger, and Bill Hobbs got the nod for the defense, and the latter was all-American for a second straight season.

A&M's 2-5 record for conference play and 3-7 season in 1968 was duplicated in 1969, the lone conquests being over Army, Baylor, and SMU.

The record was not that good in 1970, although the prospects were most encouraging after the first two games. Wichita State was beaten handily, then came one of the more memorable comebacks in A&M's football history.

Louisiana State grabbed a 12-0 lead before the sophomore-loaded Aggies scratched in the third quarter. Pat McDermott kicked two field goals and Lex James hit Homer May with an 11-yard scoring pass, and with McDermott's conversion the Aggies moved in front, 13-12, midway of the fourth quarter.

The Tigers struck back with a pair of field goals, the last one coming after A&M had gambled to retain possession deep in its own territory. LSU was in front, 18-13, with only 45 seconds remaining.

Dave Elmendorf returned the LSU kickoff to the A&M 20, and after two James passes fell incomplete, it was third down, 79 yards to go, and only 22 seconds left. Fans were heading for the exit when James dropped back and speared the 5-8 Hugh McElroy near midfield. When two LSU defenders went for the ball and missed, McElroy grabbed it and outran his pursuers for a 79-yard touchdown play and a startling 20-18 decision when McDermott's placement was true for the fourth time that night. Elmendorf, headed for consensus as all-American defensive back, sealed LSU's doom with an interception on the final play at A&M's 8.

Dave Elmendorf gained the unique distinction of being an all-America baseball player as well as all-America in football in his senior year. He also was a post-graduate scholarship honoree of the National Collegiate Athletic Association and the National Football Foundation and Hall of Fame. After graduation he joined the Los Angeles Rams and became an instant star in his rookie season as a defensive halfback.

The Aggies were not to win another game that season, although they came near upsetting mighty Michigan. The Aggies jumped to a 10-0 lead in the second quarter, but bowed, 14-10, after giving the Wolverines a cheap touchdown

Lex James gets set to complete a 79-yard scoring aerial to Hugh McElroy to give the Aggies a 20-18 lead and ultimate 1970

victory over LSU with only 13 seconds remaining.

on a fumble at the A&M 8-yard line. Elmendorf broke for 56 yards on the kickoff following Michigan's go-ahead touchdown, but the Wolverines took over on downs when Lex James' passes misfired.

The 1971 Aggies opened with a decisive victory over Wichita State, then lost five in a row before reversing the trend with a 10-9 victory over Baylor. Senior Joe Mac King, who was a third stringer in the season opener, had taken command at quarterback, and he sparked the Aggies to their first conference victory in 12 straight tests.

The following week the Aggies parlayed sound defense, expert punting by Mitch Robertson, and decisive running by Mark Green to upset Arkansas, 17-9, before a full house at War Memorial Stadium in Little Rock. Pat McDermott added a 35-yard field goal to Green's two touchdown runs.

Arkansas had defeated title-defending Texas to become a heavy favorite for the conference championship. A&M's defense was so effective, however, that the Razorbacks were denied their only touchdown until after A&M had taken a 17-3 lead. The loss cost Arkansas a share of the title, as the Razorbacks were later tied by Rice.

"This has got to be the greatest victory ever for me," Coach Stallings acknowledged at the time.

The Green-King-McDermott trio continued to spark the Aggies as they ran their winning streak to four by adding SMU and Rice as victims. "If we beat Texas, we go to the Liberty Bowl," Stallings remembers, "but Texas won (35-14) and I was summoned to the president's house." Stallings had another year on his contract, but his eight-season tenure was terminated.

"It's a great university," he says in retrospect. "And I feel like I made some contributions while I was there: an upper deck to the stadium, Astroturf on both the playing field and the practice field, and we got that new dorm project going."

Gig 'Em! Edd Hargett

"If you hadn't been there before, you couldn't find it the first time." That is how Elmer Smith, former recruiter and assistant coach at Texas A&M, described the remoteness of Edd Hargett's home in the Cass County boondocks of East Texas.

Smith had been there before. In late 1959 and early 1960 he had traveled the farm-to-market road back into the woods to recruit George Hargett, Edd Hargett's older brother. George, a stubby halfback with quickness and a tough disposition, was to distinguish himself at Aggieland as a pass receiver, returner of kicks, and ball-hawking defensive back. He never played on an Aggie team that won as many games as it lost, however. Nor did he attain the fame of younger brother Edd.

When Elmer Smith was recruiting George for A&M coach Jim Myers back in 1959-60, he first saw the prospect's 12-year old brother. "As I was leaving," Smith recalled, "I saw Edd kinda hanging back. He was about this high"—he held his hand at belt-buckle level—"and a little old timid boy. I bent down and put my arm around his shoulder and said, 'Edd, I'll be back here someday to sign you, too.'"

Six years later Elmer drove back down that winding, bumpy road to remind Edd Hargett of that promise he had made the day he signed George to a letter-of-intent. By this time a lot of rival recruiters had found their way to the Hargett home, because Edd had fashioned himself quite a reputation as a quarterback for Linden-Kildare.

Meantime, A&M had made a coaching change, and Gene

Stallings had been called back to serve as foreman of the restoration. It was a development that offered an exciting challenge; so, Edd Hargett signed his name when Smith proffered the letter-of-intent.

Edd missed his entire freshman season at A&M because of a knee injury and resulting surgery during his senior season at Linden-Kildare. After the torn ligaments were repaired, Hargett reported for baseball and reinjured the knee charging a fly ball. A second operation was endured before he entered A&M, and recovery did not come until after the 1965 football season.

Edd Hargett took over as the starting quarterback before the opening game of his sophomore season in 1966 and demonstrated his artistry as a forward passer early. He threw two touchdown passes in each victory over Texas Tech and TCU, then directed the Aggies to a share of the conference leadership by upsetting Baylor, 17-13.

It was in the final minutes of the Baylor game that young Hargett demonstrated his ability to take charge in a critical situation. Baylor had cut A&M's early 17-0 lead to 17-13, and the Aggies were bottled up inside of their own 20-yard line. Hargett entered the huddle and exclaimed—in what for him was a major speech—"let's get the hell out of here." The Aggies cranked up and moved.

As a sophomore, Hargett established five A&M game records in passing and total offense and rewrote six season records in the same categories that had been shared by Ray Graves, Charles Milstead, and Don Ellis.

In 1967 Hargett rewrote all of the A&M passing and total offense records as he led the Aggies to a dramatic championship after enduring losses in the first four games. In just two seasons he had wiped out the career records in the passing and total offense categories that had been shared by Milstead and Dick Gardemal.

When he concluded his career, Edd Hargett's name was inscribed 21 times among the A&M game, season, and career standards.

His reputation as a forward passer and as a leader were stamped more indelibly in the memories of rival coaches who watched with awe as he gained consensus all-Conference recognition in 1967 and 1968.

John Bridgers, the former Baylor coach who lived by the forward pass, was impressed with Hargett in each confrontation. After the 1966 meeting Bridgers observed, "He can throw it any way you want it. Long or short. He can burn it or lob it. He's a fine one."

The following year Bridgers said, "We rushed him off his feet. Got to him and put him on the ground eight times but he got up and beat us. One of his touchdown passes was unbelievable."

Bo Hagan, then the head coach at Rice, proclaimed that "No team is better than its quarterback, and Edd Hargett is the best." Reviewing the 1967 championship season Hagan said, "He made the big play for them all year. The great impromptu play. Time after time he would go back on third-and-long, and we would rush him and have him boxed in, and yet he would slip away and make the play."

It was under a comparable situation that Edd Hargett teamed with Bob Long in the 1967 game with Texas Tech. They collaborated on a pass play that turned things around for the Aggies and headed them toward the championship in a Silky Sullivan finish.

Only 11 seconds of play remained, and A&M had the ball on the Texas Tech 45 in a fourth-and-fifteen circumstance. Hargett announced in the huddle after calling the play: "...and if I get in trouble I'm just going to throw it up there."

Long answered, "Well, I guess I will play for the tip."

Long made the catch, a habit of his in such situations, and Hargett ran it across as time ran out on the next play to give A&M a 28-24 victory, the first in a string of seven.

In any recital of Hargett's attributes Gene Stallings points out that, "One of his greatest assets was the ability to turn a bad play into a real good one. And don't forget that he had to have a lot of courage, or he wouldn't even have been on the field in his sophomore season playing on that leg."

Asked what kind of precautions were taken to protect Hargett's knee, Stallings answered: "The trainer taped it, and I held my breath."

As for Edd Hargett, he recalled a circumstance that enabled him to appreciate tolerance of pain: "Gary Kovar played most of one season with a bad hip pointer, and was one

Edd Hargett rewrote the record book in leading the Aggies to a remarkable comeback to win the 1967 championship.

of our best blockers. I got a hip pointer in the Rice game, and it hurt enough that I was really impressed with Kovar. The thing is you know you can count on the guy in front of you, or next to you."

Everyone learned at Aggieland that he could count on Edd Hargett.

Return Of The Native

Born in Paris, Texas, March 2, 1935, Gene Stallings grew up wanting to be a football coach. Along the way he encountered a couple of architects in that profession whom he credits for his love of and dedication to football.

At Paris High School he played under Raymond Berry, Sr., and proved early leadership by serving as captain of the football, basketball, and golf teams in his senior season. When Gene was a sophomore at Paris, there was a senior end on the squad named Raymond Berry, Jr., who was destined for all-Southwest Conference in 1954 and later to become one of the greatest pass receivers in professional football history.

When Gene Stallings entered Texas A&M in the fall of 1953, he insists he had never heard of Paul (Bear) Bryant. A few months later Ray George was dismissed as head coach at Aggieland, and Stallings recalls that "The players wanted Mike Michalske to be considered for head coach." Michalske had been line coach for George in 1953 after serving in the same capacity for three years at Baylor on George Sauer's staff.

Bryant, of course, was A&M's choice to succeed Ray George as head coach, and in the spring of 1954 the second architect of Gene Stallings' coaching career took command. It was the beginning of a relationship that eleven years later was to be a big factor in Stallings' return to his alma mater as head football coach in 1965.

That is getting ahead of the story, however. As a player Stallings was a sophomore in the 1954 Junction saga that fashioned the foundation for an undefeated championship team two seasons later. Gene was a star end and one of the tri-captains of that 1956 eleven.

Looking back on his playing days Stallings recognized the great ones—stars like Jack Pardee, John David Crow, Charley Krueger, Dennis Goehring, et al—but he also remembered the contributions of the unheralded ones like Bobby Keith and Richard Gay. "You don't hear so much about Richard Gay, but he was truly an outstanding player."

As for outstanding individual performances, Stallings recalled: "Loyd Taylor's performance against Rice and (Jack) Pardee's play against Texas stand out in my mind. I also remember how much Bennie Sinclair meant to us during my sophomore year."

Back in his sophomore season Stallings started keeping a notebook in which he recorded meticulously everything Bear Bryant said or thought or did involving football. This gesture of faith may not have been an influence, but a decade later Bryant was to tab his devoted protege "the top young college coaching prospect in America."

Stallings started his coaching career in 1957, serving as freshman coach at A&M in Bryant's final year with the Aggies. When Bryant left A&M for Alabama, he took Gene with him, and "Bebes"—as Bear calls him—was to serve seven seasons on the Alabama staff before being summoned back to A&M. Alabama finished in the nation's Top Ten in six of those seven seasons and claimed the national championship twice (1961 and 1964).

Bear Bryant was in New York at the time A&M announced it was hiring Stallings as its head coach. When tracked down and pressed for his reaction to his aide's advancement, Bryant acknowledged, "It was the first time I cried in 30 years."

Bob Curran, a freelance writer, walked into Bryant's hotel room as the coach was hanging up the telephone while tears rolled down his leathery cheeks.

Curran turned to a friend of Bryant's and whispered, "What's wrong with Paul?"

"He just lost an assistant coach," the friend replied.

"Oh," said Curran, "I'm sorry. How old was he?"

"Twenty-nine."

"My gosh," exclaimed Curran, "that's an awfully young age to be passing away."

"Oh, he didn't die," hurriedly explained the friend. "He went to A&M."

Stallings' rehabilitation program at A&M did not move as briskly as Bryant's had a decade earlier, but, like his teacher, he did achieve a championship in his third season at the helm. The 1967 title was the first for A&M since 1956 and brought the first Cotton Bowl participation in a quarter of a century.

"We will win the championship within three years or you can have the job back," Stallings had told the A&M Board of Directors in December, 1964. When the Aggies lost their first four games in 1967, Stallings must have second-guessed his talent as a prophet. It was the finish that counted, however.

When Stallings' Aggies squared off against Bryant's Crimson Tide in the 1968 Cotton Bowl Classic, Mickey Herskowitz of the *Houston Post* wrote: "This might be called the Xerox Bowl, because the teams are identical copies. They look alike, sound alike, play the same style of football and, indeed, share many of the same formations and tactics, the result of Bear Bryant's unique relationship with Gene Stallings.

"As they go through this week's preliminaries, the Bear sees much of himself in the young activist who played for him at Aggieland and worked for him at Tuscaloosa. He sees the intense, restless, impatient, almost excessively proud young coach that Paul William Bryant was 20 years ago."

Dee Powell and Don Watson, who played with Stallings for three seasons at A&M and joined his coaching staff when he returned to Aggieland, attest to the fact that their friend and boss was a hard-working perfectionist. Looking back on that 1967 championship season, Powell recalled: "We would get to work before dawn and stay until after dark."

"It was so demanding, we wouldn't even go out for coffee," Watson said in corroboration.

Looking back on that championship season, Bill Hobbs, the all-America linebacker, remembered: "There was a time when nobody loved us but us. That's when you either fall apart or pull tighter together. Because of Coach Stallings there wasn't any chance we'd fall apart."

Before that championship campaign Gene Stallings had

Like Teacher, Like Pupil
Paul (Bear) Bryant, who coached Gene Stallings at Texas A&M, lifted his former pupil in a rare demonstration of mixed emotions at the 1968 Cotton Bowl game. Gene's Aggies beat Bear's Alabama Crimson Tide, 20-16.

declared: "It is easy for me to try to sell a boy on coming to A&M for three reasons. First, it is a school where you can get an excellent education. Second, it is a place where you will learn what loyalty means. Third, it is a place where a boy can play for a good football team."

Convinced that his opponents would have his team out-manned Stallings said, "We'll have to rely on conditioning, determination, and effort."

Competitiveness was Stallings' No. 1 requisite in a player. "I think that in his lifetime a boy should be four points behind with four minutes to play, and he should win a few. He should be four up with four to go and lose a few. But the most important thing is that he should compete.

"It doesn't have to be football, but a boy should compete in something, because athletics is just about the last place where discipline is taught. They don't get it at home and they don't get it in church, and when they get it in school their parents call the school board and want to fire the teacher."

Appreciative of the Twelfth Man both as a player and as a coach, Stallings says: "The yell leaders are mighty important at A&M. The head yell leader has a responsible position. He always travels with the team, and while I was head coach there, the head yell leader came out for football in the early fall practice and he practiced until school started. He wanted to go through what the players went through and wanted to know the players so he could relate better to the students in gaining strong support of the team."

When Gene Stallings left A&M after the 1971 season, only two—Homer Norton and Dana X. Bible—had served Texas A&M longer as head coach. Norton served 14 seasons, Bible 11, and Stallings 7.

Stallings switched to professional football coaching on leaving A&M. He joined another former head coach of the Aggies, Jim Myers, on the Dallas Cowboys staff.

Freshmen Add Fresh Flavor

When Emory Bellard became the seventh head football coach at Texas A&M over a 25-year span, freshmen had been declared eligible for varsity football, starting with the 1972 season, his first at the helm.

Coaches and other close observers who thought freshmen would contribute noticeably were in the minority, but Bellard, whose first recruiting campaign had put an accent on speed, believed otherwise. Neither he nor rival recruiters expected such a sensational debut by his freshmen that season, however.

After all, *Texas Football* magazine had forecast a third-place finish in the 1972 Southwest Conference race for the Aggies with this thumbnail observation: "The coach is new, the schedule is tough, the team's breakaway speed is uncertain. But what seniors!"

What went wrong? The exclamatory observation about the seniors perhaps. Of course the evaluation of the seniors was construed as complimentary, but it was based more on quantity than quality. True, Bellard was to greet 24 senior lettermen, 17 of whom had lettered twice. Ten of them had started either offensively or defensively the previous year, but not one had gained consensus all-Conference recognition. The only senior who had been among the Top Ten statistical leaders in 1971 was Bob Murski, a pass receiver who was switched to defense and became the team's punter.

After his first spring training session, Coach Bellard was far from ecstatic. "We aren't there yet, but we're headed in the right direction. The biggest plus factor was the attitude of the players. We have some who have indicated they can play and play well. Others need to improve to meet the competition we'll face."

The new A&M coach who had created the Wishbone backfield alignment while assistant coach at Texas was much more enthusiastic about the incoming freshmen: "Whatever our freshmen do, they're going to do it in a great hurry because they have great speed. We have 10 freshmen coming in who have run 10 flat or better. And some of them are the kind of prospects you dream about if you are a coach."

Bellard learned early that other teams could do things in a hurry also. Wichita State took the season-opening kickoff and ran it back 85 yards against the Aggies, then after A&M tied the score 6-all, the Kansan ran the subsequent kickoff back 96 yards for a 13-6 lead. A 24-point second quarter, featuring Mark Green, enabled the Aggies to fashion a 36-13 victory.

Carl Roaches, one of 10 freshmen lettering in the 1972 season, returned a kickoff 97 yards against LSU, but the Tigers erupted with a second-half aerial barrage to win, 42-17. The young Aggies had held LSU to a 14-10 half time margin.

Mistakes and turnovers plagued the Aggies most of the season, yet their only decisive loss in conference competition came in the season finale with Texas. They dropped their first three league games by a total of only eight points. Brad Dusek surpassed the 100-yard mark in rushing against both Texas Tech and TCU, and both foes had to come from behind to triumph with three-point decisions.

Meantime, sophomore Don Dean had relieved senior Lex James of the quarterbacking duties, and he was looking to Dusek and freshman Skip Walker, Bubba Bean, and Ronny Hubby for the ball-carrying punch. His favored targets were Richard Osborne and Carl Roaches, the Mutt and Jeff pass-receiving duo, and senior Homer May.

Baylor jumped to a 15-0 lead before the Aggies found the scoring range late in the third quarter at Waco. Roaches broke the ice with a 61-yard punt return, and Bean's 54-yard scamper featured an 80-yard drive that took up all but two points of the deficit, as the Aggies demonstrated their ability to keep battling.

The comeback against Baylor inspired a 10-7 conquest of

Arkansas the following week, marking the first time in 15 years that A&M had put victories over Arkansas back to back. Defense keyed the victory, as Aggie ballhawks picked off six of Joe Ferguson's passes. Ralph Murski and Larry Ellis stole two each, and the latter set up A&M's only touchdown with a 26-yard runback in the third quarter.

A&M whipped SMU, 17-7, for its third and final victory of the 1972 season, with Skip Walker scoring twice to join Pat McDermott in the heroics. McDermott kicked a 54-yard field goal to better the school record for distance (53 yards) made against Baylor in 1971.

An 84-yard punt return by Roaches and a Dean-to-Osborne scoring pass propelled the Aggies into a 14-0 lead over Rice, but the Owls fought back for a 20-14 victory. Roaches emerged as A&M's only individual leader in conference statistics as he led the league in punt return yardage and finished as runner-up in kickoff returns.

The eager, inexperienced Aggies lost the ball to the opposition a total of 41 times through fumbles and interceptions, while the foes committed only 24 turnovers. As a result A&M ranked last in total offense among its conference rivals but managed to rank fourth in defense with its determination.

The long-range scoring tendencies demonstrated in 1972 exploded in the opening game of the 1973 season, when the Aggies introduced a new offense—called the T-Bone—guided by a new quarterback. Mike Jay, not long out of his U. S. Marines uniform, directed the Aggies to a 48-0 victory over Wichita State in that inaugural.

It was A&M's most lopsided victory in a dozen years, and it featured a 77-yard scoring run by Malcolm Bowers, a 51-yard pass interception runback by Pat Thomas for a score, and two touchdowns by Skip Walker that measured 28 and 19 yards.

The pattern for distance became an earmark for the Aggies. Mike Jay and Carl Roaches collaborated on a 60-yard scoring aerial against LSU, and the Aggies threatened until the final minute in what had been billed as a runaway for the Tigers. LSU won the squeaker, 28-23, as Aggie Randy Haddox set a school record of three field goals for a single game.

Roaches opened the Boston College game with a 100-yard kickoff return, and the situation appeared under control when

Richard Osborne pulls in a "bean-bag" pass that worked so successfully in the 1973 game with Texas.

A&M held a 24-17 lead early in the fourth quarter. Boston College exploited a short Aggie punt and a pass interception to rally for a 32-24 victory.

Clemson, facing A&M on the gridiron for the first time, jumped to a 9-0 lead over the Aggies the following week. A&M turned it around, however, with a 78-yard run by Bubba Bean on a pitch-out, and moved on to a 30-15 decision as 17-year old David Walker subbed for Mike Jay at quarterback. Walker scored the final touchdown, and Ronny Hubby contributed two others.

Four pass interceptions and two lost fumbles denied the Aggies a chance at victory in their conference inaugural with Texas Tech, but they bounced back the following week to wham TCU, 35-16. The victory broke a TCU winning streak of four over A&M.

David Walker made his first start at quarterback against the Frogs and was so impressive he took over as the regular. The Aggies rushed for 353 yards against TCU, with the Walker boys leading the way. Skip gained 122 and David 81.

The revitalized A&M offense grabbed a 21-0 lead over Baylor in the third quarter before the Neal Jeffrey-Charley Dancer passing combination found the range for the Bears. Bucky Sams of the Aggies tempered that rally with a 28-yard scoring run, and the Aggies prevailed, 28-22.

Tied for the runner-up spot in the conference standings as the race headed into November, the Aggies could only break even in their last four games and wound up in sixth place. Highlights of their late games included a 71-yard punt return by Carl Roaches for a touchdown against SMU, a 20-point rally that wiped out Rice's early 17-0 lead, and a season record of 10 field goals by Randy Haddox that gave him a total of 66 points from placement, fifth highest season total in SWC history.

A&M took a 20-17 lead over Rice with only 2:27 to play, but the Owls' Carl Swierc ran the subsequent kickoff back 95 yards to give Rice a 24-20 decision.

Ed Simonini, a punishing sophomore linebacker, was A&M's only consensus all-Conference player in the 1973 season, but four members of the offensive unit gained second team acclaim: back Skip Walker, center Ricky Seeker, guard Bruce Welch, and split end Carl Roaches. A&M led the league in pass defense and improved its offense by 11 points per game over the previous season.

Emory Bellard was to start his third season at the helm

with 21 of the 22 players who were considered regulars at the close of the 1973 campaign.

"We should be a better football team than we have been," Bellard says, "and we have a chance to be an outstanding team. We've developed depth, especially on the defensive units, but we could use more running backs. We hope to find more depth there among our incoming freshmen."

Looking beyond the 1974 campaign Bellard observed, "I think our program is developing to the point that by 1975 we will have solid talent in each of our four classes." Bellard's recruiting has achieved a good store of freshmen, sophomores, and juniors, but it will take another good year of talent searching to give A&M the balance it needs.

"Of course, we will have more maturity in 1974 than we

Carl Roaches (18) and young speedsters like him will be the keys to Emory Bellard's hopes of restoring success to A&M in a hurry.

had the previous season. We will have ten seniors this time in contrast to only five a year ago."

Bellard lists a number of contributing factors to successful recruiting at A&M. "I think the attitude on our campus is outstanding as a starting point" he says. "Our student body is one of the finest there is. That is not implying there are not other fine student bodies, but I think our students are really outstanding in that they are interested in all activities that are representative of Texas A&M. They have a tremendous loyalty and feeling for the school and everyone that represents it. Consequently, we have an outstanding spirit and attitude that prevails here, and I think the support of the former students of Texas A&M has been what I figured it would be. Nonetheless the tremendous loyalty and interest of the people who have graduated from Texas A&M never ceases to amaze me."

Appendix

THE FIGHTIN' TEXAS AGGIE BAND

Friends and foes alike are in general agreement that Texas A&M "has never lost a half time show" simply because of its great precision-marching band.

The combined sight and sound of the 300-man Texas A&M Band defies description, although it has been attempted with "thunder and blazes under tasteful restraint." It is the largest military marching band in the nation and has thrilled millions of television viewers over the years at half time of football games and in major parades.

First formed by Joseph F. Halick (Class of '98), a Czechoslovakian cobbler in 1894, the band sounds the pulse of athletic events, reviews, parades and other functions. Holick and Arthur N. Jenkins formed the original band, a 13-man group who wore Texas Militia uniforms and played their own or borrowed instruments.

By the 1930s the band had grown to a 100-man marching unit, and in the post-World War II years grew even more rapidly to become a 267-member band in 1968. For nearly three decades the band was under the direction of Lieutenant Colonel E. V. Adams, who was the dean of the Southwest Conference bandmasters when he retired in 1973. The band's unique band hall has been named in his honor.

Colonel Adams was succeeded by Major Joe T. Haney, who served one year of apprenticeship before taking command.

The astonishing feature of the great band is three-fold: (1) no scholarships, (2) no auditions, and (3) no music majors. The only prerequisites are previous marching and previous playing experience.

The band is a military unit within the Corps of Cadets at A&M.

Members come from most of the 50 states, several foreign countries and major in courses from aerospace engineering to zoology. The unit, 12 men wide and 20 to 24 men long, cover 35 yards of gridiron and can march in one direction on the football field a maximum of 43 seconds before turning or countermarching. Three drum majors are required for control.

From spread entrances performed to the notes of "The Aggie War Hymn" to its traditional drill-ending block "T," the band plays the entire time it is on the gridiron, while performing intricate maneuvers from regular block band and company front formations.

Because the Aggie Band performs primarily outdoors, it employs heavy brass and percussion sections. Typical organization includes 60 trumpets, 55 trombones and baritones, 18 Sousaphones, 22 drums and 50 woodwinds.

Organized within the band last year were the 75-member Aggie Concert Band and Aggie Stage Band of 17 musicians who perform popular and modern music for dances, dinners and other events.

The band is supported by the Texas Aggie Band Association, organized by former bandsmen in 1966.

Although music has not been a part of the Texas A&M curriculum, the band, the traditions, and the deep sense of school loyalty have inspired several famous school songs and an outstanding choral group known as "The Singing Cadets." They are directed by Robert Boone and in recent years have made national tours and national television show appearances.

"The Spirit of Aggieland," the official school song, reflects the history, traditions and deep affection of students and former students for their alma mater. It was written in 1925 by Marvin H. Mimms, while a junior at A&M. The music was composed by Bandmaster Richard J. Dunn, and the song was played to the student body for the first time during the 1925 football season.

THE SPIRIT OF AGGIELAND

Some may boast of prowess bold,
Of the school they think so grand,
But there's a spirit can ne'er be told,
It's the spirit of Aggieland.
Chorus
We are the Aggies—the Aggies are we,
True to each other as Aggies can be,

We've got to FIGHT, boys,
We've got to FIGHT!
We've got to fight for maroon and white.
After they've boosted all the rest,
They will come and join the best,
For we are the Aggies—the Aggies so true.
We're from Texas A. M. U.
Second Chorus
T-E-X-A-S, A-G-G-I-E,
Fight! Fight! Fight-fight-fight!
Fight! Maroon! White-White-White!
A-G-G-I-E, Texas! Texas! A-M-U!
Gig'em, Aggies! 1! 2! 3!
Farmers Fight! Farmers Fight!
Fight-Fight-Fight
Fight-Fight-Fight
Farmers, Farmers, Fight!

THE AGGIE WAR HYMN

When J. V. "Pinky" Wilson, member of the Class of 1920, was standing a lonely watch in the Meuse-Argonne area after World War I his thought traveled back to the Texas Aggie campus and the love he had for his school. It was then he decided to write a Fight Song for the Texas Aggies. That song became the Aggie War Hymn and is considered one of the most spirited college songs ever written. It really gets the adrenalin flowing and all Aggies anywhere sing out the words as the music is played.

Having been truly indoctrinated as a Texas Aggie in his freshman year, Wilson did not have to grope for a despised adversary to identify in his hymn. Texas University came to mind, naturally.

Here are the words which made "Pinky" an immortal:

> Hullabaloo, Canek! Canek!
> Hullabaloo, Canek! Canek!
> Goodbye to Texas University
> So long to the Orange and White.
> Good luck to dear old Texas Aggies,

They are the boys that show the real old fight.
The eyes of Texas are upon you,
That is the song they sing so well,
So good-bye to Texas University,
We're going to beat you all to — —
Chig-ga-raa-gar-em!
Chig-ga-raa-gar-em!
Rough! Tough!
Real Stuff! Texas A&M.

When asked by a member of the State Legislature for a translation of "Hullabaloo, Canek! Canek!," Dr. Jack Williams, president of A&M, answered: "Beat the Hell out of Texas University."

YELL PRACTICE

The origin of yell practice at Texas A&M can not be pin-pointed for time or place, but those aware of customs at Aggieland know the beginning had to come before the turn of the century. Early players like Josh Sterns, Hal Moseley, and Andrew Wilkler surely inspired the support that has become another of A&M's treasured traditions.

Yell practice became ritualized in the early football championship years, and until this day freshman members of the Cadet Corps meticulously follow the ritual. The sites have varied through the years, but former students will recall such places as the steps of the YMCA, in front of Goodwin Hall, the Grove, in front of Sbisa Hall, and today on Kyle Field. Special or impromptu sessions happen wherever and whenever yell leaders deem appropriate.

R. P. Marshall (Class of '33), an executive of the King Ranch in Texas, his seven brothers and two sons attended yell practices of their vintage in an era that spanned three decades and encompassed the tenures of six head coaches. A freshman in 1929, Marshall recalls the standard of performance expected of him and his Fish comrades at the time James A. (Hop) Reynolds was the head yell leader: "If a freshman could talk after a game or after yell practice, he had some licks coming."

James Kirk of still another era recalls being confronted by

upperclassmen the morning following games or practices with: "Fish Kirk, how is your voice?" If Freshman Kirk had enough voice to be understood, it was obvious he "had not yelled his heart out" and was subject to the consequences.

Through the years former football heroes have been invited back to the campus to make appearances at yell practices, especially before the game with Texas. R. P. Marshall remembers that Dutch Hohn was a frequent visitor in the Matty Bell era. Tommie Vaughn and other members of the 1939 national championship teams have been speakers through the years, and Hank Foldberg invited all of the 1940 team back in 1963 when he was getting his Aggies ready for Texas. Coach Foldberg hoped the Aggies who had missed a second straight national championship by losing to Texas might help inspire his team to knock off the Longhorns who had their sights on a national title. It almost came to pass. (See Chapter 34)

"Pinky Downs," Arnold Hayes (Class of '52) remembers as being "exceptionally inspirational at the midnight yell practice during the bonfire before the Texas game."

Like Pinky Downs, Judson E. (Lou) Loupot was present for every major event that happened on the campus through the years. It was through Loupot's thoughtfulness and generosity that members of the Corps were provided transportation and sometimes lodging for games away from home. Arnold Hayes remembers the occasion when Lou invited nine cadets to share his room with him at a game in San Antonio.

Loupot's benefaction is unique and unforgettable among those who were treated to free bicycle transportation in their days at A&M.

The Cadence, a 1947-48 handbook for freshmen, offered the following "instructional" paragraphs concerning yell practice:

> Whenever the team plays a game away from the college the whole corps turns out to see them off and assures them of the students' support. The team is escorted to the train by the band and the cadet corps and a yell practice is held around the train. When the team returns, the cadet corps gives them a riotous welcome regardless of the score of the game and escorts them back to the campus.

At midnight of the day before every home conference game, the band members stream out of their dormitory with glowing torches playing the Aggie War Hymn. Immediately from every dormitory on the campus come students who fall in line behind the band as it marches to Goodwin Hall and climbs on the steps for yell practice.

After a victorious game on Kyle Field, the entire corps falls in line behind the band as it marches to the fish pond in Prexy's Triangle. Here the cadets celebrate the victory by throwing yell leaders into the pond. After this the band and corps proceed to the steps of Goodwin Hall where, for a few minutes, the yell leaders lead the group in rejoicing over the events of the afternoon.

THE BONFIRE

Bonfires to stimulate enthusiasm for football were on the scene as early as the Charley Moran era (1909-1914), but they did not become traditional until the 1920s. From that time until the present one has been burned annually during Thanksgiving Week in preparation for the game with the University of Texas. It started as a custom, but tremendous enthusiasm and participation made it a tradition.

Colonel Frank G. Anderson, who served as assistant football coach in the Dana X. Bible era and later as Commandant, remembers the bonfires quite well, especially after 1935 when bonfire building was placed under the control of the Commandant. By this time the enthusiastic cadets were becoming highly competitive in their search for lumber scraps, boxes, limbs, community trash and another debris that would burn. Community outhouses were frequent prey in the early days.

"On the morning following the 1935 bonfire," Colonel Andy recalled, "a very irate farmer came to my office to say that some boys had carried off his log barn, lock, stock, and barrel." The farmer demanded payment for his barn, and the Commandant assessed each company to raise the money.

The following year Colonel Andy directed the cadets to a

grove of dead cottonwood trees near the area that is now Easterwood Airport. The College provided saws and axes and trucks for hauling. The 1936 bonfire became the first "legal" one, as it was built entirely of logs from the cottonwood area.

"It wasn't a big one," Colonel Andy recalls, "but it got the job done."

The building of bonfires became an even bigger ritual after World War II, and a center pole for a mountain of logs was raised for the first time in 1946. Two logs were strapped together the following year to create an even higher pile.

The Cadence, a 1947-48 handbook for freshmen, gave the following report on the Thanksgiving bonfire:

> On the night before the annual football game with the University of Texas, the Corps stands at attention to the strains of "The Spirit of Aggieland" while a gigantic bonfire burns...A nightly guard is mounted around the drill field to protect the materials from being set aflame by students from the rival school. All passers-by are questioned to see that no person other than loyal members of the Aggie Cadet Corps is allowed to go near the huge pile of inflammable materials.
>
> The bonfire symbolizes two things: a burning desire to beat the team from the University of Texas, and an undying flame of love that every Aggie carries in his heart for his school.

Meantime, the bonfires, and the opposition to them, have been getting bigger and taller. Power equipment is now needed to hoist the timbers to great heights, and utility companies that are civic-minded provide the necessary equipment.

A number of years ago someone allegedly from Austin attempted to light the bonfire prematurely, but the abortive effort ended in a forced landing of the plane that was unsuccessful in an incendiary bombing.

RECORD OF THE 22 AGGIE COACHES
1894-1973

Coach	Year	Won	Lost	Tied	A&M	Opp.	Win Pct.
F. D. Perkins							
1 season	1894	1	1	0	14	44	.500
	1895 - No Team Fielded						
A. M. Soule and H. W. South							
1 season	1896	2	0	1	50	4	.833
C. W. Taylor							
1 season	1897	1	2	0	10	40	.333
H. W. Williams							
1 season	1898	4	2	0	117	60	.667
W. A. Murray							
3 seasons	1899	4	2	0	150	16	
	1900	2	2	1	61	22	
	1901	1	4	0	12	112	
		7	8	1	223	150	.469
J. E. Platt							
3 seasons	1902	7	0	2	128	11	
	1903	7	3	1	92	59	
	1904	4	2	0	104	51	
		18	5	3	324	121	.750
W. E. Bachman							
2 seasons	1905	7	2	0	180	83	
	1906	6	1	0	170	42	
		13	3	0	350	125	.813
L. L. Larson							
1 season	1907	6	1	1	125	27	.813
H. A. Merriam							
1 season	1908	3	5	0	76	117	.375
Charley Moran							
6 seasons	1909	7	0	1	130	14	
	1910	8	1	0	203	24	
	1911	6	1	0	134	17	
	1912	8	1	0	366	26	
	1913	3	4	2	53	76	
	1914	6	1	1	205	33	
		38	8	4	1091	190	.800
E. H. Harlan							
2 seasons	1915	6	2	0	182	34	
	1916	6	3	0	188	66	
		12	5	0	370	100	.706
D. V. Graves for D. X. Bible							
1 season	1918	6	1	0	123	19	.857
D. X. Bible (In service in 1918) 11 seasons SWC Champs	1917	8	0	0	270	0	

270

SWC Champs	1919	10	0	0	275	0	
	1920	6	1	1	229	7	
SWC Champs	1921	6	1	2	110	57	
	1922	5	4	0	166	69	
	1923	5	3	1	135	23	
	1924	7	2	1	229	35	
SWC Champs	1925	7	1	1	191	25	
	1926	5	3	1	184	59	
SWC Champs	1927	8	0	1	262	32	
	1928	5	4	1	205	77	
		72	19	9	2,256	384	.765
Matty Bell							
5 seasons	1929	5	4	0	203	65	
	1930	2	7	0	66	100	
	1931	7	3	0	137	34	
	1932	4	4	2	75	78	
	1933	6	3	1	160	89	
		24	21	3	641	366	.531
Homer Norton							
14 seasons	1934	2	7	2	84	186	
	1935	3	7	0	125	121	
	1936	8	3	1	156	74	
	1937	5	2	2	117	59	
	1938	4	4	1	137	71	
National & SWC Champs	1939	11	0	0	212	31	
SWC Co-champs	1940	9	1	0	183	46	
SWC Champs	1941	9	2	0	281	75	
	1942	4	5	1	130	79	
	1943	7	2	1	184	65	
	1944	7	4	0	289	87	
	1945	6	4	0	179	103	
	1946	4	6	0	125	107	
	1947	3	6	1	169	185	
		82	53	9	2,371	1,289	.622
Harry Stiteler							
3 seasons	1948	0	9	1	123	247	
	1949	1	8	1	92	267	
	1950	7	4	0	344	206	
		8	21	2	559	720	.290
Ray George							
3 seasons	1951	5	3	2	213	179	
	1952	3	6	1	137	187	
	1953	4	5	1	128	186	
		12	14	4	478	552	.467
Paul Bryant							
4 seasons	1954	1	9	0	97	177	
	1955	7	2	1	160	89	
SWC Champs	1956	9	0	1	223	81	
	1957	8	3	1	158	50	
		25	14	2	638	397	.634
Jim Myers							
4 seasons	1958	4	6	0	124	217	

		1959	3	7	0	101	141	
		1960	1	6	3	73	117	
		1961	4	5	1	184	118	
			12	24	4	482	593	.350
Hank Foldberg								
3 seasons		1962	3	7	0	61	155	
		1963	2	7	1	90	153	
		1964	1	9	0	88	162	
			6	23	1	239	470	.207
Gene Stallings								
7 seasons		1965	3	7	0	80	170	
		1966	4	5	1	145	183	
SWC Champs		1967	7	4	0	211	153	
		1968	3	7	0	196	184	
		1969	3	7	0	116	192	
		1970	2	9	0	170	304	
		1971	5	6	0	144	212	
			27	45	1	1,062	1,299	.377
Emory Bellard								
2 seasons		1972	3	8	0	165	243	
		1973	5	6	0	292	231	
			8	14	0	457	474	.363
Totals for 22 Coaches		1894-1973	387	289	45	12,056	11,541	.570

TEXAS AGGIE RECORDS
ALL-TIME STANDINGS WITH 95 FOES

Opponent	W	L	T	Pts.	Opp.
Alabama	1	1	0	41	45
Arizona	1	0	0	17	13
Arkansas	17	27	3	613	677
Arkansas A&M	1	0	0	40	0
Arlington (NTAC/UT-Ar)	1	0	1	61	0
Army	1	1	0	34	37
Auburn (API)	1	0	0	16	0
Austin College	12	0	0	344	26
Baylor	40	23	7	980	649
Boston College	0	1	0	24	32
Bryan Air Field	2	0	0	87	6
Camp Mabry	1	0	0	19	6
Camp Travis	1	0	0	12	6
C. C. Travis Remount	1	0	0	60	0
Centenary	3	6	0	34	62
Centre	1	0	0	22	14
Cincinnati	0	1	0	0	17
Clemson	1	0	0	30	15
Corpus Christi NAS	0	1	0	7	18
Dallas University	3	0	0	142	6
Daniel Baker	3	0	0	194	0

Ellington Field AFB	1	0	0	54	0
Florida	0	1	0	6	42
Florida State	0	2	0	32	39
Fordham	1	0	0	13	12
Fort Worth University	2	0	0	62	0
Galveston High	1	0	1	14	6
Georgia	3	0	0	60	32
Georgia Tech	1	1	0	17	48
Hardin-Simmons	1	0	0	3	0
Haskell Institute	5	3	0	86	80
Henry College	1	0	0	44	0
Houston High	3	2	0	122	16
Houston	6	5	3	183	165
Houston YMCA	1	0	0	29	0
Howard Payne	3	1	0	54	20
Iowa	1	0	0	29	0
Kansas City Medics	0	0	1	6	6
Kansas State	1	2	0	29	25
Kentucky	1	1	0	14	16
LSU	12	22	3	520	546
Manhattan	2	0	0	27	13
Marshall School	1	0	0	48	0
Maryland	2	0	0	35	23
Miami	1	0	0	70	14
Michigan	0	1	0	10	14
Michigan State	1	2	0	28	81
Mississippi	2	0	0	31	7
Mississippi Southern	1	0	0	7	3
Mississippi State	2	2	0	55	20
Missouri	2	0	0	40	0
Missouri Mines	2	0	0	110	3
Nebraska	1	4	0	41	98
Nevada	1	0	0	48	18
New Mexico	1	0	0	63	0
New York University	1	0	0	49	7
North Texas	2	0	0	91	0
Ohio State	0	2	0	13	73
Oklahoma University	5	7	0	184	207
Oklahoma (A&M) State	6	2	0	162	31
Ouachita	1	0	0	19	6
Phillips	1	0	0	47	0
Polytechnic (Fort Worth)	1	0	0	19	6
Purdue	0	1	0	20	24
Ream Field	1	0	0	6	0
Rice	29	26	3	738	639
St. Edward's	1	0	0	11	0
Sam Houston State	9	0	0	413	20
San Francisco	2	0	0	80	14
Santa Clara	1	1	0	7	10
School for the Deaf	1	0	0	49	0
SMU	26	24	6	802	614
Sewanee	5	2	1	125	36

Southwestern	18	0	0	488	13
Southern California	0	1	0	7	31
Southwest Texas State	1	0	0	28	0
S. F. Austin State	2	0	0	91	6
John Tarleton State	2	0	0	61	0
Temple	0	2	0	6	54
Tennessee	0	1	0	0	3
Texas A&I	5	0	1	164	14
TCU	33	29	7	1024	726
Texas	18	57	5	634	1357
Texas Tech	17	14	1	596	419
Transylvania	1	1	0	39	20
Trinity	18	1	2	602	42
Tulane	10	5	0	276	119
Tulsa	2	1	0	71	19
UCLA	2	1	0	28	35
Utah	1	0	0	20	7
Villanova	2	2	0	66	76
VMI	1	0	0	52	0
Washington State	2	0	0	28	0
Waxahachie A. C.	1	0	0	11	0
Wichita State	4	0	0	166	34
TOTALS	387	289	45	12,056	11,541

WINNING PERCENTAGE .570

TEXAS A&M UNIVERSITY
YEAR-BY-YEAR FOOTBALL RECORD
A&M Score Listed First

1894
Coach: F. D. Perkins

14 Galveston High School 6
0 Texas 38
14   (1-1)   44

1895
No Team Fielded This Year

1896
Coach: A. M. Soule & H. W. South

0 Galveston High School 0
22 Austin College 4
28 Houston High School 0
50   (2-0-1)   4

1897
Coach: C. W. Taylor

0 Houston High School 10
6 TCU 30
4 Austin College 0
10   (1-2)   40

1898
Coach: H. W. Williams

51 Houston High School 0
0 Texas 48
0 Houston High School 6
16 TCU 0
22 Austin College 6
28 Fort Worth U 0
117   (4-2)   60

1899
Coach: W. A. Murray

43	Houston High School	0
0	Sewanee	10
22	Tulane	0
52	LSU	0
33	Baylor	0
0	Texas	6
150	(4-2)	16

1900
Coach: W. A. Murray

6	Kansas City Medics	6
0	Texas	5
0	Texas	11
11	Waxahachie Ath. Club	0
44	Henry College	0
61	(4-2-1)	22

1901
Coach W. A. Murray

6	Baylor	0
6	Baylor	17
0	Texas	17
0	Texas	32
0	Baylor	46
12	(1-4)	112

1902
Coach: J. E. Platt
Southern Champs

11	St. Edwards	0
0	Trinity	0
11	Baylor	6
22	Baylor	0
0	Texas	0
17	Tulane	5
22	TCU	0
34	Trinity	0
11	Texas	0
128	(7-0-2)	11

1903
Coach: J. E. Platt

16	Trinity	0
11	TCU	0
6	Arkansas	0
0	Oklahoma	6
0	Baylor	0
18	Baylor	0
16	TCU	0
0	Trinity	18
5	Baylor	0
6	Texas	29
14	TCU	6
92	(7-3-1)	59

1904
Coach: J. E. Platt

49	School for the Deaf	0
5	Baylor	0
29	TCU	0
5	Sewanee	17
6	Texas	34
10	Baylor	0
104	(4-2)	51

1905
Coach: W. E. Bachman

29	Houston YMCA	0
20	TCU	0
42	Baylor	0
24	Trinity	0
18	Austin College	11
24	TCU	11
6	Transylvania	29
17	Baylor	5
0	Texas	27
180	(7-2)	83

1906
Coach: W. E. Bachman

42	TCU	0
34	Daniel Baker	0
22	TCU	0
18	Tulane	0
32	Haskell Institute	6
22	LSU	12
0	Texas	24
170	(6-1)	42

1907
Coach: L. L. Larson

34	Ft. Worth University	0
0	Texas	0

11 LSU	5
5 Haskell Institute	0
32 TCU	5
18 Tulane	6
19 Oklahoma	0
6 Texas	12
125 (6-1-1)	27

1908
Coach H. A. Merriam

6 Trinity	0
5 Baylor	6
0 LSU	26
13 TCU	10
8 Texas	24
0 Haskell Institute	23
32 Southwestern	0
12 Texas	28
76 (3-5)	117

1909
Coach: Charley Moran

17 Austin College	0
0 TCU	0
15 Haskell Institute	0
9 Baylor	6
23 Texas	0
47 Trinity	0
14 Oklahoma	8
5 Texas	0
130 (7-0-1)	14

1910
Coach: Charley Moran

48 Marshall School	0
27 Austin College	5
35 TCU	0
33 Transylvania	0
0 Arkansas	5
23 TCU	6
14 Texas	8
6 Southwestern	0
17 Tulane	0
203 (8-1)	24

1911
Coach: Charley Moran

22 Southwestern	0
33 Austin College	0
16 Auburn	0
17 Mississippi	0
0 Texas	6
22 Baylor	11
24 Dallas University	0
134 (6-1)	17

1912
Coach: Charley Moran

50 Daniel Baker	0
59 Trinity	0
27 Arkansas	0
57 Austin College	0
28 Oklahoma	6
41 Mississippi State	7
41 Tulane	0
10 Kansas State	13
53 Baylor	0
366 (8-1)	26

1913
Coach: Charley Moran

7 Trinity	0
6 Austin College	0
19 Polytechnic College	6
0 Mississippi State	6
0 Kansas State	12
0 Oklahoma A&M	3
0 Haskell Institute	28
14 Baylor	14
7 LSU	7
53 (3-4-2)	76

1914
Coach: Charley Moran

32 Austin College	0
0 Trinity	0
40 TCU	0
0 Haskell Institute	10
63 LSU	9
32 Rice	7
24 Oklahoma A&M	7
14 Mississippi	7
205 (6-1-1)	33

276

1915
Coach: E. H. Harlan

40	Austin College	0
62	Trinity	0
13	TCU	10
33	Missouri Sch. Mines	3
21	Haskell Institute	7
0	Rice	7
13	Texas	0
0	Mississippi State	7
182	(6-2)	34

1916
Coach: E. H. Harlan

6	Southwestern	0
20	Dallas University	6
0	LSU	13
62	SMU	0
13	Haskell Institute	6
0	Rice	20
3	Baylor	0
77	Missouri Sch. Mines	0
7	Texas	21
188	(6-3)	66

1917
Coach: D. X. Bible
Southwest Conference Champs

66	Austin College	0
98	Dallas University	0
20	Southwestern	0
27	LSU	0
35	Tulane	0
7	Baylor	0
7	Texas	0
10	Rice	0
270	(8-0)	0

1918
Coach: D. V. Graves

6	Ream Field	0
12	Camp Travis	6
19	Baylor	0
7	Southwestern	0
19	Camp Mabry	6
0	Texas	7
60	C. C. Travis Remount	0
123	(6-1)	19

1919
Coach: D. X. Bible
Southwest Conference Champs

77	Sam Houston State	0
28	Southwest Texas State	0
16	SMU	0
12	Howard Payne	0
42	Trinity	0
28	Oklahoma A&M	0
10	Baylor	0
48	TCU	0
7	Southwestern	0
7	Texas	0
275	(10-0)	0

1920
Coach: D. X. Bible

110	Daniel Baker	0
3	SMU	0
0	LSU	0
47	Phillips	0
35	Oklahoma A&M	0
24	Baylor	0
7	Rice	0
3	Texas	7
229	(6-1-1)	7

1921
Coach: D. X. Bible
Southwest Conference Champs

14	Howard Payne	7
13	SMU	0
0	LSU	6
17	Arizona	13
23	Oklahoma A&M	7
14	Baylor	3
7	Rice	7
0	Texas	0
*22	Centre College	14
110	(6-1-2)	57

*Dixie Classic

1922
Coach: D. X. Bible

7	Howard Payne	13
10	Tulsa	13
33	Southwestern	0
46	LSU	0

19 Ouichita College	6
7 Baylor	13
6 SMU	17
24 Rice	0
14 Texas	7
166 (5-4)	69

1923
Coach: D. X. Bible

53 Sam Houston State	0
21 Howard Payne	0
13 Southwestern	0
14 Sewanee	0
28 LSU	0
0 SMU	10
0 Baylor	0
6 Rice	7
0 Texas	6
135 (5-3-1)	23

1924
Coach: D. X. Bible

40 John Tarleton State	0
33 Trinity	0
54 Southwestern	0
7 Sewanee	0
40 Arkansas A&M	0
7 SMU	7
7 Baylor	15
28 TCU	0
13 Rice	6
0 Texas	7
229 (7-2-1)	35

1925
Coach: D. X. Bible
Southwest Conference Champs

20 Trinity	10
23 Southwestern	6
6 Sewanee	6
7 SMU	0
77 Sam Houston State	0
13 Baylor	0
0 TCU	3
17 Rice	0
28 Texas	0
191 (7-1-1)	25

1926
Coach: D. X. Bible

26 Trinity	0
35 Southwestern	0
6 Sewanee	3
63 New Mexico	0
7 SMU	9
9 Baylor	20
13 TCU	13
20 Rice	0
5 Texas	14
184 (5-3-1)	59

1927
Coach: D. X. Bible
Southwest Conference Champs

45 Trinity	0
31 Southwestern	0
18 Sewanee	0
40 Arkansas	6
0 TCU	0
47 Texas Tech	6
39 SMU	13
14 Rice	0
28 Texas	7
262 (8-0-1)	32

1928
Coach: D. X. Bible

21 Trinity	0
21 Southwestern	0
69 Sewanee	0
0 Centenary	6
0 TCU	6
12 Arkansas	27
44 North Texas State	0
19 SMU	19
19 Rice	0
0 Texas	19
205 (5-4-1)	77

1929
Coach: Matty Bell

54 Southwestern	7
10 Tulane	13
19 Kansas State	0
7 TCU	13
13 Arkansas	14

54	S. F. Austin State	0
7	SMU	12
26	Rice	6
13	Texas	0
203	(5-4)	65

1930
Coach: Matty Bell

43	Southwestern	0
0	Nebraska	13
9	Tulane	19
0	Arkansas	13
0	TCU	3
7	Centenary	6
7	SMU	13
0	Rice	7
0	Texas	26
66	(2-7)	100

1931
Coach: Matty Bell

33	Southwestern	0
21	John Tarleton State	0
0	Tulane	7
29	Iowa	0
0	TCU	6
33	Baylor	7
7	Centenary	0
0	SMU	8
7	Rice	0
7	Texas	6
137	(7-3)	34

1932
Coach: Matty Bell

7	Texas Tech	0
14	Tulane	26
26	Sam Houston State	0
14	Texas A&I	0
0	TCU	17
0	Baylor	0
0	Centenary	7
0	SMU	0
14	Rice	7
0	Texas	21
75	(4-4-2)	78

1933
Coach: Matty Bell

38	Trinity	0
13	Tulane	6
34	Sam Houston State	14
17	Texas A&I	0
7	TCU	13
14	Baylor	7
0	Centenary	20
0	SMU	19
27	Rice	0
10	Texas	10
160	(6-3-1)	89

1934
Coach: Homer Norton

28	Sam Houston State	0
14	Texas A&I	14
6	Temple	40
0	Centenary	13
0	TCU	13
10	Baylor	7
7	Arkansas	7
0	SMU	28
6	Rice	35
0	Texas	13
13	Michigan State	26
84	(2-7-2)	186

1935
Coach: Homer Norton

37	S. F. Austin State	6
25	Sam Houston State	0
0	Temple	14
6	Centenary	7
14	TCU	19
6	Baylor	14
7	Arkansas	14
10	Rice	17
20	Texas	6
0	SMU	24
125	(3-7)	121

1936
Coach: Homer Norton

39	Sam Houston State	6
3	Hardin-Simmons	0
3	Rice	0

| 18 TCU 7
| 0 Baylor 0
| 0 Arkansas 18
| 22 SMU 6
| 38 San Francisco 14
| 20 Utah 7
| 0 Centenary 3
| 0 Texas 7
| 13 Manhattan....................6
| 156   (8-3-1)   74

1937
Coach: Homer Norton

| 14 Manhattan....................7
| 14 Mississippi State 0
| 7 TCU 7
| 0 Baylor 13
| 13 Arkansas 26
| 14 SMU 0
| 6 Rice 6
| 7 Texas 0
| 42 San Francisco 0
| 117   (5-2-2)   59

1938
Coach: Homer Norton

| 52 Texas A&I....................0
| 20 Tulsa 0
| 0 Santa Clara 7
| 6 TCU 34
| 13 Arkansas 7
| 7 SMU 10
| 6 Texas 7
| 27 Rice 0
| 137   (4-4-1)   71

1939
Coach: Homer Norton
Southwest Conference Champs
NATIONAL CHAMPIONS

| 32 Oklahoma A&M 0
| 14 Centenary 0
| 7 Santa Clara 3
| 33 Villanova 7
| 20 TCU 6
| 20 Baylor 0
| 27 Arkansas 0
| 6 SMU 2
| 19 Rice 0
| 20 Texas 0

| *14 Tulane......................13
| 212   (11-0)   31
*Sugar Bowl

1940
Coach: Homer Norton
Southwest Conference Co-Champs

| 26 Texas A&I....................0
| 41 Tulsa 6
| 7 UCLA 0
| 21 TCU 7
| 14 Baylor 7
| 17 Arkansas 0
| 19 SMU 7
| 25 Rice 0
| 0 Texas 7
| *13 Fordham 12
| 183   (9-1)   46
*Cotton Bowl

1941
Coach: Homer Norton
Southwest Conference Champs

| 54 Sam Houston State 0
| 41 Texas A&I....................0
| 49 New York University 7
| 14 TCU 0
| 48 Baylor 0
| 7 Arkansas 0
| 21 SMU 10
| 19 Rice 6
| 0 Texas 23
| 7 Washington State 0
| *21 Alabama 29
| 281   (9-2)   75
*Cotton Bowl

1942
Coach: Homer Norton

| 7 LSU 16
| 19 Texas Tech 0
| 7 Corpus Christi NAS 18
| 2 TCU 7
| 0 Baylor 6
| 41 Arkansas 0
| 27 SMU 20
| 0 Rice 0
| 6 Texas 12
| 21 Washington State 0
| 130   (4-5-1)   79

280

1943
Coach: Homer Norton

48	Bryan AFB	6
13	Texas Tech	0
28	LSU	13
13	TCU	0
0	Arlington (NTAC)	0
13	Arkansas	0
22	SMU	0
20	Rice	0
13	Texas	27
*14	LSU	19
184	(7-2-1)	65

*Orange Bowl

1944
Coach: Homer Norton

39	Bryan AFB	0
27	Texas Tech	14
14	Oklahoma	21
7	TCU	13
7	LSU	0
61	Arlington (NTAC)	0
6	Arkansas	7
39	SMU	6
19	Rice	6
0	Texas	6
70	Miami	14
289	(7-4)	87

1945
Coach: Homer Norton

54	Ellington Field AFB	0
16	Texas Tech	6
19	Oklahoma	14
12	LSU	31
12	TCU	13
19	Baylor	13
34	Arkansas	0
3	SMU	0
0	Rice	6
10	Texas	20
179	(6-4)	103

1946
Coach: Homer Norton

47	North Texas State	0
0	Texas Tech	6
7	Oklahoma	10
9	LSU	33
14	TCU	0
17	Baylor	0
0	Arkansas	7
14	SMU	0
10	Rice	27
7	Texas	24
125	(4-6)	107

1947
Coach: Homer Norton

48	Southwestern	0
29	Texas Tech	7
14	Oklahoma	26
13	LSU	19
0	TCU	26
24	Baylor	0
21	Arkansas	21
0	SMU	13
7	Rice	41
13	Texas	32
169	(3-6-1)	185

1948
Coach: Harry Stiteler

14	Villanova	34
14	Texas Tech	20
14	Oklahoma	42
13	LSU	14
14	TCU	27
14	Baylor	20
6	Arkansas	28
14	SMU	20
6	Rice	28
14	Texas	14
123	(0-9-1)	247

1949
Coach: Harry Stiteler

0	Villanova	35
26	Texas Tech	7
13	Oklahoma	33
0	LSU	34
6	TCU	28
0	Baylor	21
6	Arkansas	27
27	SMU	27
0	Rice	13
14	Texas	42
92	(1-8-1)	267

1950
Coach: Harry Stiteler

48	Nevada	18
34	Texas Tech	13
28	Oklahoma	34
52	VMI	0
42	TCU	23
20	Baylor	27
42	Arkansas	13
25	SMU	20
13	Rice	21
0	Texas	17
*40	Georgia	20
344	(7-4)	206

*Presidential Cup

1951
Coach: Ray George

21	UCLA	14
20	Texas Tech	7
14	Oklahoma	7
53	Trinity	14
14	TCU	20
21	Baylor	21
21	Arkansas	33
14	SMU	14
13	Rice	28
22	Texas	21
213	(5-3-2)	179

1952
Coach: Ray George

21	Houston	13
14	Oklahoma A&M	7
7	Kentucky	10
6	Michigan State	48
7	TCU	7
20	Baylor	21
31	Arkansas	12
13	SMU	21
6	Rice	16
12	Texas	32
137	(3-6-1)	187

1953
Coach: Ray George

7	Kentucky	6
14	Houston	14
14	Georgia	12
27	Texas Tech	14
20	TCU	7
13	Baylor	14
14	Arkansas	41
0	SMU	23
7	Rice	34
12	Texas	21
128	(4-5-1)	186

1954
Coach: Paul Bryant

9	Texas Tech	41
6	Oklahoma A&M	14
6	Georgia	0
7	Houston	10
20	TCU	21
7	Baylor	20
7	Arkansas	14
3	SMU	6
19	Rice	29
13	Texas	22
97	(1-9)	177

1955
Coach: Paul Bryant

0	UCLA	21
28	LSU	0
21	Houston	3
27	Nebraska	0
19	TCU	16
19	Baylor	7
7	Arkansas	7
13	SMU	2
20	Rice	12
6	Texas	21
160	(7-2-1)	89

1956
Coach: Paul Bryant
Southwest Conference Champs

19	Villanova	0
9	LSU	6
40	Texas Tech	7
14	Houston	14
7	TCU	6
19	Baylor	13
27	Arkansas	0
33	SMU	7

21	Rice	7
34	Texas	21
223	(9-0-1)	81

1957
Coach: Paul Bryant

21	Maryland	13
21	Texas Tech	0
28	Missouri	0
28	Houston	6
7	TCU	0
14	Baylor	0
7	Arkansas	6
19	SMU	6
6	Rice	7
7	Texas	9
*0	Tennessee	3
158	(8-3)	50

*Gator Bowl

1958
Coach: Jim Myers

14	Texas Tech	15
7	Houston	39
12	Missouri	0
14	Maryland	10
8	TCU	24
33	Baylor	27
8	Arkansas	21
0	SMU	33
28	Rice	21
0	Texas	27
124	(4-6)	217

1959
Coach: Jim Myers

14	Texas Tech	20
9	Michigan State	7
7	Mississippi Southern	3
28	Houston	6
6	TCU	39
0	Baylor	13
7	Arkansas	12
11	SMU	14
2	Rice	7
17	Texas	20
101	(3-7)	141

1960
Coach: Jim Myers

0	LSU	9
14	Texas Tech	14
14	Trinity	0
0	Houston	17
14	TCU	14
0	Baylor	14
3	Arkansas	7
0	SMU	0
14	Rice	21
14	Texas	21
73	(1-6-3)	117

1961
Coach: Jim Myers

7	Houston	7
7	LSU	16
38	Texas Tech	7
55	Trinity	0
14	TCU	15
23	Baylor	0
8	Arkansas	15
25	SMU	12
7	Rice	21
0	Texas	25
184	(4-5-1)	118

1962
Coach: Hank Foldberg

0	LSU	21
3	Houston	6
7	Texas Tech	3
6	Florida	42
14	TCU	20
6	Baylor	3
7	Arkansas	17
12	SMU	7
3	Rice	23
3	Texas	13
61	(3-7)	155

1963
Coach: Hank Foldberg

6	LSU	14
0	Ohio State	17
0	Texas Tech	10
23	Houston	13
14	TCU	14
7	Baylor	34
7	Arkansas	21

283

7	SMU	9
13	Rice	6
13	Texas	15
90	(2-7-1)	153

1964
Coach: Hank Foldberg

6	LSU	9
0	Houston	10
12	Texas Tech	16
7	Southern California	31
9	TCU	14
16	Baylor	20
0	Arkansas	17
23	SMU	0
8	Rice	19
7	Texas	26
88	(1-9)	162

1965
Coach: Gene Stallings

0	LSU	10
14	Georgia Tech	10
16	Texas Tech	20
10	Houston	7
9	TCU	17
0	Baylor	31
0	Arkansas	31
0	SMU	10
14	Rice	13
17	Texas	21
80	(3-7)	170

1966
Coach: Gene Stallings

3	Georgia Tech	38
13	Tulane	21
35	Texas Tech	14
7	LSU	7
35	TCU	7
17	Baylor	13
0	Arkansas	34
14	SMU	21
7	Rice	6
14	Texas	22
145	(4-5-1)	183

1967
Coach: Gene Stallings
Southwest Conference Champs

17	SMU	20
20	Purdue	24
6	LSU	17
18	Florida State	19
28	Texas Tech	24
20	TCU	0
21	Baylor	3
33	Arkansas	21
18	Rice	3
10	Texas	7
*20	Alabama	16
211	(7-4)	154

*Cotton Bowl

1968
Coach: Gene Stallings

12	LSU	13
35	Tulane	3
14	Florida State	20
16	Texas Tech	21
27	TCU	7
9	Baylor	10
22	Arkansas	25
23	SMU	36
24	Rice	14
14	Texas	35
196	(3-7)	184

1969
Coach: Gene Stallings

6	LSU	35
0	Nebraska	14
20	Army	13
9	Texas Tech	13
6	TCU	16
24	Baylor	0
13	Arkansas	35
20	SMU	10
6	Rice	7
12	Texas	49
116	(3-7)	192

1970
Coach: Gene Stallings

41	Wichita State	14
20	LSU	18
13	Ohio State	56

10	Michigan	14	36	Wichita State	13
7	Texas Tech	21	7	Nebraska	37
15	TCU	31	17	LSU	42
24	Baylor	29	14	Army	24
6	Arkansas	45	14	Texas Tech	17
3	SMU	6	10	TCU	13
17	Rice	18	13	Baylor	15
14	Texas	52	10	Arkansas	7
170	(2-9)	304	27	SMU	17
			14	Rice	20
			3	Texas	38
			165	(3-8)	243

1971
Coach: Gene Stallings

1973
Coach: Emory Bellard

41	Wichita State	7	48	Wichita State	0
0	LSU	37	23	LSU	28
7	Nebraska	34	24	Boston College	32
0	Cincinnati	17	30	Clemson	15
7	Texas Tech	28	16	Texas Tech	28
3	TCU	14	35	TCU	16
10	Baylor	9	28	Baylor	22
17	Arkansas	9	10	Arkansas	14
27	SMU	10	45	SMU	10
18	Rice	13	20	Rice	24
14	Texas	34	13	Texas	42
144	(5-6)	212	295	(5-6)	231

1972
Coach: Emory Bellard

RECAP 1894-1972
(No Team in 1895)

Number of Teams 79
Number of Coaches* 22
Games Played 721
Games Won 387
Games Lost 289
Games Tied 45
Total Points A&M 12,056
Total Points Opp 11,541
Winning Percentage   .570
   *Co-Coaches in 1896

SOUTHWEST CONFERENCE HIGHS AND LOWS

	WON		LOST	
(1942)	41-0	Arkansas	6-45	(1970)
(1912)	53-0	Baylor	0-46	(1901)
(1933)	27-0	Rice	7-41	(1947)
(1916)	62-0	SMU	0-33	(1958)
(1925)	28-0	Texas	0-48	(1898)
(1919)	48-0	TCU	6-39	(1959)
(1927)	47-6	Texas Tech	9-47	(1947)

TEAM RECORDS

SEASON OFFENSE RECORDS

RUSHING:
Most Attempts	605	1973
Most Yardage	2920	1973
Average Per Rush (527 for 2682)	5.1	1950
Average Per Game	268.2	1950

PASSING:
Most Attempts	351	1968
Most Completions	171	1968
Most Intercepted	30	1941
Best Completion Percentage (38 of 70)	543	1956
Most Yardage	2337	1968
Most Touchdowns	16	1968
Average Yards Per Game	233.7	1968

TOTAL OFFENSE:
Most Plays	775	1970
Most Yardage	4064	1973
Average Yards Per Game	369.5	1973

PUNTING:
Most Punts	92	1946
Best Average	43.6	1965

PUNT RETURNS:
Average Per Return	17.6	1950

KICKOFF RETURNS:
Average Per Return	25.3	1939

INTERCEPTIONS:
Most Intercepted	30	1941
Most Yardage Returns	475	1941

MISCELLANEOUS RECORDS:
First Downs, Rushing	143	1973
First Downs, Passing	113	1968
Total First Downs	208	1973
Total Penalties	75	1955
Total Yards Penalized	716	1955
Average Penalty Yards Per Game	71.6	1955
Total Fumbles	45	1972
Total Fumbles Lost	26	1972

SEASON DEFENSE RECORDS

RUSHING:
Fewest Attempts	272	1939
Fewest Yards	399	1940
Lowest Average Per Rush	1.3	1940
Lowest Average Per Game	41.5	1939

PASSING:
Fewest Attempts	98	1954
Fewest Completions	33	1954
Fewest Yards	*348	1939
Fewest Touchdowns	0	1957
Lowest Percentage of Completions (33 of 138)	.239	1943
Lowest Average Per Game	*34.8	1939

TOTAL DEFENSE:
Fewest Plays	447	1939
Fewest Yards	763	1939
Lowest Average Per Game	76.3	1939

PUNTING:
Most Punts by Foes	114	1939
Lowest Average by Foes	34.4	1949
Most Punts Blocked	5	1941

PUNT RETURNS:
Lowest Average Per Return	1.3	1973
Lowest Total Yards Returned (SWC Record)	24	1973

KICKOFF RETURNS:
Lowest Average For Return	13.9	1955

MISCELLANEOUS RECORDS:
Fewest Total First Downs	54	1939
Highest Average Penalty Yard For Foes	69.2	1949
Most Fumbles By Foes	42	1952, 1955
Most Fumbles Lost By Foes	26	1952, 1955

*National Records

SINGLE GAME OFFENSE RECORDS

RUSHING:
Most Attempts	Arkansas	76	1956
Most Yardage	SMU	432	1973

PASSING:
Most Attempts	SMU	58	1968
Most Completions	SMU	32	1968
Most Intercepted	Texas	7	1943
	Rice	7	1953
Best Completion Percentage (9 of 11)	SMU	.818	1944
Most Yardage	SMU	376	1968
Most Touchdowns, Passing	VMI	3	1950

(Also 3 against Tech, '50; UCLA, '51; Arkansas, '52; Arkansas, '67; Tech, SMU, '68)

TOTAL OFFENSE:
Most Plays	SMU	94	1968
Most Yardage	Wichita State	550	1970

PUNTING:
Most Punts	SMU	17	1945
Best Average	SMU	49.6	1965

PUNT RETURNS:
Most Returns	NTAC	12	1943
Most Yards Returned	North Texas	319	1946

KICKOFF RETURNS:
Most Returns	Ohio State	8	1970
	LSU	8	1971
Most Yardage	Boston College	226	1973

INTERCEPTIONS:
Most Intercepted	NTAC	6	1944

(Also 6 against Arkansas, '50 and '52)

Most Yardage Returned	Bryan Field	150	1943

MISCELLANEOUS RECORDS:
First Downs, Rushing	Arkansas	21	1956
	Wichita State	21	1972
First Downs, Passing	SMU	22	1968
Total First Downs	SMU	29	1968
	Baylor	29	1926
Total Penalties	Texas Tech	14	1949
Total Yards Penalized	Texas Tech	167	1949
Total Fumbles	Ellington Field	10	1945
	Texas Tech	10	1954
Total Fumbles Lost	Ellington Field	9	1945

SINGLE GAME DEFENSE RECORDS

RUSHING:
Fewest Attempts	Baylor	23	1955
Fewest Yards	Bryan Field	-23	1943

PASSING:
Fewest Attempts	Oklahoma State	3	1954

(Also 3 by Rice, '57; Arkansas, '58)

Fewest Completions	Ellington Field	0	1945

(Also 0 by Oklahoma State, '54; Arkansas, '56)

Fewest Yards	Ellington Field	0	1945

(Also 0 by Oklahoma State, '54; Arkansas, '56)

TOTAL DEFENSE:
Fewest Plays	Ellington Field	38	1945
Fewest Yards	Ellington Field	-19	1945

PUNTING:
Most Punts By Foes	Texas Tech	17	1943
Lowest Average Per Punt	(9 by TCU)	22.1	1944

MISCELLANEOUS RECORDS:
Fewest Total First Downs	Ellington Field	0	1945
Most Times Foe Penalized	Villanova	14	1945

(Also Texas, '51; Arkansas, '53 and '65)

Most Yards Foe Penalized	Arkansas	136	1953
Most Fumbles by Foe	Texas Tech	8	1944

(Also 8 by Texas, '45; Baylor, '52)

Most Fumbles Lost By Foes	Baylor	5	1945

(Also 5 by Trinity, '51; Baylor and Kentucky, '52; SMU, '55; Wichita State, '73)

MISCELLANEOUS TEXAS AGGIE RECORDS

Greatest Winning Margin, Non-Conference 110-0 (Daniel Baker 1920)
Greatest Winning Margin, Conference 48-0 (Baylor 1941)
Worst Defeat, Non-Conference 48-0 (Texas 1898)
Worst Defeat, Conference 52-14 (Texas 1970)
Most Games Foe Held Scoreless, One Season 10 (1919)
Least Points Scored by Foes, One Season 0 (1917 & 1919)
Least Points A&M Scored, One Season 10 (1897)
Most Points A&M Scored, One Season 366 (1912)
Most Points Foe Scored, One Game 56 (Ohio State 1970)
Longest TD Run From Scrimmage: 81 (Bob Smith, Texas Tech 1949)
Longest Kickoff Return: 100 (Bob Smith, Georgia 1950)
Longest Kickoff Return: 100 (Dan McIlhaney, Texas Tech 1962)
Longest Punt Return for TD: 98 (Bob Goode, Ellington Field 1945)
Longest Intercepted Pass Runback for TD: 100 (Bill Hobbs, TCU 1967)
Longest Pass for TD: Jim Kauffman to Ken McLean 91 (Texas 1965)
Longest Punt: 86 (Bobby Goff, Texas Tech 1944)
Longest Field Goal; 54 (Pat McDermott, SMU 1972)
Longest Winning Streak: 19 (11 in 1939, 8 in 1940)
Longest Streak of Blanking Foes: 18 (1918 final game, 1919, 7 games in 1920)

ALL-TIME TEXAS AGGIE FOOTBALL RECORDS
1894-1973
(Official Southwest Conference Statistics Were Not Kept Prior to 1937. Earlier Records Are From Annuals, Etc.)

INDIVIDUAL RECORDS
CAREER

RUSHING:
Most Attempts	463	Larry Stegent	1967-68-69
Most Yardage	2415	Bob Smith	1949-50-51

PASSING:

Most Attempts	821	Edd Hargett	1966-67-68
Most Completions	403	Edd Hargett	1966-67-68
Most Intercepted	40	Edd Hargett	1966-67-68
Best Completion Percentage	.520	Ray Graves (141 of 271)	1950-51-52
Most Yardage	5379	Edd Hargett	1966-67-68
Most Touchdowns	40	Edd Hargett	1966-67-68

PASS RECEIVING:

Most Caught	91	Barney Harris	1967-68-69
Most Yardage	1298	Barney Harris	1967-68-69
	1298	Bob Long	1967-68-69
Most Touchdowns	19	Bob Long	1967-68-69

TOTAL OFFENSE:

Most Plays	1092	Edd Hargett	1966-67-68
Most Yardage	5411	Edd Hargett	1966-67-68

PUNTING:

Most Punts	212	Steve O'Neal	1966-67-68
Best Average	41.9	Phil Scoggin (161 for 6739)	1964-65
Most Yardage	8854	Steve O'Neal	1966-67-68

PUNT RETURNS:

Most Returned	70	Derace Moser	1939-40-41
Most Yardage	878	Derace Moser	1939-40-41

INTERCEPTIONS:

Most Intercepted	12	Dave Elmendorf	1968-70
Most Yardage Returned	288	Ross Brupbacher	1967-68

KICKOFF RETURNS:

Most Returns	39	Larry Stegent	1967-68-69
Most Yardage Returned	852	Carl Roaches	1972-73

SCORING:

Touchdowns	30	Joel Hunt	1925-26-27
Total Points	224	Joel Hunt	1925-26-27
Field Goals	20	Pat McDermott	1970-71-72
PAT Attempts	83	Darrow Hooper	1950-51-52
PAT Made	62	Darrow Hooper	1950-51-52
Kick Points (20 FG & 42 PAT)	102	Pat McDermott	1970-71-72

SEASON

RUSHING:

Most Attempts	199	Bob Smith	1950
Most Yardage	1302	Bob Smith	1950
Best Average Carry	6.8	Glenn Lippman (118 for 801)	1951

PASSING:

Most Attempts	348	Edd Hargett	1968
Most Completions	169	Edd Hargett	1968
Most Intercepted	19	Derace Moser	1941
	19	Edd Hargett	1966
Best Completion Percentage	.567	Ray Graves (93 of 164)	1952
Most Yardage	2321	Edd Hargett	1968
Most Touchdowns	16	Edd Hargett	1968

PASS RECEIVING:

Most Caught	60	Ken McLean	1965

289

| Most Yardage | 835 | Ken McLean | | 1965 |
| Most Touchdowns | 8 | Bob Long | | 1967 & 1968 |

TOTAL OFFENSE:
| Most Plays | 433 | Edd Hargett | | 1968 |
| Most Yardage | 2330 | Edd Hargett | | 1968 |

PUNTING:
| Most Punts | 88 | Phil Scoggin | | 1965 |
| Best Average | 43.6 | Phil Scoggin | | 1965 |

PUNT RETURNS:
| Most Returned | 49 | Marion Flanagan | | 1943 |
| Most Yardage | 475 | Marion Flanagan | | 1943 |

INTERCEPTIONS:
| Most Intercepted | 10 | Bill Sibley | | 1941 |
| Most Yardage | 167 | Ross Brupbacher | | 1967 |

KICKOFF RETURNS:
| Most Returns | 23 | Dave Elmendorf | | 1970 |
| Most Yardage Returned | 457 | Dave Elmendorf | | 1970 |

SCORING:
Touchdowns	19	Joel Hunt		1927
Total Points	128	Joel Hunt		1927
Field Goals	10	Randy Haddox		1973
PAT Attempts	45	Darrow Hooper		1950
PAT Made	34	Darrow Hooper		1950
Total Kicking Points	62	Randy Haddox		1973

SINGLE GAME

RUSHING:
| Most Attempts | 41 | Mark Green | SMU | 1971 |
| Most Yardage | 297 | Bob Smith | SMU | 1950 |

PASSING:
Most Attempts	58	Edd Hargett	SMU	1968
Most Completions	32	Edd Hargett	SMU	1968
Most Intercepted	5	Jim Cashion	LSU	1948
	5	Edd Hargett	Texas	1968
Best Completion Percentage	.800	J. L. (Babe) Hallmark	Arkansas	1943
Most Yardage	376	Edd Hargett	SMU	1968
Most Touchdowns	3	Delmar Sikes	Texas Tech	1950
	3	Ray Graves	Arkansas	1952
	3	Edd Hargett	Texas Tech	1967

(Also Arkansas, '67; SMU and Arkansas, '68)

PASS RECEIVING:
Most Caught	13	Ken McLean	Texas	1965
	13	Barney Harris	SMU	1968
Most Yardage	250	Ken McLean	Texas	1965
Most Touchdowns	3	Don Ellis	Arkansas	1952

TOTAL OFFENSE:
| Most Plays | 70 | Edd Hargett | SMU | 1968 |
| Most Yardage | 418 | Edd Hargett | SMU | 1968 |

PUNTING:
| Most Punts | 17 | Bob Goode | SMU | 1945 |
| Best Average | 49.6 | Phil Scoggins | SMU | 1965 |

PUNT RETURNS:

Most Returned	7	Marion Flanagan	SMU	1943
	(Also Tech, TCU, NTAC in '43)			
Most Yardage	96	Carl Roaches	SMU	1973

INTERCEPTION:

Most Intercepted	4	Joe Boring	Arkansas	1952
Most Yards Returned	132	Bill Hobbs	TCU	1967

KICKOFF RETURNS:

Most Returns	5	Glenn Lippman	Villanova	1949
	5	Bob Smith	TCU	1949
	5	Don Ellis	Michigan State	1952
Most Yardage Returned	193	Carl Roaches	Boston College	1973

SCORING:

Touchdowns	7	Jelly Woodman	New Mexico	1926
Total Points	44	Jelly Woodman	New Mexico	1926
Field Goals	3	Randy Haddox	LSU	1973
PAT Attempts	8	Darrow Hooper	VMI	1950
PAT Made	6	Randy Haddox	Wichita State	1973
	6	Darrow Hooper	TCU	1950
	(Also Arkansas, Nevada, '50)			
	6	John Ballentine	Southwestern	1947

HONORED TEXAS AGGIE FOOTBALL MEN

NATIONAL FOOTBALL HALL OF FAME

1951	Coach Dana X. Bible	1967	Joel Hunt, quarterback
1954	John Kimbrough, fullback	1971	Coach Homer Norton
1955	Coach Matty Bell	1974	Joe Utay, halfback
1962	Joe Routt, guard		

JOHN HEISMAN TROPHY WINNER

1957 John David Crow
(John Kimbrough finished second to Nile Kinnick, Iowa, in 1939)

TEXAS AGGIE ALL-AMERICAS

Year	Player	Year	Player
1936	Joe Routt, guard	1956	Charlie Krueger, tackle
1937	Joe Routt, guard	1957	Charlie Krueger, tackle
1939	Joe Boyd, tackle	1957	John David Crow, halfback
1939	John Kimbrough, fullback	1966	Maurice Moorman, tackle
1940	John Kimbrough, fullback	1967	Bill Hobbs, linebacker
1940	Marshall Robnett, guard	1968	Bill Hobbs, linebacker
1950	Bob Smith, fullback	1968	Rolf Krueger, tackle
1951	Jack Little, tackle	1968	Tommy Maxwell, safety
1952	Jack Little, tackle	1968	Steve O'Neal, punter
1956	Jack Pardee, fullback	1970	Dave Elmendorf, safety
1956	Dennis Goehring, guard		

TEXAS SPORTS HALL OF FAME

Coach Matty Bell
Coach Dana X. Bible
Joel Hunt, quarterback
John Kimbrough, fullback

Coach Homer Norton
Joe Routt, guard
Dick Todd, halfback

TEXAS A&M UNIVERSITY ATHLETIC HALL OF FAME

Frank G. Anderson, coach
James W. Aston
Tyree Bell, deceased
Dana X. Bible, coach
Joe Boyd
John David Crow
Charlie DeWare, Sr., deceased
King Gill
R. W. (Jitterbug) Henderson, deceased
R. G. Higginbotham, deceased
Caesar (Dutch) Hohn, deceased
Darrow Hooper
Joel Hunt
Barlow (Bones) Irvin
Bill James, coach, deceased
L. S. (Tiny) Keen
John Kimbrough
Charlie Krueger

Yale Lary
Jack Mahan, deceased
Tommy Mills
Charley Moran, coach, deceased
Homer Norton, coach, deceased
Jack Pardee
Marion Pugh
Marshall Robnett, deceased
J. W. (Dough) Rollins
J. E. Routt, deceased
Earl Rudder, deceased
S. H. (Sammy) Sanders
J. V. (Siki) Sikes, deceased
R. L. (Bob) Smith
Herbie Smith, deceased
Jim Thomason
Dick Todd
Joe Utay

TEXAS AGGIE ALL-SOUTHWEST CONFERENCE

Year	Player	Year	Player
1915	John Garrity, end		Jack Mahan, fullback
	Nick Braumiller, guard		T. F. (Puny) Wilson, end
1916	Newt Settegast, Sr., tackle	1921	Sammy Sanders, halfback
	Jim Crow, tackle		T. F. (Puny) Wilson, end
1917	Tim Greisenbeck, end		W. E. (Cap) Murrah, guard
	Ox Ford, tackle	1922	T. F. (Puny) Wilson, end
	E. S. Wilson, guard		W. D. (Bull) Johnson, guard
	Rip Collins, halfback	1923	W. D. (Bull) Johnson, guard
	Jack Mahan, fullback		A. J. Evans, end
1918	No Conference Teams Picked	1924	Neely Allison, end
1919	Scott Alexander, end		W. W. (Mule) Wilson, halfback
	E. S. Wilson, guard	1925	Joel Hunt, quarterback
	W. E. (Cap) Murrah, guard		L. G. (Ox) Dieterich, tackle
	C. R. Drake, tackle		W. M. Dansby, guard
	R. G. Higginbotham, halfback		Barlow (Bones) Irvin, tackle
	Jack Mahan, fullback		W. W. (Mule) Wilson, halfback
1920	W. E. (Cap) Murrah, guard	1926	Joel Hunt, quarterback
	C. R. Drake, tackle		L. G. (Ox) Dieterich, tackle
	R. G. Higginbotham, halfback		J. A. Rektorik, guard

	J. V. (Siki) Sikes, end		Goble Bryant, tackle
	C. D. Watts, center		Jim Hallmark, quarterback
1927	Joel Hunt, quarterback	1944	Monte Moncrief, tackle
	J. V. (Siki) Sikes, end		Paul Yates, fullback
	J. G. (Klepto) Holmes, guard		Clarence Howell, end
	A. C. Sprott, tackle	1945	Monte Moncrief, tackle
	E. E. Figari, guard		Grant Darnell, guard
	W. S. Lister, tackle		Bob Goode, fullback
1928	Willie Bartlett, center		Preston Smith, halfback
	Herschel Burgess, fullback	1946	Monte Moncrief, tackle
	S. J. (Red) Petty, end	1947	Jim Winkler, tackle
1929	Tommy Mills, quarterback	1948	Odell Stautzenberger, guard
	Charlie Richter, guard		Jim Winkler, tackle
1930	Adrain Tracey, end		Bob Goode, fullback
1931	Carl Moulden, guard		Andy Hillhouse, end
	Cliff Domingue, quarterback	1949	Bob Smith, fullback
	Charlie Malone, end	1950	Bob Smith, fullback
1932	Willis Nolan, center		Max Greiner, tackle
	Charley Cummings, tackle		Carl Mohlberg, guard
1933	Ted Spencer, fullback		Andy Hillhouse, end
	Ray Murray, end	1951	Jack Little, tackle
	W. T. Jordan, tackle		Glenn Lippman, halfback
1934	John Crow, guard		Hugh Meyer, center
1936	Joe Routt, guard		Billy Tidwell, halfback
	Charlie DeWare, Jr., center		Yale Lary, def. halfback
	Roy Young, tackle	1952	Jack Little, tackle
1937	Joe Routt, guard		Ray Graves, quarterback
	Roy Young, tackle		Joe Boring, safety
	Dick Todd, halfback	1953	Don Ellis, quarterback
	Virgil Jones, guard	1954	Bennie Sinclair, end
1938	Dick Todd, halfback		Elwood Kettler, quarterback
	Joe Boyd, tackle	1955	Dennis Goehring, guard
1939	Joe Boyd, tackle		Gene Stallings, end
	John Kimbrough, fullback	1956	Jack Pardee, fullback
	Marshall Robnett, guard		Charlie Krueger, tackle
	Herbie Smith, end		John David Crow, halfback
	Jim Thomason, halfback		Loyd Hale, center
1940	John Kimbrough, fullback		Dennis Goehring, guard
	Marshall Robnett, guard		John Tracey, end
	Jim Thomason, halfback		Roddy Osborne, quarterback
	Ernie Pannell, tackle	1957	Charlie Krueger, tackle
	Jim Sterling, end		John David Crow, halfback
1941	Jim Sterling, end		Bobby Marks, end
	Derace Moser, halfback	1958	Charlie Milstead, quarterback
	Bill Sibley, center		John Tracey, end
	Martin Ruby, tackle	1960	Sam Byer, fullback
1942	Jitterbug Henderson, end	1961	Jerry Hopkins, center
	Leo Daniels, halfback	1962	Jerry Hopkins, center
	Cullen Rogers, halfback	1963	Ronney Moore, guard
	Felix Bucek, guard	1964	Ray Gene Hinze, tackle
1943	Marion Settegast, Jr., tackle		Mike Pitman, def. back
	Marion Flanagan, halfback	1965	Ken (Dude) McLean, end

1966	Joe Wellborn, linebacker Maurice Moorman, tackle Gary Kovar, guard Wendell Housley, halfback		Larry Stegent, off. halfback Lynn Odom, def. guard Mike DeNiro, def. end Ross Brupbacher, off. end
1967	Edd Hargett, quarterback Bob Long, off. end Tommy Maxwell, safety Rolf Krueger, def. tackle Bill Hobbs, linebacker Grady Allen, def. end Larry Stegent, off. halfback Steve O'Neal, punter Dan Schneider, off. tackle	1970 1971 1972	Dave Elmendorf, safety Homer May, off. end Leonard Forey, off. guard David Hoot, safety Boice Best, def. tackle Grady Hoermann, linebacker Buster Callaway, off. tackle Mark Green, off. halfback Boice Best, def. tackle
1968	Edd Hargett, quarterback Rolf Krueger, def. tackle Bill Hobbs, linebacker Mike DeNiro, def. end Steve O'Neal, punter	 1973	Grady Hoermann, linebacker Robert Murski, safety Ed Simonini, linebacker Don Long, def. end Skip Walker, halfback
1969	Dave Elmendorf, safety		

HOUSTON POST
MOST VALUABLE PLAYER AWARD

1939	John Kimbrough, fullback Marshall Robnett, guard	1957	John David Crow, wingback Charlie Krueger, tackle
1941	Martin Ruby, tackle Derace Moser, tailback	1967	Edd Hargett, quarterback Bill Hobbs, linebacker
1956	Jack Pardee, fullback	1973	Ed Simonini, linebacker

This much desired trophy was first awarded in 1928 and went to one man each year until 1937 when it was enlarged to include one back and one lineman. It was not awarded in World War II years.

TEXAS AGGIE HEART AWARD

The Aggie Heart Award is awarded to a senior player by a vote of the varsity squad on the basis of effort, desire, determination and dedication for the good of the team.

Year Player
1965 Joe Wellborn
1966 Dan Westerfield
1967 Grady Allen
1968 Tom Buckman
1969 Jack Kovar
1970 Winston Beam
     Mike DeNiro, posthumously
1971 Joe Mac King
1972 Boice Best
1973 Larry Ellis

POST-GRADUATE SCHOLARSHIP AWARDS
National Football Foundation

1970 Dave Elmendorf

National Collegiate Athletic Association

1968 Edd Hargett
1970 Dave Elmendorf

UNITED SAVINGS–HELMS ATHLETIC FOUNDATION HALL OF FAME

John Kimbrough	Coach Homer Norton
Coach Charley Moran	Coach J. W. Rollins
Coach Dana X. Bible	Trainer Lil Dimmitt
Coach Matty Bell	H. B. (Mac) McElroy, S.I.D.

TEXAS AGGIE FOOTBALL CAPTAINS
1894-1973

Year	Captain	Year	Captain
1894	A. P. Watts	1925	Fay Wilson
1895	No Team	1926	L. G. Dieterich
1896	F. D. Perkins	1927	Joel Hunt
1897	Josh Sterns	1928	Willie Bartlett
1898	Hal Moseley	1929	Tommy Mills
1899	Hal Moseley	1930	J. G. Floyd
1900	R. M. Brown	1931	Carl Moulden
1901	C. F. Schultz	1932	Jimmy Aston
1902	Tom Blake	1933	C. M. Cummings
1903	Tom Blake	1934	E. O. Fowler
1904	R. B. Boettcher	1935	Taylor Wilkins
1905	G. T. Haltom		Nick Willis
1906	Felix Puckett	1936	Charlie DeWare, Jr.
1907	Joe Utay		Les Cummings
1908	Charlie DeWare, Sr.	1937	Joe Routt
1909	Louie Hamilton		Dick Vitek
1910	George Barnes	1938	Dick Todd
1911	Dutch Hohn		Owen Rogers
1912	Tyree Bell	1939	Joe Boyd
1913	W. B. Beasley		Cotton Price
1914	Tyree Bell		Herbie Smith
1915	Johnny Garrity	1940	Jim Thomason
1916	J. W. Rollins		Tommie Vaughn
1917	M. X. Ford	1941	Martin Ruby
1918	Scott Alexander		Marshall Spivey
1919	E. S. Wilson	1942	Cullen Rogers
1920	Jack Mahan		Elvis Simmons
1921	W. C. Weir	1943	Goble Bryant
1922	T. F. Wilson		Marion Flanagan
1923	W. D. Johnson	1944	Monte Moncrief
1924	T. L. Miller		Damon Tassos
	Charlie Waugh	1945	Monte Moncrief

295

	Bob Butchofsky		Wayland Simmons
1946	Monte Moncrief	1962	Jerry Hopkins
	Willie Zapalac		Sam Byers
1947	Bob Gary	1963	Ray Kubala
	Barney Welch		Ronnie Carpenter
1948	Jim Cashion	1964	John Brotherton
	Jim Winkler		Ronney Moore
	Odell Stautzenberger	1965	Joe Wellborn
1949	Bobby Goff		Jerry Nichols
	Wray Whittaker	1966	Dan Westerfield
1950	Max Greiner		Ken Lamkin
	Carl Molberg	1967	Grady Allen
1951	Bob Smith		Dan Schneider
	Hugh Meyer		Robert Cortez
1952	Jack Little	1968	Edd Hargett
	Ray Graves		Tom Buckman
1953	Durwood Scott	1969	Larry Stegent
1954	Bennie Sinclair		Ross Brupbacher
	Norbert Ohlendorf		Buster Adami
1955	Billy Huddleston	1970	Dave Elmendorf
1956	Gene Stallings		Jimmy Sheffield
	Jack Pardee		Winston Beam
	Lloyd Hale		Jim Parker
1957	John David Crow	1971	David Hoot
	Charlie Krueger		Joe Mac King
1958	John Tracey		Van Odom
	Richard Gay	1972	Todd Christopher
	Ken Beck		Brad Dusek
1959	Charlie Milstead		Boice Best
	Gale Oliver		Grady Hoermann
1960	Roy Northrup	1973	Larry Ellis
	Powell Berry		Ed Simonini
1961	Wayne Freiling		Mike Jay

TEXAS A&M IN BOWL GAMES

Date	Bowl	Teams			Coach
1/2/22	Dixie Classic	Texas A&M	22 - Centre	14	D. X. Bible
1/1/40	Sugar Bowl	Texas A&M	14 - Tulane	13	Homer Norton
1/1/41	Cotton Bowl	Texas A&M	13 - Fordham	12	Homer Norton
1/1/42	Cotton Bowl	Texas A&M	21 - Alabama	29	Homer Norton
1/1/44	Orange Bowl	Texas A&M	14 - LSU	19	Homer Norton
12/9/50	Presidential Cup	Texas A&M	40 - Georgia	20	Harry Stiteler
12/28/57	Gator Bowl	Texas A&M	0 - Tennessee	3	Paul Bryant
1/1/68	Cotton Bowl	Texas A&M	20 - Alabama	16	Gene Stallings

Won 5 - Lost 3 - Tied 0
(The Dixie Classic was the forerunner of the Cotton Bowl)

CONFERENCE CHAMPIONSHIPS

Year	Conference	Won	Lost	Tied	A&M	Opp.	Coach
1917	Southwest Conference	8	0	0	270	0	D. X. Bible
1919	Southwest Conference	10	0	0	275	0	D. X. Bible
1921	Southwest Conference	6	1	2	110	57	D. X. Bible
1925	Southwest Conference	7	1	1	191	25	D. X. Bible
1927	Southwest Conference	8	0	1	262	32	D. X. Bible
1939	Southwest Conference	11	0	0	212	31	Homer Norton
1940*	Southwest Conference	9	1	0	183	46	Homer Norton
1941	Southwest Conference	9	2	0	281	75	Homer Norton
1956**	Southwest Conference	9	0	1	223	81	Paul Bryant
1967	Southwest Conference	7	4	0	211	154	Gene Stallings

* - Co-Champion with SMU
** - On Probation and ineligible for bowl games
Teams of 1917 & 1919 were undefeated, untied and unscored on.
Team of 1939 was undefeated and untied.
Teams of 1902, 1927, and 1956 were undefeated but were tied.

SOUTHWEST CONFERENCE CHAMPIONS

Following are the names of Southwest Conference Champion players and coaches who are pictured by year earlier in the book. To match an individual with his name, select the corresponding year in which he is shown from the list below, identifying him by row, reading from left to right, from front row to back.

1917 Southwest Conference Champions

Assistant Coach D. V. Graves, Coach Dana X. Bible.

Bob Patillo, Bryan Gouger, Bill Sparks, Abe Price, Leon Gilmore, Neil Klock.

J. B. Sims, Sawyer Wolston, Jewell (Mule) Davis, Albert McHenry, Jack Mahan, L. F. Dinan, R. G. Higginbotham, G. D. Williamson.

Clint Copeland, Scott Alexander, Dick Furman, Carl Fabian, Rip Collins, Frank Boriskie, W. G. McMillan, George Anderson, Harmon Egger.

Kyle Elam, Jim Garth, Captain Ox Ford, J. D. McMurrey, Jack McClintock, C. T. Griesenbeck, John McKnight, George Martin, Frank Wendt.

1919 Southwest Conference Champions

Ben Baskin, Nick Askey, A. M. (Bugs) Morris, Jack Mahan, R. H. (Chick) Harrison, A. B. Knickerbocker, Heinie Weir, Oscar Frazier, Johnny Pierce.

B. L. Crocker, Bob Carruthers, W. E. (Cap) Murrah, Captain Woody Wilson, A. S. Vandervoort, Bill Touchstone, R. G. Higginbotham, Scott Alexander, Carl Scudder, M. H. Anglin.

Assistant Coach D. V. Graves, George Martin, Ed Forrest, Jewell (Mule) Davis, C. R. Drake, Frank Wendt, Tiny Keen, Roger Simpson, F. A. Murray, Bob Patillo, Coach Dana X. Bible, (Not shown: Bryan Gouger).

1921 Southwest Conference Champions

A. F. Dieterich, R. G. Neely, Sam Pinson, Jim Y. Forgason, A. B. (Bugs) Morris, Sammy Sanders, Roger Simpson, Lacy Shifflett, Floyd Buckner, H. C. Dillingham.

W. E. (Cap) Murrah, M. V. Smith, Ben Beesley, Frank Judd, H. W. McClelland, Captain Heinie Weir, King Gill, Jewell (Mule) Davis, Harry Pinson, Bull Johnson, John N. Askey, T. L. Miller.

Coach Dana X. Bible, Sam Cowan, Bob Carruthers, Puny Wilson, R. A. Brown, Jim Crawford, Tiny Keen, Dick Wilson, Sam Leiper, Jack Evans, Frank Wendt, Ted Winn, Line Coach C. J. Rothgeb.

1925 Southwest Conference Champions

Jelly Woodman, Bob Berry, Bob Edgar, Taro Kishi, D. C. Arnold, Captain Mule Wilson, Joel Hunt, Hugh McConaughey, Pee Wee Turner, P. C. Colgin, J. D. (Dutch) McGuire.

Simon Utay, Herb Beutel, H. P. (Sis) Wylie, Carleton Speed, H. S. Woodland, John Braselton, Hack Willis, J. D. Wyman, George Curry, Norman Dansby.

Coach Dana X. Bible, Bones Irvin, Henry Eitt, L. G. Dieterich, W. S. Lister, A. C. Sprott, Siki Sikes, Babe Watts, John Deffebach, A. C. Bryant, Assistant Coach Claud Rothgeb.

Bill Kuykendall, Wilbur Ochterbeck, Bill Bethea, H. W. Townsend, Gillam Morris, Phil Price, G. L. Hart, Irvy Burney, Ernie Figari, Dutch Rektorik.

1927 Southwest Conference Champions

Ross Martello, Dutch Rektorik, Tommy Mills, R. R. Dorsey, Frank Ish, Zeke Snead, Herschel Burgess, J. G. Holmes, R. A. (Bill) Cody, Walter Ewell.

H. P. (Sis) Wylie, Willie Bartlett, Roy Varnell, Pinky Alsobrook, Captain Joel Hunt, Siki Sikes, Red Petty, W. E. Davis, Charley Richter.

Coach Dana X. Bible, Johnny Deffebach, Ed J. (Gut) Mosher, Joe Brown, W. S. Lister, A. C. Sprott, Joe Holleran, Ernie Figari, Brooks Conover, Assistant Coach Chuck Bassett.

1939 National Champions

Herbie Smith, Marland Jeffrey, Ed Robnett, Cotton Price, Marion Pugh, Frank Wood, Bill Henderson, Les Richardson, Joe Rothe.

Mack Browder, Muley White, Charles Henke, Marshall Robnett, Tommie Vaughn, Euel Wesson, Jim Thomason, John Kimbrough, Bud Force, 'Bama Smith.

Cullen Rogers, Bill Conatser, Derace Moser, Odell Herman, Bill Miller, Hugh Boyd, Bill Buchanan, Jim Sterling, Cotton Williams, Bubba Reeves, Martin Ruby.

Ernie Pannell, Marshall Spivey, Bill Duncan, John Abbott, Zolus Motley, Bill Blessing, Leon Rahn, Harold Cowley, Dog Dawson, Rock Audish.

Leonard Joeris, Joe Parish, Howard Shelton, Jo Jo White, Jack Kimbrough, Chip Routt, Carl Geer, Chester Heimann, Joe Boyd, Gus Bates, Willard Clark.

Roy Bucek, Henry Hauser, Pinky Williams.

Charles Deware, Marty Karow, Bill James, Hub McQuillen, Homer Norton, Lil Dimmitt, Manning Smith, Harry Faulkner, Dough Rollins.

1940 Southwest Conference Champions

Odell Herman, 'Bama Smith, Bill Conatser, Derace Moser, Bill Henderson, Harold Cowley, Les Richardson, Dub Sibley, Pete Henry.

Marion Pugh, Marland Jeffrey, Charles Henke, Ernie Pannell, Co-Captain Tommy Vaughn, Co-Captain Jim Thomason, John Kimbrough, Marshall Robnett.

Sam Rankin, Bill Buchanan, Chip Routt, Dog Dawson, Euel Wesson, Leon Rahn, Joe Rothe, Howard Shelton, Bud Force.

Harold Tuebner, Jamie Wilson, Knubby Thompson, Henry Hauser, Kyle Drake, Bubba Reeves, Bill Blessing, Leonard Joeris.

Jake Webster, Jim Brewer, Bob Mansfield, Marshall Spivey, Woodrow Bando, Bill Gregory, John Abbott.

Zolus Motley, Martin Ruby, Jimmy Knight, Felix Bucek, Fount Wade, Willie Zapalac, Cotton Williams.

Mack Browder, Jim Sterling, Ray Mulhollan, Mgr. Jimmie Parker, Pinky Williams, Roy Bucek, Elvis Simmons.

Coach Homer Norton, Manning Smith, Lil Dimmitt, Harry Faulkner, Bill James, Charles DeWare, Dough Rollins, Hub McQuillen, Marty Karow. (Not shown: Jack Kimbrough).

1941 Southwest Conference Champions

Dub Sibley, Jim Sterling, Co-Captain Marshall Spivey, Derace Moser, Don Luethy, Jim Montgomery, Bill Henderson, Les Richardson, Bob Tulis.

Leo Daniels, 'Bama Smith, Sam Porter, Bobby Williams, Felix Bucek, Leonard Holder, Leonard Dickey, Jack Swank.

A. J. Mercer, Cotton Williams, Sam Rankin, Richard Skarke, Truman Cox, Freddy Wolters, Dennis Andricks, Jake Webster, Paul Cheatham, Willie Zapalac.

Charles Miller, Tom Pickett, Cullen Rogers, Lincoln Roman, Pete Slaughter, Boots Simmons, Fount Wade, Harold Cowley.

Jamie Dawson, Co-Captain Martin Ruby, Zolus Motley, Jimmy Knight, Roy Bucek, Bill Andrews, Owen Moore.

John Stout, Dan Levy, Ray Mulhollan, Euel Wesson, Weldon Maples, Wayne Cure, Leonard Wagner.

Coach Homer Norton, Marty Karow, Bill James, Dough Rollins.

1956 Southwest Conference Champions

Bobby Lockett, George Gillar, Dennis Goehring, Jack Pardee, Gene Stallings, Lloyd Hale, Dee Powell, Bob Clendennon, Bobby Keith, Don Watson.

Manager Gary Rollins, John Tracey, John Gilbert, Bill Appelt, Loyd Taylor, Bobby Marks, Roddy Osborne, Murry Trimble, Carl Luna, Allen Goehring, Carlos Esquivel, Manager Joe Schmid.

Jim Stanley, Jim Wright, John Crow, A. L. Simmons, Ken Beck, Jim Langston, Don Smith, Charles Krueger, Dick Goff, Dick Steadman, Tommy Howard.

Richard Gay, Luther Hall, Bobby Conrad, Henry Pearson, Ray Doucet, Leo Wotipka, Don McClelland, Ed Dudley, Lloyd Wasserman, John Polk, Stan Roper.

1967 Southwest Conference Champions

Ronald Cole, Ross Brupbacher, Larry Stegent, Barney Harris, Mark Weaver, Bill Sallee, Robert Cortez, Grady Allen, Dan Schneider, Billy Hobbs, Curley Hallman, Bill Kubecka, Roy Gunnels, Charlie Riggs.

Gary Gruben, Jack Whitmore, Sammy Williams, John Turney, George Walker, Lynn Fister, Leroy Hauerland, Pat Shannon, Winston Beam, Harvey Aschenbeck, Bob Long, Edd Hargett, Buster Adami, Bill Seely, Tommy Maxwell, Jimmy Adams, Tom Sooy, Jerry Campbell, Steve O'Neal.

George Resley, Wayne King, Tom Gergeni, Doug Valois, Jim Piper, Ray Morse, Lynn Odom, Arthur Cooley, James Reynolds, Tom Chaffee, Jim Kazmierski, Jack Kovar, Danny Eckermann, Wendell Housely, Ronnie Rudloff, Mike Stinson, Danny Owens, Steve Mullen.

Manager Robert Power, Vance Brack, Robert Stansbury, Rusty Stallings, Ronald Reagan, Tom Buckman, Javier Vela, Leslie Dickson, Terry Brewster, Ivan Jones, Joe Shaw, Bill Gilliam, Phil McAnelly, Gary Kitchens, Rolf Krueger, Cliff Golden, Carl Gough, Mike Caswell, Gaddy Wells, Carl Engleman, Walter Mohn.

FOOTBALL T-MEN SINCE 1894

The Athletic Department at Texas A&M University, College Station, TX. 77843 will welcome additions or corrections to this list.

A

Abbey, Dan '29, '30
Abbott, John A. '39
Abraham, Arthur A. '44, '45
Adami, Buster, '67, '68, '69
Adams, Jimmy '67, '68, '69
Alexander, Scott '17, '18, '19
Allen, Grady L. '65, '66, '67
Allison, J. Neely '23, '24
Alsabrook, O. D. '27, '28, '29
Altgelt, George A. '10, '11
Anderson, Gary Lee '50
Anderson, George D. '17
Anderson, Gerald R. (Mgr) '53
Anderson, P. Jennings '47
Andricks, Dennis B. '41
Angermiller, Roy L. '49
Anglin, M. H. '20
Armbrister, Gary '69
Arndt, Charles '73
Arnold, D. C. '26
Arnold, W. J. '13
Aschenbeck, Harvey '66, '67, '68
Askey, N. '19
Astin, Erwin H. '96, '97, '98, '99
Aston, James W. '30, '31, '32
Audish, William '37, '38, '39

B

Balenti, Michael R. '09
Ballard, William R. '51
Ballentine, John R. '45, '46, '47
Barfield, R. F. '31
Barker, William O. '65
Barnes, George W. '09, '10, '11
Barnett, Billy Bob '69
Barnett, Ray R. '52, '53, '54
Barnett, Robert W. '65, '66
Bartlett, Z. W., Jr. '26, '27, '28
Bartley, Arthur N. '02
Barton, Dorbandt '49, '50
Bateman, A. R. '10, '11
Bates, Gus '39
Bates, Larry E. '64
Bates, Robert G. '48, '49, '50
Baty, Robert B., '46, '47, '48
Baumgarten, Charles, '97, '98
Bayless, Frederick '32
Bean, Ernest '72, '73
Beam, Winston '67, '70
Beard, Glenn G. '45
Beasley, Wyatte G. '10, '11, '12, '13
Beck, Kenneth '56, '57, '58
Beeman, Del S. '04
Beesley, Ben B. '21
Beesley, Earl G. '43
Beilharz, William '01, '02
Bell, Luther E. '31
Bell, Tyree L. '10, '11, '12, '14
Bellar, Mike '69, '70, '71
Belville, Vernon R. '42
Bennett, Gary L. '62
Bernay, Camp L. '03
Berry, Murry P. '58, '59, '60
Berry, Robert H. '24, '25
Best, Boice W. '70, '71, '72
Best, Bruce A. '70
Beutel, H. W. '24, '25
Bible, Hollis U. '28
Billingsley, Charles '71
Bird, Max D. '70, '71, '72
Black, Marc '69, '70, '71
Blackburn, George S. (Mgr) '39

302

Blair, W. G. '52
Blake, Robert E. '05
Blake, Thomas M. '01, '02, '03
Blessing, William '39
Boettcher, Reinhardt B. '96, '03, '04
Bonner, H. L. '13
Booth, Ellison S. '03
Boring, Joseph '52, '53
Boswell, James R. '48
Bounds, James Y. '62, '63, '65
Bowers, Alvin '72, '73
Bowler, Sam E. '12
Boyce, C. William, Jr. '05
Boyd, Hugh F., Jr. '39
Boyd, Joe M. '37, '38, '39
Boyd, William O. '35, '36
Brack, Vance '67
Bradford, J. B. '23
Bransom, George E., Jr. '37, '38
Braselton, J. W. '24
Braumiller, Nick M. '14, '15
Breding, Edward V. '64, '65, '66
Breedlove, H. M. '32, '33
Brice, Roland G. '60, '61, '62
Britt, A. Rankin '36, '37, '38
Broaddus, Larry G. '59, '60
Brooks, Hugh '14
Brotherton, John R. '62, '63, '64
Broussard, Fred E. '53
Browder, Harris Mack '39
Brown, Charles W. '14
Brown, Darrell W. '54, '55, '57
Brown, J. E. '28, '29
Brown, J. S. '09
Brown, Reaville M. '00, '01, '04
Brupbacher, Ross '67, '68, '69
Bruton, Alfred L. (Mgr) '54
Bruton, Mike '73
Bryant, Goble W. '43
Bucek, Felix A. '41, '42
Bucek, Roy E. '39, '40, '41
Buchanan, A. B. '39, '40
Buckman, Tom '66, '67, '68

Buckner, F. K. '21
Bujnoch, Glenn '73
Bull, A. C. '15
Bunger, Mike '69, '70, '71
Buntin, R. F. (Mgr) '42, '47
Burditt, Jesse N. '43, '44, '45, '46
Burgess, Edwin B. '94
Burgess, Herschel E. '26, '27, '28
Burks, Steve '69, '70, '71
Burleson, Russell W. '94
Burney, John W. '94
Burns, Darnace B. '14, '15, '16
Burton, Alan M. (Mgr) '51
Butchofsky, R. L. '43, '44, '45
Butler, Marvin N. '14
Byer, Sam A. '60, '61, '62

C

Caffey, Kenneth D. '64, '65, '66
Caffey, Lee Roy '60, '61, '62
Callahan, A. Paul '34
Callaway, David Earl '70, '71, '72
Callcott, George V. (Trnr) '62
Callcott, William H. (Trnr) '64, '65
Callender, Richard '48, '49
Campbell, Jerry '66, '67, '68
Capt, Louis E. '52, '53
Cardwell, John E. '13
Carlin, William J. '09
Carpenter, Miles '99, '00, '01
Carpenter, Ronnie D. '61, '62, '63
Carruth, Dennis P. '70, '71, '72
Carruthers, R. L. '19, '20, '21
Carson, C. '94
Caruthers, B. V. '05
Cashion, James T. '44, '45, '46, '47
Caskey, Robert D. '60, '61
Caswell, Mike '67, '68, '69
Cauthorn, Sidney W. '58
Cawthorn, Frank W. '14
Chaffee, Tom '67
Chapin, R. Tuck '48, '49, '50

Childress, Jay '94
Chiles, H. T. '94
Christensen, John L. '49
Christian, J. P. '29, '30, '31
Christopher, Todd D. '70, '71, '72
Church, Warren E. '37
Clark, Henry F. '55
Clark, Michael V. '60, '61, '62
Clark, Willard W. '39
Clendennan, Robert J. '55, '56
Coleman, Wiley L. '14
Colgin, P. C. '26
Collins, H. W. '14, '15
Collins, Bubba J. '64, '65
Collins, William A. '14, '15
Conatser, William E. '38, '39, '40
Connelley, R. E. '32
Conoley, Odell M. '33, '34
Conover, Brooks W. '28, '29
Conrad, Bobby Joe '55, '56, '57
Cooley, Arthur '67, '68
Cooper, Jeff (Trnr) '72
Copeland, Cedric D. K. '48, '49
Cornell, Albert L. '05, '06, '07
Cortez, Roberto '65, '66, '67
Coston, Fred M. '36, '37, '38
Coulter, Hiram T. '94
Couser, William L. '33, '34
Cousins, R. W. '98
Cover, Robert J. '03
Cowley, Harold E. '39, '40, '41
Cox, Truman D. '42
Cox, William E. '96
Craig, George W. '60, '61
Craig, James W., Jr. '62, '63
Cretcher, J. C. '08, '09, '10
Crossman, Jerry M. '50, '51, '52
Crow, Floyd A. '14
Crow, John David '55, '56, '57
Crow, John W. '32
Crow, Marion O. '34, '35
Crutsinger, Larry L. '61
Cummings, Charley M. '31, '32, '33

Cummings, Leslie L. '34, '35, '36
Cure, Wayne O. '42
Currington, Lloyd D. '64, '65, '66
Cushman, Cecil A. '12
Cuthrell, J. H. '28

D

Dale, Ivan '06, '07
Dale, Jesse D. '05, '06, '07
Daniel, Edwin R. '46, '47, '48
Daniel, Thomas C. '44, '45
Daniels, James '73
Daniels, Leo H. '41, '42, '46
Dansby, M. W. '24
Dansby, N. J. '23, '24, '25
Darbyshire, Russell O. '08
Darnell, Grant S. '43, '44, '45
Darwin, William B. '57, '58, '59
Davis, James M. '02
Davis, Jewel '19
Davis, Robin '69
Davis, W. E. '27, '28
Davis, W. E. '30, '31
Dawkins, Marvin H. '63, '64
Dawson, Oran '31
Dawson, William H. '38, '39, '40
Dean, James S. (Mgr) '05
Dean, Jimmy '73
Deaton, Thomas W. '70
DeBusk, Kelly S. '64
Decker, Jack (Trnr) '68
Deere, Donald R. '43
Deffebach, J. A. '26, '27
Delery, H. B. '28, '29
DeLong, Raleigh '14
Dendy, Billy G. '55
Denton, Dean M. '45
Devin, Michael D. '64
Dew, Bobby W. '47
DeNiro, Mike '68, '69
DeWare, Charles A., Sr. '05, '06, '07, '08
DeWare, Charles A., Jr. '34, '35, '36

304

DeWare, Robert R. '99, '00, '01
DeWitt, Bernard John, III '70
Dickey, Leonard M. '41, '45, '46
Dickie, Byron H. '14
Dieterich, A. F. '20, '21
Dieterich, L. G. '24, '25, '26
Dillon, Paul G. '62
Dittman, Henry '37, '38
Dixon, Robert H. '51, '52
Domingue, G. C. '31, '32, '33
Dorsey, R. R. '27, '28, '29
Doucet, Raymond L. '57, '58
Dowell, George S. '97
Drake, C. R. '18, '19, '20
Dreiss, Ed., Jr. '10, '11
Drennan, James L. '62, '63, '64
Dubcak, James L. '70, '71
DuBois, H. V. '21, '22, '23
Dudley, Edward R. '55, '58
Duncan, William M. '38, '39
Dunn, Ralph B. '03
Dupree, Calvin R. '47, '48
Dusek, Ed. D. '42, '46, '47
Dusek, John Bradley '70, '71, '72
Dwyer, Tom J. '08, '09, '10
Dwyer, W. F. '97, '98

E

Easley, Robert A., Jr. '53, '54
Eberle, A. A. '43, '44
Ebrom, Edwin '69, '70, '71
Eilers, Joseph A. '60, '61
Eitt, Henry W. '22
Elam, K. C. '17, '18
Elder, Jim M. '02
Elledge, Jerry R (Trnr) '61
Ellis, Donald E. '52, '53
Ellis, Herbert W. '44, '45, '47, '48
Ellis, J. P. (Mgr) '66
Ellis, Larry '71, '72, '73
Ellis, Oscar L. '07
Elmendorf, Dave '68, '69, '70

Endsley, Lindon C. '64
Engle, William F. '45
Erhard, Earl '00
Erickson, Jalmer L. '61, '62
Ermis, Harvey J. '64
Eschenberg, Arthur C. '14, '15
Esquivel, Carlos '56, '57
Estes, Teddy J. '58, '59, '60
Evans, A. J. '21, '22, '23
Everett, G. Dudley '12, '13, '14
Ewell, W. L. '28

F

Faber, Benny H. '14
Farr, Reso '96, '97
Few, Jon W. '58, '60
Figari, E. E. '27
Fields, Mike '69, '70
Fisher, Franklin C. '60, '61
Fister, Lynn '67, '68
Flanagan, Marion D. '43, '46
Fletcher, Pierce H. '63, '65, '66
Flinchem, James M. '07, '10
Flowers, James L. '48, '49, '50
Floyd, J. G. '28, '29, '30
Foldberg, Henry C. '42
Foldberg, John Dan '45
Foote, J. M. '11, '12
Force, Henry H. '39
Ford, M. H. '17
Ford, William J. '62, '63, '64
Forey, Leonard '69, '70, '71
Forgason, J. Y. '22, '23, '24
Forgsard, Charles H. '09
Foster, Edmund J. '02, '03, '04, '05
Foster, H. '99, '00
Fowler, Odell '32, '34
Fowler, James B. '49, '50, '51
Franklin, Carter L. '58, '59, '60
Frazelle, Billy J. (Trnr) '51
Freiling, Wayne E. '59, '60, '61
Frey, Richard H. '50, '51, '52

G

Gardemal, Richard D. '49, '50, '51
Gardner, John '69, '70, '71
Garner, Robert A. '58
Garrett, T. H. '97, '98, '99, '00
Garrity, Johnny '13, '14, '15
Garth, J. W. '18
Gary, Robert J. '43, '44, '46, '47
Gay, Richard G. '56, '57, '58
Gebhart, P. C. '99, '00
Geer, Carl E. '39
Geer, W. E. '43, '44, '45
Geraismowicz, Robert W. '70, '71
Gibson, Charles B. '43
Gilbert, John R. '55, '56, '57
Gilbert, Warren A. (Mgr) '07
Gilbert, Warren A., Jr. (Mgr) '46, '47
Gilfillan, Max D. '14, '15, '16
Gill, E. King '22, '23
Gillar, George E. '55, '56
Gilmore, L. M. '17
Glendenning, Craig '73
Godwin, W. G. '33
Godwin, William H., Jr. '57, '58, '59
Goehring, Allen G. '57, '58, '59
Goehring, Dennis H. '54, '55, '56
Goff, Robert E. '44, '48, '49
Golasinski, Joe A. '32
Goode, Robert L. '45, '46, '47, '48
Goodwin, Tommy '70, '71
Gosney, Robert R. '53
Gouger, G. Bryan '17, '19, '20
Gough, Carl '67, '68
Graham, M. C. '16
Grant, Donald G. '55
Graves, Henry L. '31, '32
Graves, Ray D. '51, '52
Gray, Frank M. '00, '02
Gray, George W. '44, '45
Gray, George William '58
Gray, Tim '73
Green, Mark '71, '72
Greene, Taylor H. (Mgr) '54
Greeno, David '73
Greisenbeck, C. T. '17
Gregory, J. C. '33
Greiner, Max G. '47, '48, '49, '50
Grissom, Roy J. '10
Gruben, Gary '68
Gunnels, Roy '67
Guseman, Oliver J. '31
Gwin, Clinton D. '50

H

Haas, Raymond A., Jr. '52
Haddox, Randy '72, '73
Hail, George (Trnr) '59
Hale, Lloyd R. '54, '55, '56
Hall, Charles L. '52, '54
Hall, Luther H. '58
Hall, Robert L. '38
Hallman, Curley '66, '67, '68
Hallmark, James L. '43, '46
Hallmark, Kenzy D. '50
Haltom, Bart U. '48
Haltom, Guy V. '04, '05
Hamilton, Louis '06, '07, '08, '09
Hammer, Stayton W. '02, '03
Hand, Floyd '42
Hanick, C. F. '05
Hanna, Howard E. '03, '05
Hanna, T. W. '22, '23
Hanson, Allan '68, '69
Hardman, J. J. '22
Hargett, Edd '66, '67, '68
Hargett, George W. '61, '62, '63
Harper, James L. '60, '61, '62
Harris, Barney '67, '68, '69
Harris, David B. (Mgr) '05, '09
Harrison, R. H., Jr. '18, '19
Hart, Lilliard D. '45
Hart, William T. '45
Hartman, Jim '73
Hauerland, Leroy '67, '68
Hauser, Henry '38, '39, '40

Hayes, Lester '73
Heidelberg, Frank T. '07, '08
Heimann, Chester F. '39
Henderson, Daniel E. '55
Henderson, R. Wm. '40, '41, '42
Henke, Charles E. '38, '39, '40
Henry, Peter C. '39
Herman, Odell C. '38, '39, '40
Hernandez, Frank P. (Mgr) '58
Herr, Joey '69, '70, '71
Herring, Julian C. '50
Hewitt, W. W. '30, '31, '32
Higginbotham, G. H. '12
Higginbotham, R. G. '17, '19, '20
Higgins, Norton '44, '45, '46, '47
Hill, Carl R. '49
Hill, Russell E. '59, '60, '61
Hill, Walter R. '50, '51, '52
Hillhouse, Andy L. '48, '50
Hinnant, Barb '69, '70
Hinze, Ray Gene '62, '63, '64
Hitt, Lee Ellison '70, '71
Hobbs, Bill '66, '67, '68
Hodge, Charles H. '50, '51
Hodges, Gene (Mgr) '71
Hoermann, Grady '70, '71, '72
Hogan, George A. '60, '61
Hohn, Caesar '09, '10, '11, '12
Hohn, Charles M. '43
Holder, Leonard D. '41
Holditch, Murry W. '49, '50
Holliday, T. C. '11
Hollmig, Stanley E. '46, '47
Holmes, J. G. '27
Holmes, Robert C. (Mgr) '47, '48
Honore, Jerry '73
Hooker, Roger M. '07, '08, '09
Hooper, Clarence D. '50, '51, '52
Hoot, David '69, '70, '71
Hope, George N. '02
Hopkins, Jerry W. '60, '61, '62
Hornsby, H. R. '30, '31
Housley, Wendell '66, '67, '68

Howard, Albert L. '64, '65, '66
Howard, Thomas V., Jr. '56, '57, '58
Howell, John C. '44, '46, '47
Hoyl, Basil L. (Mgr) '42
Hubby, Ronnie '72, '73
Huddleston, Billy P. '53, '54, '55
Hudeck, Russel R. '49, '50, '51
Hudgins, Charles M. '50
Huff, Leslie N. (Mgr) '07
Hulin, Paul '72, '73
Hull, Burt E. (Mgr) '04
Hunt, O. Joel '25, '26, '27
Huntington, Bobby N. '60, '61, '62
Hyde, Walter '00, '01

I

Irvin, Barlow '23, '24, '25
Irwin, B. M. '32

J

James, Lex F. '70, '71, '72
Janner, Calvin F. '61
Jay, Mike '73
Jeffrey, William Marland '38, '39, '40
Jenkins, Jerry S. '60, '61
Jenkins, Joseph S. (Mgr) '64
Joeris, Leonard '39, '42
Johnson, A. L. '16
Johnson, B. L. '46
Johnson, Chris '69, '70, '71
Johnson, F. S. (Mgr) '03
Johnson, George R. '55
Johnson, Joe B. '60
Johnson, Wilbur G. '45
Johnson, William D. '22, '23
Jones, Donald H. (Mgr) '60
Jones, Ivan '66, '67, '68
Jones, Virgil B. '36, '37
Jordan, W. T. '32, '33, '34

K

Kachtick, Jerry V. '63, '64, '65
Kachtik, Edward Don '52, '53, '54
Kamp, Charles H. '70
Kauffman, James H. '65
Kazmierski, Jim '68
Keeling, Thomas D. '60, '61
Keen, Lowell S. '21, '22
Keese, Mike '73
Keith, Robert D. '54, '55, '56
Keller, James L. '61, '62, '63
Kelley, Victor M. '05, '06, '07, '09
Kemph, Gary S. '65
Kenderdine, J. M. '33
Kendrick, J. M. '15
Kendrick, Robert T. '04, '05
Kennon, Paul A. '54
Kern, R. A. '10, '12
Kesey, David A. (Stats) '69
Kettler, Elwood N. '53, '54
Kildow, P. C. '99
Kimbrough, Jack C. '39, '40
Kimbrough, John A. '38, '39, '40
Kimbrough, William R. '33, '34
King, Joe Mac '69, '70, '71
Kipp, Kenneth W. '60, '61, '62
Kirby, Selmer M. '34, '35
Kirchmer, John T. '64
Kirkpatrick, Roy '69
Kishi, Taro '24, '25
Kitchens, Gary '67
Knickerbocker, A. B. '19
Knickerbocker, H. W. '22, '23
Knight, Charles J. '64
Koehn, Donald W. '64, '65, '66
Kohlman, Joe M. '62, '64
Kovar, Gary W. '64, '65, '66
Kovar, Jack '67, '68, '69
Kramm, Raymond F. '62
Krenek, Benedict J. '60, '61, '62
Krueger, Charlie A. '55, '56, '57
Krueger, Rolf '66, '67, '68
Krug, William '94

Kubala, Raymond G. '61, '62, '63
Kubecka, Bill '67
Kubesch, Raymond A. '62
Kuehn, Russell '71, '72

L

Labar, Harry W. '58, '59, '60
LaBauve, Dwight '71, '72
LaGrange, Charles R. '63, '64, '65
LaGrone, Walter A. '60, '61
Lambert, H. G. '10, '11, '12
Lamkin, Kenneth A. '64, '65, '66
Langford, Alvin L. '50, '51, '52
Langston, James E. '56
Lary, Robert Yale '49, '50, '51
Latham, Joel P. '60, '61, '62
Lawson, Clarence O. '49
Lazarine, Marshall M. '50
League, Thomas '44
LeBoeuf, Gordon E. '57, '58, '59
Ledbetter, Harry L. '65, '66
Ledbetter, Ronald P. '60, '61, '62
Lee, Larry L. '65, '66
Lee, Robert G. '63
Leggett, Charles W. '09
Leiper, Sam E. '22
Lemmons, Bernard '50
Lemmons, Billy '73
Lillard, Steve T. '09
Lindsey, Ernest Martin '35
Lindsey, Glynn '64, '65, '66
Lindsey, Ronald L. '64, '65, '66
Linnstaedter, James A. '61, '62, '63
Lippman, Glenn E. '49, '50, '51
Lister, W. Sprott '26, '27
Little, Jack H. '50, '51, '52
Litterst, Frank C. '16
Lockett, Bobby J. '56
Long, Bob '66, '67, '68
Long, Don '72, '73
Long, Eldon W. '43
Lord, George P. '30, '31
Lord, Mike '69, '70, '71

Love, Andrew C. '94, '98
Love, J. N. '32
Love, Richard L. '59
Loving, James W. '04
Luebbehusen, Steve '69, '70, '71
Luethy, Don R. '42
Luna, Otie C. '57, '58
Lutrick, J. A. '11
Lyles, John V. '12

M

Maddox, Randy '69
Magouirk, Conrad W. '51, '52, '53
Magrill, O. B. '29, '30, '31
Mahan, Jack '17, '19, '20
Malone, Charles '30, '31
Maltz, Herschel (Mgr) '47
Manning, Waylon E. '35, '36
Maples, Weldon '41, '42
Marks, Robert E. '55, '56, '57
Marquette, Leo J. '52
Marshall, Tank '73
Martin, G. W. '18, '19, '20
Martin, Harry '94
Martin, Sidney T. '34
Masterson, L. '02
Matthews, Mason L. '44, '45
Mauk, Albert '03, '05
Maxwell, Stapp N. '32
Maxwell, Tommy '66, '67, '68
May, Homer H. '70, '71, '72
Mayeaux, Hayden E. '51, '52
Mayfield, John D., Jr. (Mgr) '49, '50
McAllister, G. T. '43, '44
McAnelly, Phil '68
McArthur, O. A. '12
McCaffrey, Gary '70
McCarley, Robert E. '52
McClelland, Don A. '57, '60
McClelland, H. W. '22
McClintock, J. R. '17
McCrumbly, John '73

McDermott, Pat '70, '71, '72
McDonald, Charles N. '49, '50, '51
McDonald, Hugh F. '94
McDonald, Pace '18
McDonald, William A. '09
McDowell, Charles H. '10
McElroy, Hugh '70, '71
McFadden, P. M. '30, '31
McFarland, Arthur '03, '04
McFarland, H. F. '93, '94
McFarland, James L. '11
McGinnis, Francis K. '00
McGonagill, J. D. '94
McGowan, Billy Joe '52, '54
McGregor, Flint '02
McGuire, Joseph D. '24, '25
McIllhaney, Joe D. '62, '63, '64
McKaughan, Edward W. '64, '65
McKnight, J. B. '15, '17
McLean, Ken J. '62, '63, '65
McMahan, Billy M. '53
McMahan, James T. '50
McMillan, M. Blaisdale '94
McMillan, W. G. '21, '22
McMurray, J. D. '17
McNeil, J. G. '94
Meeks, Thomas E. '62, '63, '64
Meitzen, J. B. '24
Mercer, Arthur J. '41, '42
Merka, Jeremiah H. '33
Meyer, D. '02
Meyer, William H. '49, '50, '51
Miller, A. R. '12
Miller, Eric K. '51, '52, '53
Miller, L. '02
Miller, T. L. '21, '22
Miller, Thomas Bill '39
Miller, Vance W. '12, '13
Milligan, Wayne '03, '07
Mills, J. Kenneth '37
Mills, Thomas W. '27, '28, '29
Millsap, Leonard '70
Milstead, Charles F. '57, '58, '59

Minnock, William A. '37, '38
Mitchell, Merlin '15, '16
Mohn, Walter '67
Molberg, Carl '48, '49, '50
Moncrief, Monte P. '43, '44, '45, '46
Montgomery, J. B. '42
Montgomery, Roark '12
Moore, A. A. '30, '31
Moore, Doyle H. '49
Moore, George F. '07, '08
Moore, William R. '62, '63, '64
Moore, W. Scott '07, '08, '09, '10
Moorman, Maurice '66
Morris, A. B. '20, '21, '22
Morrison, D. E. '12
Morrison, P. M. '96
Morrow, Johnnie '35, '36
Mortensen, James E. '45
Moseley, Hal '97, '98, '99, '00
Moser, R. Derace '39, '40, '41
Moses, Sam F. '49, '50, '51
Mossenburg, W. G. '94
Motley, Zolus C. '39, '40
Moulden, Carl D. '29, '30, '31
Mulhollan, Ray W. '40, '41, '42
Mullen, Steve '68
Munson, George (Mgr) '72
Munson, Joe U., Jr. '57, '58
Murname, Tommy (Mgr) '44, '45, '46
Murphy, Alton L. (Mgr) '52, '53
Murphy, James L. '59, '60, '61
Murrah, Thomas F. '63, '64, '65
Murrah, W. E. '18, '19, '20, '21
Murray, Ray L. '31, '32, '33
Murski, Robert '70, '71, '72
Myers, O. W. '97, '98, '99

N

Neece, Clarence M. '08, '09
Neely, Roy G. '22, '23
Neff, Asa J. '02
Nelms, Milton R. '12
Nelson, Freddie Ted '65
Neill, Doug '69, '70, '71
Nesrsta, J. O. '35, '36, '37
Netardus, Jaro G., Jr. '49, '51
Neville, Henry A. '43
Nicholas, Don R. '49
Nichols, Jerry D. '64, '65
Niland, T. K. '51, '52
Nilson, John H. '63, '64, '65
Noble, Elton '99, '00
Nohavitza, Elo E. '49, '50, '51
Nolan, Willis '30, '31, '32
Nolen, Lockhart (Mgr) '48
Northrup, Roy F. '58, '59, '60

O

Ochterbeck, W. J. '24, '25
Odom, Lynn '67, '68, '69
Odom, Van '69, '70, '71
Ogdee, Edward '42
Ohlendorf, Norbert K. '52, '53, '54
Olbrich, Alvin P. '38
Oliver, Gale G. '57, '58, '59
O'Neal, Hard E. '02
O'Neal, Steve '66, '67, '68
Osborne, Carl R. '55, '56, '57
Osborne, Richard '72, '73
Overly, Charles R. '43, '46, '47
Overly, James A. (Tmr) '48, '49
Overshiner, E. M. '96
Overton, Andrew '63, '64

P

Pannell, Ernie W. '38, '39, '40
Pardee, John P. '54, '55, '56
Parish, Joseph M. '39
Park, Mike '70, '71, '72
Parker, James H. (Mgr) '39, '40
Parker, Jim '68, '69, '70
Parker, William E. '08, '09, '10, '12
Parmer, James R. '44

Payne, Howard '57, '58, '59
Payne, Lawrence J. '45
Payne, W. O. '42
Pearson, Henry A. '57
Peoples, Dan '71
Perkins, Frank D. '94, '96, '97
Persons, David H. '13
Peter, Philip '61
Petty, S. J. '26, '27
Philley, Andy '69, '70, '71
Phillips, H. D. '30
Phillips, James D. '60, '61, '62
Phillips, Michael L. '64
Phillips, Robert H. '59, '60
Phythian, Walter R. '35, '36
Pickett, Tom '41, '46
Pierce, J. A. '18
Pinson, C. T. '23
Pinson, Harry T. '21
Piper, Jim '67, '68, '69
Piper, Paul K. '59, '60
Pirie, James E. '01, '02, '03
Pitman, Mike J. '62, '63, '64
Pitner, H. M. '34, '35, '36
Pizzitola, Michael J. '61, '62
Polasek, Billy Joe '69, '71
Pollock, Oscar L. '47
Pool, Rusty '71
Poss, John M. '65, '66
Powell, Jack E. '53, '55
Powell, Louis H. '14
Powell, William Dee '54, '55, '56
Power, Robert (Mgr) '67
Price, C. Walemon '37, '38, '39
Price, Harold L. '56
Price, P. M. '25
Prokop, Merl A. '47
Puckett, Felix S. '05, '06
Puckett, John W. '02, '03
Pugh, Marion C., Sr. '38, '39, '40
Pyburn, Jack H. '64, '65, '66

R
Ragsdale, Robert '97, '98
Rahn, Leon F. '39, '40
Rawlins, Harry E. '97
Reagan, Travis H. '61, '62, '63
Rees, W. Nelson '31
Reeves, John R. '39, '40
Rektorik, J. A. '26
Resley, George '68
Reynolds, James '68
Reynolds, John W. '65
Richardson, Lester S. '39, '41
Richenstein, Charles A. '05
Richter, Charles E. '27, '28, '29
Rickman, Ricky (Mgr) '68
Ridenhower, Ray '01, '02
Riggs, Charlie '66, '67, '68
Roach, James B. '33
Roaches, Carl '72, '73
Robbins, Cooper P., Jr. '52, '53
Robbins, Donald '55
Robbins, Doug '70
Roberts, F. A. (Mgr) '13
Roberts, William C. '08
Robertson, Art Mitchell '70, '71
Robertson, John E. '31, '33
Robnett, Edward '39
Robnett, Marshall F. '38, '39, '40
Roepke, Robert E. (Mgr) '61
Rogers, Cullen J. '39, '41, '42
Rogers, Gerald G. '61, '62, '63
Rogers, Joe C. '15, '16
Rogers, Owens A. '36, '37, '38
Rollins, Charles H. '34
Rollins, Gerald D. (Mgr) '56
Rollins, John W. '14, '15, '16
Roper, James S. '58
Roquemore, Michael A. '62
Ross, James B. '06, '07
Rothe, Joe H. '39, '40
Routt, Joe E. '35, '36, '37
Routt, William A. '38, '39, '40
Royalty, Charlie A. '48, '49

Ruby, Martin O. '39, '40, '41
Rudder, James Earl '31
Rugel, Dan F. '07, '08, '09
Rush, Marshall N. '51, '52
Rush, William T. '49, '50, '51
Rushing, Eli '37, '38
Rylander, E. W. '15

S

Sacra, Joseph R., Jr. '70, '71, '72
Sacra, Joseph R., Sr. '44, '46, '47
Sallee, Bill D. '65, '66, '67
Salyer, Johnny A. '51, '52, '53
Sams, Bucky, '73
Sammons, Thomas B. '04
Sanders, Augie W. '50, '51
Sanders, Robert W. '57, '58, '59
Sanders, Sam H. '21
Saxe, Charles S. '51, '52
Scarborough, J. S. '08
Schaedel, Charles T. '10, '11
Schero, Joe E. '52, '53, '54
Schmid, Joe H. (Mgr) '57
Schmidt, Hubert '06, '07
Schneider, Daniel W. '65, '66, '67
Schroeder, Bruno E. '35, '37, '38
Schroeder, William H. '53, '54
Schultz, Earl '00, '01, '02, '03
Schwarz, Blake '72, '73
Scoggin, Phillip C. '64, '65
Scott, Herbert B. '52
Scott, Johnny D. '52, '53
Scott, Joseph O. '44, '46
Scott, Richard E. '49
Scott, Verne A. '14
Scovell, J. Field '28
Scudder, Carl F. '18, '19, '20
Seago, H. W. '36
Seeker, Rickey '72, '73
Seely, Bill '68, '69
Self, Rocky '69
Settegast, Marion E., Jr. '43

Settegast, Marion E., Sr. '14, '15, '16
Shaeffer, Robert J. '49, '50, '51
Shaw, Joe '69
Sheffield, Corky '69, '70
Sheffield, Jimmy '68, '69, '70
Shefts, Morton '44, '46
Shelton, J. Howard '39, '40
Shippex, F. '09
Shira, Charles N. '43, '44
Shockey, Jacob C. '35, '36, '37
Sibley, William R. '41, '42
Sikes, Delmar D. '50
Sikes, Jules V. '25, '26, '27
Simmons, A. L. '56, '57
Simmons, Elvis A. '40, '41, '42
Simmons, J. A. '26
Simmons, Melvin D. '62, '63, '64
Simmons, Wayland A. '59, '60, '61
Simonini, Ed. '72, '73
Simpson, J. V. '02, '03, '04
Simpson, O. M. '97, '98, '99
Sims, A. Randy '58, '59, '60
Sims, M. W. '94
Sinclair, Bennie C. '53, '54
Singleton, James M. '65, '66
Skinner, Ben S. (Mgr) '52
Slaughter, Marion Pete '42
Smelaer, Dennis '73
Smith, Bland '70, '71
Smith, Don G. '56, '57, '58
Smith, Earl L. '39, '40
Smith, Gilbert '66
Smith, Herbert E. '37, '38, '39
Smith, Langston M. '14, '15
Smith, M. V. '20, '21
Smith, Preston W. '45, '46, '47, '48
Smith, Ralph '58, '59, '60
Smith, Robert L. '49, '50, '51
Smith, Ted '69, '70, '71
Smitham, Verner R. (Mgr) '14
Sooy, Tom '67, '68, '69
Spadora, Joseph (Mgr) '65
Spake, W. E. '12

Speed, Carleton D. '25
Spencer, Michael F. '49, '50
Spencer, Oliver F. '14
Spencer, Rick '71
Spencer, Ted L. '31, '32, '33
Spires, Truman E. '45
Spivey, Marshall '39, '40, '41
Sprott, Alton C. '26, '27
Stabler, James M. '64, '65
Stach, Stanfield A. '33, '35
Stages, William F. '36
Stallings, Eugene C. '54, '55, '56
Stallings, Rusty '68, '69
Stanley, James L. '55, '56, '57
Stanley, Mark '73
Stansberry, Robert '69
Stautzenberger, W. Odell '46, '47, '48
Steffens, Karl K. '38
Stegent, Larry '67, '68, '69
Sterling, James R. '39, '40, '41
Sterns, James B. '96, '97, '98
Steymann, Walter R. '42
Stinson, Mike '68, '69
Stiteler, R. Harry '30
Stratton, Kenny '72, '73
Street, Gus C. '99, '01, '03, '04
Street, Robert L. (Mgr) '48, '49
Stringfellow, Jack C. '33
Sturcken, Edward B. '42
Surovik, John H. (Mgr) '52, '53
Swan, Michael K. '63
Swedeen, John '70
Swilley, Dennis '73
Symes, Clarence '06, '07

T

Taliaferro, Darrell '73
Tassos, Damon G. '43, '44
Tate, Marvin P. '52, '53, '54
Taylor, Arthur W. '08, '09
Taylor, Loyd F. '55, '56, '57
Teague, Foster S. '53

Teague, Sammie R. (Mgr) '59
Ten Napel, Garth '73
Tewell, Dennis (Trnr) '67
Theriot, Sidney J. '52, '53, '54
Thomas, Clifford '69
Thomas, Clifton '70
Thomas, Edwin W. '13, '14
Thomas, Pat '72, '73
Thomason, James N. '38, '39, '40
Thompson, Nash O. '34
Thompson, Thomas E. '09
Thompson, William '73
Thornton, Penn B. '16
Thrower, John D. '99, '00
Thurmond, Al '72, '73
Tidwell, Billy R. '49, '50, '51
Todd, Dick S. '36, '37, '38
Torno, Frank V. '46
Tracey, John '56, '57, '58
Tracy, Carroll A. '28, '29, '30
Tracy, H. H. '97
Tracy, Henry '72, '73
Trammell, Bud '73
Trimble, Murry H. '55, '56
Trew, Robert L. '13
Trimmier, Tim '73
Trott, Bobby (Trnr) '66, '67
Tucker, M. Dwayne '48, '49, '50
Tulis, Robert F. '41, '46, '47
Turley, Herbert R. '43, '46, '47, '48
Turner, Joe G. '37
Turner, Stanley S. '43
Turney, John '68

U

Ullrich, Charles E. '13
Utay, Joe '05, '06, '07
Uzzell, William J. '63, '64

V

Vaden, Frank S. (Mgr) '55

Vandervoort, A. S. '18, '19
Van Dyke, Lewis E. '60, '62
Van Pelt, Thomas E. (Trnr) '60
Van Zandt, Roscoe L. '28, '29
Vassar, William C. (Mgr) '63
Vaughn, Tommie '38, '39, '40
Veckert, Herman H. '96, '97
Vela, Javier '67, '68
Vesmirovsky, E. '10, '11, '12, '13
Vick, Richard P. '54
Vitek, Richard D. '35, '36, '37
Voss, Kenneth R. '48

W

Walker, Alvin '72, '73
Walker, David '73
Walker, George '66
Walker, L. E. '18
Walker, Weldon F. '35
Walker, William E. '44
Walker, William T. '02, '03, '04, '05
Ward, Arland L. '09
Ward, C. E. '09, '10
Ward, Waylon O. '63, '64
Ward, William R. '63
Warnke, Carl '73
Washington, William H. '12
Watson, Donald A. '54, '55, '56
Watts, Arthur P. '94
Watts, Claude D. '25, '26
Watts, Dale '68, '69
Waugh, C. A. '23, '24
Weaver, Mark '66, '67
Webster, Jake D. '40, '41, '42
Weinert, Arthur '00, '08
Weir, H. B. '17
Weir, W. C. '19, '20, '21
Weiss, Joe H. '64, '65, '66
Welch, F. Barney, '42, '46, '47
Welch, Bruce '73
Wellborn, Joseph H. '63, '64, '65
Wells, Gaddy '67

Wendt, F. T. '21
Wesson, T. Euel '39, '40, '41
West, Donald E. '64
Westbrook, William A. (Mgr) '62
Westerfield, Ira Dan '64, '65, '66
Whatley, Richard E. '63, '64, '65
Wheat, Wayne '69
White, Finis L. '39
White, Joe R. '37, '38, '39
White, Oscar M. '45
Whithead, Gary '71, '72
Whitfield, John T. '35, '36
Whitmore, Jack '67, '68, '69
Whittaker, Wray W. '46, '47, '48, '49
Whyte, James A. '10
Wickerham, James B. '64
Wiebold, Bill '71, '72
Wiley, J. E. '43
Wilkerson, Grady '73
Wilkins, W. Taylor '34, '35
Willenborg, James C. '62, '63, '64
Williams, George '39
Williams, Jackie '73
Williams, J. Maurice '39
Williams, Reggie '73
Williams, Robert H. '41, '42
Williams, Sammy '68
Williams, T. J. '05
Williams, W. B. '31, '32
Willis, Nicholas W. '34, '35
Willoughby, Jack (Mgr) '71
Wilson, E. S. '16, '17, '18, '19
Wilson, Fay '23, '24, '25
Wilson, Richard O. '22, '23
Wilson, Roy D. (Trnr) '63
Wilson, T. F. '20, '21, '22, '23
Wilson, W. W. '24
Winkler, Andrew '97, '98
Winkler, James C. '45, '46, '47, '48
Winkler, Lawrence E. '52, '53, '54
Winn, W. E. '21
Wolf, Herbert J. '54, '55
Wolf, William M. '30

Wood, Frank M. '39
Wood, Joe '66
Woodland, Sully S. '32, '33
Woodman, Cony N. '04, '06
Woodman, James O. '30
Woodman, V. W. '25, '26
Worthing, Evan E. '01, '02
Wright, Charlie E. '43, '46, '47, '48
Wright, Fred G. '35
Wright, James '55, '56, '57
Wright, Larry '73
Wright, R. C. '43, '46
Wright, Richard H. '32
Wylie, H. P. '26

Y

Yates, Paul T. '44
Yeargain, C. W. '44, '45
Yeoman, William F. '45
Yocum, Bill '71
Young, Roy O. '35, '36, '37

Z

Zapalac, Willie F. '41, '42, '46
Zarafonetis, George H. '28, '29
Zedler, Otto F. (Mgr) '16
Zuch, Howard W. '51, '52

The following names were not included in the original list of lettermen and should be added.

Benjamin, Joseph W. '02, '03
Dollar, Roy I. '52

Finley, Bruce K. '70, '71
Saxe, Augie W. '50, '51

Prior to 1906 the letter award at Texas A&M was a "C" instead of the "T", the "C" representing College and to distinguish it from Texas University which awarded the "T".

Upon petition of the players the Texas A&M Administration granted the change and also approved the formation of the T-Association, which includes all lettermen regardless of the sport in which they lettered.

Credits for photographs used in this book are the following: Texas A&M Athletic Department; The Association of Former Students, Texas A&M University; *Football History,* Inc.; *The Dallas Morning News*; *The Dallas Times Herald*; *Fort Worth Star-Telegram*; *Waco News-Tribune*; Dr. Sam H. Sanders; Joel Hunt; John Kimbrough; Will Grimsley; John David Crow; Dana X. Bible; Dr. King Gill; Harry W. Thompson; Dwight H. McAnally; Cotton Bowl Athletic Association; Jim Bradley; Tom Nelson, Association of Former Students, E. W. Buchtien, and W. H. Dawson.